Socrates and Subtitles

Socrates and Subtitles

*A Philosopher's Guide to
95 Thought-Provoking Movies
from Around the World*

WILLIAM G. SMITH

McFarland & Company, Inc., Publishers
Jefferson, North Carolina, and London

Library of Congress Cataloguing-in-Publication Data

Smith, William G.
     Socrates and subtitles : a philosopher's guide to 95 thought-
provoking movies from around the world / William G. Smith.
          p.   cm.
     Includes bibliographical references and index.

     ISBN 978-0-7864-4380-2
     softcover : 50# alkaline paper 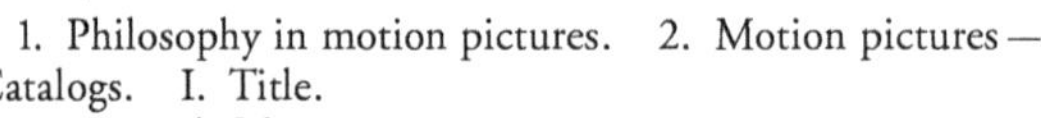

     1. Philosophy in motion pictures.   2. Motion pictures —
Catalogs.   I. Title.
     PN1995.9.P42S65   2010
     791.43'684 — dc22   2009052751

British Library cataloguing data are available

Front cover: *A Clockwork Orange* (1971, Warner Bros./Photofest)

Manufactured in the United States of America

McFarland & Company, Inc., Publishers
   Box 611, Jefferson, North Carolina 28640
      www.mcfarlandpub.com

To Donna

Ganser Library, catching leaves,
Nessun Dorma, *Billy Elliot*,
three minutes, Galway...

TABLE OF CONTENTS

Spain

France

Scandinavia

Germany

Eastern Europe

Italy

Africa

Israel

Iran

India

China, Hong Kong and Nepal

Preface

After the publication of my previous book, *Plato and Popcorn* in 2004, I was pleased that numbers of people contacted me to say they had organized film-watching groups and were utilizing my book as a guide. In addition, I have been using *Plato and Popcorn* as the central text in the course "Philosophy in Film" I offer at Millersville University in Pennsylvania.

That book categorized movies under philosophical labels. Very early after the publication of *Plato and Popcorn*, I started thinking about a follow-up book that would be similar in style. Instead of dividing the next book by philosophical topics, I decided I wanted to "travel around the world via world cinema." Though I decided to include some movies made in the United States, the majority of movies covered would be from foreign countries. With the exception of films from English-speaking countries, the majority of films included in this book utilize subtitles. (The dubbing of voices is almost invariably an atrocity.) I continue being the philosopher who likes to raise probing questions. When certain noteworthy ideas from the writings of philosophers are relevant to the plot of a movie, I provide a synopsis of those philosophical ideas. Thus, for example, David Hume's arguments against the notion of life after death are presented in the section on the film *After Life*.

My thanks must again go to a number of the people mentioned in *Plato and Popcorn*. Donna Smith, who became my wife since the publication of that book, continued as the person who did all the typing, and regularly gave me good advice during the writing of the manuscript. Since I first met him in the 1960s, John Ellsworth Winter has been a central part of my life. Among other things, John has always been my midwife of ideas. Elva Winter is a prime example of how one should live as a caring person. She sees that good movies have a spiritual dimension. As in the past, Gus Meckley is a chief provider of original analyses of individual films. My son, Jason, calls me whenever he sees a new movie that excited him.

My daughter, Tess, has shown ever-more readiness to check out independent and foreign movies. Finally, I owe much to many of the students from my film class. They often see things I would have missed in films we review. I am especially grateful to Adam Woods, who proofread my entire manuscript. His corrections and suggestions were invaluable. Of course, any errors that remain are my responsibility. I owe a great deal of gratitude to Dr. John Short, dean of humanities and social sciences at Millersville University, for moral and material support. In addition, President Francine McNairy, and Vilas Prabhu, provost/vice president for academic affairs have consistently been responsible for an aura of support for faculty research without setting up a threatening "publish or perish" atmosphere at Millersville. Special thanks go the members of the Millersville University Faculty Grants Committee for their support.

INTRODUCTION: HOW TO VIEW, ENJOY, AND CRITICALLY APPRAISE MOVIES

Approximately ten years ago, when I was trying to decide whether I was going to offer a course on Philosophy in Film, I faced a quandary. I *loved* movies. At that time, I was viewing at least 52 movies a year — in theatres. (Now, with quality DVDs and Blu-ray disks, the number of films I view in a year's time is not mentionable — people will think I don't do anything other than watch movies.) I feared, however, that teaching a film course would destroy my love of film. Would I pick apart movies so much that the life would go out of them? Analysis, claimed the great philosopher Henri Bergson (1859–1941), deals with concepts that are static. Analysis stops the flow of what is being experienced and — in a sense — takes snapshots of reality. A snapshot of a person might reveal some things about the person, but it fails to capture what went on before the picture was taken, and fails to capture what occurs in the aftermath of the instant captured. Whenever I see the famous photograph of the raising of the American flag on Iwo Jima, I wonder what was occurring in the area outside the camera's eye. Mainly, I would like to experience the flow of events before, during, and after the raising of the flag. The photograph can not provide the flow of the events.

Analysis is not a snapshot in a literal sense. Analyses yield concepts — not pictures. If I try to analyze for you my experience of floating on a raft down the Colorado River in the Grand Canyon, I have no hope you will capture the essence of that experience. I am unable to capture it with words. The way to experience x is to experience x — one cannot experience x by thinking, analyzing, or talking about x. Likewise, the way to experience a film is by viewing it, immersing yourself in the images as much as you can. My fear was that analyzing films in a classroom atmosphere would suck the life out of the film and leave me with mere static words or concepts.

Fortunately, my fears were not justified. Comparing one's analysis with those of others can lead to an added appreciation of a film. You might become aware of things you missed. As it turned out, I quickly became excited to find that many students, who would never have given certain movies a chance, learn to appreciate those films when they became involved in class discussions. On their own, many people will not choose to view *Babette's Feast* (1988), because it is a foreign film. They won't watch *12 Angry Men* (1957), because it is a black and white film. They won't give *My Dinner with Andre* (1981) a chance, because there is no action in it.

It is regrettable that a good number of adults cannot enjoy films that do not contain the action they expect. When they were children, these people were bombarded with hundreds of images of violence in TV shows their parents allowed them to watch. As adults, they then judge a film to be "bad" if there is no action. The possibilities of appreciating films with no action has been cancelled out by the programming from their past. *American History X* (1998) is an excellent film. It is not certain, however, that it is a "better" film than *Whale Rider* (2002), or *Look Both Ways* (2005). The great majority of my students, nevertheless, would judge it to be the best of the three films mentioned. Why? Because it is the best? No. Because the film contains scenes of people being shot, and a scene of someone smashing the head of another person on a concrete curb. My view: there are great movies that are violent —*American History X* is one. *Reservoir Dogs* (1992) and *Funny Games* (1997 — original German version, not the remake) are two others. They are *not* excellent movies *because* they are violent. Such things as the originality of the plot, and the quality acting and directing make them excellent. Those factors constitute the excellence of many non-violent films also.

So, I am indeed discouraged when I hear people say "that film was really good!" when it is clear their judgment is based on the fact that they require the films they watch to show lots of blood. (They also demand that the "F" word be omnipresent in the film.)

Those who are programmed to expect action in a film must learn to follow "the principle of charity." I introduce all my students to that principle. In philosophy classes, students are exposed to many ideas that don't jive with their established beliefs. The principle of charity demands that criticism of a novel idea not take place until one has given the new idea a fair chance. Assume the proponent of the idea is an intelligent person who has something to say. Try to put yourself in that person's shoes and, as much as possible, see the world as he sees it. After that, criticism is justified. Don't criticize x until you have charitably given x a chance.

Using the principle of charity, a person who has a prejudice against black and white films, "old" films, foreign films or films that do not have much action must give these films a fair viewing. If he does that, he may be surprised that he likes many of the films he previously would not have given a chance.

Choosing What Movies to View

I am sympathetic to those who choose to see certain films panned by most critics, as long as they are not the only films given a chance. I am referring to movies such as *Dumb and Dumber* (1994) and *Friday the 13th, Part XVIII* (some future date). Depth of content and originality of plot are important elements of a film. A mature audience will find rewarding entertainment in movies that contain those elements.

How can a person spot what is probably an excellent film that does not pander to the tastes of those with adolescent minds? A good starting point is Rotten Tomatoes, the website that contains the judgments of a large number of critics. If you type in a movie title, a page of reviews will appear. At the top of the page, you will see a percentage number. That number summarizes the percentage of critics who passed favorable judgments on the film. Stay away from any movie that rates 60 percent or below. 80–100 percent indicates a good bet. Most of the time, if the majority of critics view a film favorably, the film is worth checking out.

A word of warning: many critics are lazy and their reviews merely summarize the plot of the films. It is easy to write a review like that. The best critics convey what is worthwhile about the production and give away little of the plot. I have met quite a few people who *want* to know what happens in a film *before* they decide to see it. For me, a good film is like life — you don't know what is around the corner, but discovering what is there provides the drama that makes life exciting.

I also recommend subscribing to *Film Comment* or some other magazine that provides up-to-date articles on films that are, or will be, causing a stir. There are also articles on films from past masters. In general, ignore magazines that only cover Hollywood blockbusters, and only contain articles on mega-stars like Brad Pitt.

The Theater vs. the TV Experience

The following was written in 1915:

> I want to tell you about the action film, the simplest, and the type most often seen. In the mind of the habitué of the cheaper theater, it is the only sort in existence. It dominates the slums, is announced there by red and green posters of the melodrama sort, and retains its original elements, more deftly handled in places more expensive. The story goes at the highest possible speed to remain credible ... you remember the first one you saw where the policeman pursues the comical tramp over hill and dale and across the town lots. You remember others where the cavalry follows the horse thief across the desert, spies him at last and chases him faster, faster, faster and faster, and finally catches him.

> • • •

> In the Action Picture there is no adequate means for the development of any full grown passion. The distinguished character-study that makes genuine the human emotions in the legitimate drama, has no chance.... The audience gossips and chews gum.
> Why does the audience keep coming to this type of photoplay if neither lust, love, hate, nor hunger, is adequately conveyed? Simply because such spectacles gratify the incipient or rampant speed-mania in every American.[1]

Things have not changed. I ask my students why they are not bothered that in movie after movie, heroes or villains will dive through windows (in slow motion) in order to escape capture. I challenge them to dive through a window and see if they will be in any shape to run away.

I am puzzled at how so many otherwise intelligent people can be entertained by such hogwash. Add the behavior of some members of a theater audience to the absurdity of the images being watched, and you have a recipe for time wasted. Why do so many people talk during the showing of a movie? Why must they spend exorbitant amounts of money for popcorn, soft drinks, and candy? Filmmaking is an art form. People don't talk and chomp on popcorn in symphony halls or museums. Recently, the number of white screens on cell phones make the theater look like it is filled with giant fireflies.

The ideal theater experience is possible only if the film is a creative work of art (that doesn't mean "boring") and the audience is attentive. I remember seeing the Danish film *Babette's Feast* (1988) in a theater filled to capacity. I think everyone in that theater immersed himself in this film, which depicts a meal prepared with love. No one left the theater as the end credits — all in Danish — rolled. When the screen went blank, there was a standing ovation. How different was that experience from the usual! How different from the one in which some stranger sat next to me, eating a sandwich that smelled of rotting fish! How different from the time I had to listen to someone behind me continually tell their friend what was going to happen next because he had already seen the movie!

When I watch a film, I become part of it. I am Frodo, a hobbit with hairy feet who lives in a hole, and is visited by a wizard named Gandolf. Why should I be pulled out of my experience of the movie by someone talking on a cell phone, or chomping on nachos? Even if people like me are in the minority, shouldn't others show respect by being quiet? One film critic has written: "We ought to visit a cinema as we would go to church."[2] While the sermon was being delivered, wouldn't the church experience suffer if the congregation were gorging themselves with food and talking about the new clothes they bought? Why should seeing a film in a theater be any different?

Watching a film on network TV is a dismal experience. Part of the film may be censored, and the countless commercials destroy the flow that should be experienced. The best way to view a film at home is to watch it on DVD (Blu-ray, if possible) without a break. That often is not possible, as interruptions invariably occur. Though it is true that the continuity can be destroyed, the ability to rewind a DVD to recapture what you previously saw, or to pick up lines not understood, has its own benefits. I have found many special features on DVDs to be insightful.

Character Development and Consistent Plotting

If I see a film that lacks originality, I will not remember the plot one week later. For the life of me, I cannot tell you anything about the plot of *There's Something About Mary* (1998), except that she got yucky stuff in her hair. If I try to remember the plot of *Spider-Man* (2002), my mind is blank, except I remember being disappointed that Tobey Maguire took a break from making quality films in order to cash in big. *Ghostbusters II* (1989)? Blank.

If I compare the above films to my experience while watching Edward Norton in *American History X*, being transformed from a nasty racist to a caring, mature person, I am stunned that anyone would settle for less. No one who appreciates Ozu's *Tokyo Story* (1953) will ever forget the impact of seeing elderly people being pushed aside by their loved ones. If you are open to it, you will begin to feel you know the characters of *The Apu Trilogy* (movies 67, 68 and 69 in this book).

If characters of a film undergo character changes that do not make sense, the film suffers. *Slumdog Millionaire* (movie 71) is an excellent film in spite of the fact that the brother of the main character irrationally flip-flops between doing good deeds and acting in a malicious way. In an early scene from Quentin Tarentino's *Inglourious Basterds* (2009) a "Jew Hunter" inexplicably allows a Jewish woman to escape his grasp. The only possible reason he did this was because the woman had a major role to play later in the film. In an otherwise powerful film from Denmark called *The Inheritance* (2003), the main character curiously fails to do something he had agreed to do.

Improbable events that occur in a film should also grate like sandpaper. In *Plato and Popcorn*, I complain about a scene in *Indiana Jones and the Temple of Doom* (1984). Indiana Jones and two companions are in an airplane that is about to crash. They are saved by jumping out of the plane with an inflatable raft, inflate the raft, and float to safety. The main plot of *The Boy with the Striped Pajamas* (2009) hinges on a German child regularly going to a barbed wire fence surrounding a concentration camp to meet a young Jewish inmate. No guards see them as they meet time after time. Right!

Watching Films

One of the joys of watching a movie is sharing the experience with friends, and then talking about what you liked and what you disliked about the film. Listening to the friends' responses often leads to a deeper appreciation of what you just viewed. Others may have seen things you missed. If you agree that a movie is a dud, it is fun to clarify why that is so. I have actually changed my appreciation of a film as a result of points made by friends' comments. I don't generally think less of a film after discussions, but I do at times generate a more favorable opinion of a film. After viewing David Lynch's *Mulholland Drive* (2001), I felt it was an interesting film without much depth. As a result of lengthy discussions with friends who helped me figure out what was going on, I came to the conclusion it is a *great* film.

In the book titled *How Movies Helped Save My Soul*, Gareth Higgins presents a few do's and don'ts of watching a film. The last two rules are especially interesting:

> 1. Don't talk during the credits.... The person sitting beside you may have been deeply affected by it.... [A]fter my third viewing of Terrence Malick's *The Thin Red Line*, as soon as the credits began to roll, I was conscious of the sound of my own epiphanic breathing for half a second before the bloke behind me said to his wife in a voice loud enough to drown out the parting of the Red Sea, "that was the biggest load of shite I've ever seen in my life." I think I made my point.
>
> 2. Observe the ten-minute-rule ... I will not discuss the film for the period of time after the credits have finished. You will have begun to integrate your response to that experience into your psyche and will be protected from attack by the ignorant.[3]

My friends and I have always been compelled to begin talking about the film the instant after leaving the theater, or immediately after viewing a DVD. I haven't sensed any problems with doing that. However, the ten-minute-rule may be helpful for you.

How to Use This Book

1. If the only thing you get out of this book is an appreciation of some of the movies covered — movies you may have otherwise missed — then I think I have served you well. There is no compelling reason to start with the first movie and progress step-by-step to movie 95. You can start at the beginning or just pick films you think will be of special interest to you.

2. Read the introductory comments before watching a movie. I will *never* give away any of the plot in such remarks. I may, however, contribute general comments about the overriding subject matter of the film — comments about issues that often should be obvious merely from the title of the movie. For example, I introduce some moral issues about sexuality prior to the movie *Kinsey* (movie 6) and issues about death and dying before *The Death of Mr. Lazerescu* (movie 50).

3. Watch the movie after you read the words "Watch the movie."

   4. After viewing a film, immediately fill out a chart like the following:

General Impression	Actors	Actresses	Director	Cinema-tography	Plot	Setting	Music	Editing	Sound

   Give values of 1 to 10 for each of the categories (10 is "can't be better"; 1 is "really sucks"). The general impression is your overall reaction to the movie-watching experience. Did you think the actors and actresses did a mediocre or an excellent job? The buck pretty much stops with the director. Was the plot original and unforgettable? What about the setting? Did the movie seem to take place in a *real place*? Did the setting seem to be a fake movie set? Did the music add or detract from the experience of "getting into" the movie? Is the editing such that any given scene flows effortlessly into the next scene? Is the sound muffled or clear?

   If you watch a movie as a member of a group, you can spend some time discussing your ratings. There are times someone will give a high rating for some or all of the categories and someone else will give low ratings.

   5. After you watch the film, read my comments and answer any questions. Such comments and questions will often involve "spoilers" that would give away some of the plot if you read them before watching the film.

   6. I will often present a list of additional movies you should try if you liked what you just viewed.

UNITED STATES

Movie 1: *Modern Times*

Director: Charlie Chaplin; 1 hour, 43 minutes; 1936

Charlie Chaplin's *Modern Times* is one of the American Film Institute's top 100 American movies of all time. Chaplin's genius is evident every moment of the film. The viewer must be in awe of his stunts and of the many brilliant scenes of slapstick. Behind the silliness stands a serious indictment of the de-humanizing mechanized world of our industrial age.

Watch the movie.

Questions to ponder:

1. At the beginning of the film, Chaplin shows sheep being herded through gates. That scene fades into another scene showing people heading for work at a factory — the workers looking much like the sheep. In the workplace, are the majority of people like sheep? Day after day, the sheep are herded the same way through the same gates, and the workers flock to the same job and the same routine. Many philosophers have criticized the mindlessness of the work routine. Does that routine have to be mindless?

In his great essay, "The Myth of Sisyphus," Albert Camus (1913–1960) recounts the story of Sisyphus, who rebelled against the gods who then condemned him by requiring him to push a heavy rock up a mountain, just to have it roll to the bottom. That routine would happen over and over again for all eternity. Many readers probably think that Camus is merely writing about a character from ancient Greek mythology, but in one sentence, he shows that he was writing about the human condition: "The workman of today works everyday in his life at the same tasks, and this fate is no less absurd (than the fate of Sisyphus)."[1] For many, a Sisyphean life would be meaningless. Camus, however, ends the essay with: "The struggle itself toward the heights is enough to fill a man's heart.

One must imagine Sisyphus happy."[2] Can a workman placed in a factory, forced to perform "mindless" chores, be "happy"? Would happiness be more attainable if we would reject the industrialized world, as does the Tramp (Charlie Chaplin) and the gamine (Pauline Goddard)?

My interpretation of Camus' "Sisyphus" is that we are all Sisyphus, both in *and* out of the workplace. Each day we wake up, go to the bathroom, eat breakfast, brush our teeth, go to work, eat lunch, work, go home, read or drink a beer, have sex (if we are lucky) and go to sleep. The next morning, we wake up, go to the bathroom, go to work ... well, you get the picture. Can we — should we — be happy with such a life?

2. Of course, to answer the above question, one must determine the nature of happiness. Too many movies make it seem that happiness is easy to find. The Tramp and the gamine just have to be together to be happy. Harry and Sally just have to realize they love one another. However, if happiness were something so easy to find, many more people would have found it by now. It seems to me the majority of people are not happy.

Charlie Chaplin fighting an industrial monster in his great classic *Modern Times* (1936).

They are miserable with their jobs. The divorce rate shows they are not happy with their married lives. So — what exactly constitutes happiness?

The main goal of Aristotle's (384–322 B.C.) great work *Nicomachean Ethics* is to discover what would constitute a happy life. According to Aristotle, all natural things have goals. An acorn has the goal of becoming an oak tree. What is the goal of human life? To make money? Making money may be good, but it cannot be the ultimate good or ultimate goal for the reason that one wants money because *it will supposedly help make one happy.* Anything a person seeks will be sought because possessing it will supposedly make the person happier. Thus happiness is the ultimate good — the goal of the human's life.

Aristotle presents a lengthy, systematic argument that happiness is possible only if one lives a life of contemplation. In fact, happiness *is* living the contemplative life. Happiness, for Aristotle, is difficult to achieve. A contemplative life is impossible if a person is not virtuous, does not do things in moderation, or does not have a broad range of knowledge about the causes of things. In addition, happiness requires what Aristotle calls "external goods." The following quote gives a partial list of external goods that are necessary if happiness is to be possible:

> Many things are done by means of friends, or wealth, or political power, as if by means of tools: and then again, there are some things the lack of which is like a stain on happiness, things like good birth, being blessed in one's children, beauty: for the person who is extremely ugly, or of low birth, or on his own without children is someone we would be not altogether inclined to call happy, and even less inclined, presumably, if someone had totally depraved children or friends, or ones who were good but dead.[3]

Which of the following elements which Aristotle claims are necessary for happiness do you think are essential?

    a. Being a contemplative person, i.e., being a philosopher?
    b. Being virtuous?
    c. Being moderate in one's desires and activities?
    d. Having friends who are virtuous and moderate?
    e. Having a certain amount of money and "political power"?
    f. Having "good birth?
    g. Being blessed in one's children?
    h. Not being "ugly"?
    i. Having living children who are virtuous?

Does the Tramp show that he possesses any, or all, of the above characteristics?

3. Returning to the problem of the tendency for industry and technology to engage in dehumanization, one critic, Christopher Smith, recently put the dilemma presented us by "Modern Times" as follows:

> Chaplin wasn't against technology — as a filmmaker, he relied upon it — but he did believe that technology should at least live up to its promise and benefit mankind. In 1935, when he began to formulate and shoot "Modern Times," it was clear to him that this wasn't the way things were going. He viewed the rise of industrialization and technology — and the men getting wealthy off each — as real dangers facing society. If left unchecked, if not confronted and questioned, these gleaming, intoxicating machines created to improve our lives might one day ruin our lives. Ironically, they would control us. Was he so far off the mark?
>
> Nearly 70 years after the film's premiere, we live in a world in which identity theft, Internet hackings, corporate streamlining, plant closings, computer viruses and kids being murdered for their iPods are the direct result of technology's hold over us. The flip side of the equation is that technology has extended our lives, and in many ways improved upon them. It's this paradox that makes "Modern Times" relevant to today. It's a movie that was for the times and ahead of its time [www.weekinrewind.com posted August 28, 2007].

In the realm of philosophic studies, *One-Dimensional Man: Studies in the Ideology of Advanced Industrial Society* by Herbert Marcuse (1898–1979), published in 1964, still contains significant relevance by warning us about the dangers of a society governed by mechanized industry and technology. Do you think what Chaplin and Marcuse saw as a threat is becoming an ever more encompassing reality? Do you agree with Marcuse that mega corporations exert control worldwide and that propaganda molds the opinions of uncritical humans, who become more and more apathetic about what should really matter? Or is such a view simply a prejudice expressed by those with an anti-industry mentality?

ADDITIONAL RECOMMENDED FILMS
BY CHARLIE CHAPLIN

The Gold Rush (1925)

City Lights (1931). One of the great love stories in film. The last scene is unforgettable.

The Great Dictator (1940). Chaplin makes fun of Adolf Hitler.

Movie 2: *Now, Voyager*

Director: Irving Rapper; 1 hour, 57 minutes; 1942

Jean-Paul Sartre (1905–1980) presented the following three word sentence that captures the central idea of the philosophic movement called Existentialism: "Existence precedes essence." What does that sentence mean? It means humans are not given any essence, but rather are responsible for their own essence. It is not the case that God, or that one's DNA, or that other people make us what we are. We are totally responsible for our own characters, decisions, and actions. There is no one human essence shared by all — there are as many human essences as there are humans. Each person is a unique individual, and that individuality results from the free choices of each person.

"Existence precedes essence" is the opposite of "Essence precedes existence." If the latter sentence were true about people, then a person's essence would be determined by some outside forces. An automobile — or any other thing — cannot choose to be anything other than what it is. An

automobile's essence is given to it by the automobile manufacturer. "Existence precedes essence" means that although we did not choose to come into existence, once we exist we are responsible for our essence.

An idea that is extremely relevant to a major theme in *Now, Voyager* follows from "existence precedes essence." The essence we choose for ourselves is of the utmost importance to us. When I choose to be a Christian, or an atheist, or a pacifist, or a terrorist, my choice makes me what I am.

Charlotte (Bette Davis) struggles in a life controlled by a dominating mother in *Now, Voyager* (1942).

When I make such choices, I am at the same time choosing what I think all other people should choose. If I choose to be a Christian, I expect everyone else to be a Christian. If I choose to be a Democrat, I expect everyone else to be a Democrat. In addition, we will relate well with those who choose the same essence we choose and not relate well to those who choose essences incompatible with what we choose. I relate well with fans of the Philadelphia Flyers, and I shun New Jersey Devils fans. A person who admires Barack Obama and a person who despises him have chosen conflicting essences, and will tend not to relate well with each other.

Humans feel threatened when they meet people who have chosen essences radically different from the ones they have chosen. Thus, they begin to engage in the process that existentialists call "leveling." In numerous ways, humans attempt to "level down" people who do not live according to what they see as essential. There are many ways to level down others, and there are many kinds of leveling. In extreme cases, violence is used to rid the world of those who are "different." The gun has often been called "the great equalizer." People will group together into what Friedrich Nietzsche called "the herd," and Søren Kierkegaard called "the crowd," and such groups will try numerous means — some nice, and some not-so-nice — to "correct" a person who is not a member of their group.

Some people choose to see themselves as the center of the universe. In *Now, Voyager*, a mother destroys the individuality of her daughter. She has "leveled down" someone whom she should be "raising up."

When someone levels down another person, they are treating that person as a *thing*. The daughter in the movie is asked if she is "one of the Vales of Boston." She answers, "One of the lesser ones." She has been reduced to thinking of herself as less important than other members of her family. She sees herself as a poor example of humanity.

Another theme stressed by the existentialist is that individuals should rebel against the forces that attempt to level them. They should fight to regain the dignity of being able to stand on their own two feet, choose their own essence, and live a life not controlled by the levelers. *Now, Voyager* captures that theme also.

Watch the movie.

Questions to ponder:

1. Charlotte (Bette Davis) is called by her mother (Gladys Cooper) "my ugly duckling." What chance does a child have of becoming a well-

balanced adult if that child has a parent like Charlotte's mother? The mother is told by Dr. Jaquith (Claude Rains) that if she "had deliberately and maliciously planned to destroy (her) daughter's life, (she) couldn't have done it more completely." She responds that she was merely exercising "a mother's rights." What "rights" do parents have over their children? What rights do children have? Dr. Jaquith says, "a person has rights — to discover her own mistakes, to make her own way, to grow and blossom in her own particular soil." Too many parents prohibit their children from developing their own distinct personalities. Charlotte, the victim of her controlling mother, puts it this way: "Dr. Jaquith says that tyranny is sometimes an expression of maternal instinct. If that's a mother's love, I want no part of it."

2. Given the fact that Charlotte can't have Jerry (Paul Henreid) but she loves him and he loves her, should she marry Elliot Livingston (John Loder)? If she doesn't marry soon, Charlotte thinks she will never have a man or a child of her own.

Movies 3 and 4: *Before Sunrise* and *Before Sunset*

Director: Richard Linklater; 1 hour, 45 minutes (1995) / 1 hour, 20 minutes (2004)

Warning: Some strong language

My Dinner with Andre is a film basically of a dinner conversation between Andre and his friend Wally. Andre is a successful playwright who wrestles with the question of whether or not there is any meaning to existence. Wally thinks if he had all Andre has, he would be happy. Memorable lines abound in the film. *Before Sunrise* contains the ruminations of two people who meet for one day in Europe, fall in love, and then go their separate ways. Nine years later, as captured in *Before Sunset,* they meet again and rekindle their relationship. Some of what they say in their philosophizing may turn viewers off, but many of the questions they raise and comments they make are extremely thought-provoking.

The Up Series (movie 13) follows the lives of real people by interviewing them every seven years. *Before Sunrise* and *Before Sunset* have captured something comparable to that offered by *The Up Series,* but with fictional people. Director Richard Linklater originally considered doing three to five films which would, as he says in an extra to the DVD of *Before Sunset,* constitute "a giant document on love and on relationships, following

Julie Delpy as Celine and Ethan Hawke as Jesse, two people who meet each other, philosophize, and fall in love in *Before Sunrise* (1995).

two actors on the course of their life." It is interesting that he uses the word "actors" and not "characters." These two films focus on two characters, Jesse and Celine, as well as the two actors who play them, Ethan Hawke and Julie Delpy. We will have to wait to see if Linklater does indeed come back with a third film on Jesse and Celine.

My "Questions to Ponder" for the two films will generally be questions brought up by Jesse and Celine.

Watch *Before Sunrise.*

Questions to ponder:

1. Traveling on a train to her home in Paris, Celine is trying to read. A loud, obnoxious, German couple forces Celine to seek a quieter section of the train. Clearly, she is verifying something Friedrich Nietzsche once wrote: "Noise destroys thought." She sits opposite Jesse, and they strike up a conversation. One of the first things Jesse says is that "as couples get older, they lose the ability to hear each other." Though his remark is a generalization, he is probably right about a large number of relationships. Why do you think lots of couples "lose the ability to hear each other"?

2. Jesse says that a dog "sleeping in the sun is so beautiful, but a guy standing at a bank machine — trying to take some money out — looks like a complete moron." Do you agree with Jesse? If so, why is the dog more beautiful than the guy?

3. Jesse has an idea for a movie made up of 365 episodes. Each day a different person from a different country would be filmed. If those persons do not know they are being filmed, it seems Jesse is correct — it would be tremendously interesting to watch. If they know they are being filmed, then they would put on a show that would not reveal the real person. Disregarding any moral issues connected to filming people without their permissions, do you think that such a series would be interesting? (For a fictionalized approximation of Jesse's idea, see *The Truman Show — Plato and Popcorn*, pages 72–74 — in which one person's life is filmed from birth on. As Truman becomes aware that his every move is being tracked by cameras, he seeks to find a way to break free.)

4. I think many people believe they are in love, but do not really know what love is. Jesse says, "I have told somebody that I loved them before, and I meant it. Was it totally an unselfish, giving love? Was it a beautiful thing? Not really." Do you think that most people who believe they are in love are really mistaking their own selfish feelings for love?

5. Jesse asks Celine to tell him what really "pisses" her off. What really pisses you off? I have a long list: tailgaters, people who talk in movie theatres, endless TV commercials, foul-mouthed people, and people who lick their fingers while eating. I once was a finalist for a college teaching position in California. The members of the Philosophy Department wanted me, and assured me that I was going to get the job. My final interview was with the president of the college. He floored me with one of his first questions: "What really pisses you off?" I wanted to appear like a rational person who is always in control, so I answered: "Nothing." That was the wrong answer. The president knew it was a lie, and I did not get the job.

In *The Color Purple* (*Plato and Popcorn*, pages 78–80) the question is raised, "What would piss God off?" The answer: God would be pissed off if you walked by a field of purple flowers and did not notice the color purple. I often think of that quote when I catch myself taking nature for granted.

6. Jesse brings up a puzzle: Given the population explosion, where

do all the souls of people come from? David Hume discusses a similar problem of where all the souls of dead people go:

> How to dispose of the infinite number of posthumous existences ought ... to embarrass the religious theory ... when it is asked whether Agamemnon, Therites, Hannibal, Nero and every stupid clown that ever existed in Italy, Scythia, Bactria or Guinea, are now alive, can any man think that a scrutiny of nature will furnish arguments strong enough to answer so strange a question in the affirmative?[1]

I personally cannot make any sense of the word "soul," except in sentences like "James Brown had soul." I don't know what the heck my soul is supposed to be. I happen to think that people who use the word "soul" have no content to the idea. They feel good when they hear soul-talk. However, assuming there is such a thing called a soul and that every person has one, are there conceptual problems about where all the souls come from and where they all go? Do animals have souls? If a soul leaves a body at death, how can Soul A be distinguished from Soul B? Various Medieval thinkers held that — because it is the body that individuates and the body is left behind at death — there must be a *spiritual* body connected with the soul after death. That way you can tell who the soul is. Does all this talk about souls make sense to you? (For more on arguments concerning life after death, see movie 81: *After Life*.)

7. Celine asks Jesse, "Do you know anyone who is in a happy relationship?" Jesse answers, "Yeah, but I think they lie to each other." Is Jesse correct that there are happy relationships, but that those relationships depend on lies? Do you know anyone who is in a happy relationship?

8. Celine says: "If there is any kind of God it wouldn't be in any of us, but just this little space in between [you and me]." She is expressing an idea that is central to Martin Buber's (1878–1965) view of the nature of God. For Buber, God is present wherever love or authentic relationships exist. God is present because God is love. God is relation. Buber was influenced by Friedrich Nietzsche's proclamation that "God is dead." However, for Buber, God does not die. At certain times when love is not present and hatred reigns, there is an "eclipse of God." At such times, it feels like God is dead. Is such a view about the nature of God meaningful to you?

9. Jesse asserts that people get "sick to death" being around themselves all the time. Do you agree? Celine agrees that such is the case except

when a person is in love. Do we think better of ourselves when we are in love?

Watch *Before Sunset*.

Questions to ponder.

1. Jesse says that "happiness is the doing, not in the getting, what you want." Do you agree with Jesse?

2. Jesse and Celine get into a debate about happiness. The debate centers on a basic Buddhist idea that suffering is eliminated if desire is eliminated. This Buddhist idea will be of central importance in *Spring, Summer, Fall, Winter ... and Spring* (movie 75.) Jesse asks whether we would be happy "if we ceased to want things." He says, "Liberate yourself from desire, and you'll find you have everything you need." Celine, on the other hand, sees nothing wrong with desire. For her, desiring — whether you desire "intimacy with another" or "a new pair of shoes" — provides the spice of life. Do you think that desire is something unhealthy? Or is it the case that only *some* desires are unhealthy?

3. In reading a diary entry written years earlier, Celine realizes she has basically been the same person at the "core," from when she wrote the entry to the present. Jesse agrees that people generally do not change: "We have these innate set points, you know, and not much that happens to us changes disposition." In what way has your character remained constant over the years? Have there been any major changes in your character?

4. Jesse asks Celine if she believes in: (a) ghosts, (b) reincarnation, (c) God, and (d) astrology. She says "no" for a, b, and c. She seems to say she believes in d when she says "that makes sense" but quickly says "no" to d also. Do you believe in a, b, c or d? In teaching Philosophy courses, I spend some time criticizing a, b, c, and d above. For example, many people seem pleased with their belief that God sees everything they do, every record of their lives. I find such an idea obscene. Whether it is "Big Brother" or a God watching over every move, a cosmic Peeping Tom seems beneath the dignity of an admirable supreme being.

Students in one of my Philosophy and Film sections spotted a possible inconsistency in my criticism of the idea of an all-seeing God. "What about Santa Claus?" they asked. Do I think it is good to program children to believe that Santa Claus sees everything they do? He will bring presents to good little boys and girls. Wouldn't it be disturbing to children to think that a bearded man in a red suit, who goes "Ho, Ho, Ho," sees everything they do? In recent years, my mother has come to believe it is immoral to tell children there is a Santa Claus, because "it is a lie." Shouldn't I be anti–Santa Claus? No. Perhaps it isn't that Santa Claus *sees* everything children do, but he knows if they have been bad or good. Maybe Mommy and Daddy tell him.

Many students in my classes announce that they fervently believe in things a philosopher would question. One student was an avid believer that Nostradamus could predict the future. I decided to use the "Socratic Method" in order to prove the student did not really have knowledge she claimed to have. If Socrates (469–399 B.C.) met someone who claimed to know x, but clearly didn't, he would not merely point out that the person did not really know x. People tend to be too bull-headed to accept criticism, even if the criticism is right on target. Socrates would give praise, saying how he was impressed with the person's wisdom. He put the individual on a pedestal, causing the person to beam at the fact that the great Socrates spotted his wisdom. Then — usually through questioning that would lead the person to a state of confusion — Socrates would pull the pedestal out from under him. Two possibilities then arose: either Socrates' opponent would stump off in anger at the trick played on him by Socrates, or would realize he did not possess the knowledge he thought he had. In the latter case, the person now was ready to seek true knowledge and wisdom — which was Socrates' goal.

I decided to play along with the student who admired Nostradamus. I brought to class a book of Nostradamus' prophesies, and praised the student for being so wise as to spot that wise man's special gift. I proceeded to read some of the prophesies, all of which are very vague in meaning. Words like "a bright flash from the East," predict the bombing of Hiroshima. "A leader cut down in his youth" refers to the assassination of John F. Kennedy. The Nostradamus fan was beaming, and several other students started to show signs of being impressed with Nostradamus. I continued to read a nonsense prophecy *I* had written, but said it was from the hand of Nostradamus. The fan continued to beam, and more and more students now started to approve of Nostradamus' accomplishment. I then told the truth about the last "prophecy." The point I had shown the students, particularly the fan, was that they *wanted* to believe Nostradamus could predict the future. They didn't know he could, because they were inspired by a nonsense prophecy they mistakenly thought he had written.

Another student once shared her belief that she could travel through space without taking as much time as the laws of nature would dictate she would have to take. She had read some Eastern mystical book that taught her how to place herself in a certain conscious state so, for example, she could walk at a normal pace a distance of one mile, but it would only take her approximately three minutes. I asked her if I could walk with her, and time her. She said, "No, the book doesn't allow that." Any suggestion used to test her claim was rejected as going against the book's rules. She was using the public notion of clock-time in her claim, and yet the public was not permitted to test her claim. There is no reason to believe she could do what she claimed.

I have had numbers of students who believe that the earth is being visited by aliens, but really have *no* evidence that such is the case. *I* have seen two UFOs, and I don't believe in them! One night in 1967, I saw a bright white light in the sky. A blue streak appeared on the right side of the white light, and a red streak appeared on the left side. Whatever it was, it lasted only for about 4 seconds. I asked people all around me if they had seen it. Nope. I called an employee of the local radio station, and asked if there were any reports of something strange in the sky. Nope. But the person I spoke with said it sounded like a good story. I should call back in about ten minutes, because he wanted to check something out. When I called back, here is what I was told: "I checked with an astronomer at a local college. The astronomer said, 'There are more UFO reports this time of year, because the North Star is at a certain elevation in the sky and light coming to earth from it does strange things. People think they are seeing a UFO.'" I had a problem with that theory! I was currently taking a course in astronomy, and I could point directly to the North Star. It wasn't near the part of the sky from which the strange white light appeared. The rest of the story? By the next morning, thousands of people from New York City to Baltimore reported seeing something strange in the sky. Many, however, described what they saw as a spaceship. I'm fairly sure I saw some strange atmospheric disturbance — and that's it!

My second UFO experience provides a strong explanation for sensationalized accounts given after people see something strange. I was one of twelve students on a field trip in Florida, accompanied by three professors. One day there was a perfectly clear bright blue sky, cloudless, except for the presence of one small cloud. We watched as white puffs broke away from the cloud. We all agreed that what we saw was strange, but we also agreed it was probably merely a cloud with condensation occurring next to it. Hours later, two of the professors and a majority of the students changed their story. According to them, we had seen a UFO! (I'm still convinced we had seen an UFC — an unidentified flying cloud.)

The latter UFO experience verifies a judgment made by David Hume. In the quote, Hume is referring to why people tend to believe in miracles. What he writes can also provide a reason for why people believe in all kinds of improbable fantastic things. "The passion of *surprise* and *wonder*, arising from miracles, being an agreeable emotion, gives a sensible tendency towards the belief of those events, from which it is derived. And they go so far, that even those who cannot enjoy this pleasure immediately ... love to partake of the satisfaction at second-hand or by rebound, and place a pride and delight in exciting the admiration of others."[2]

So, as you can tell from my comments above, I am not a believer in such things as ghosts, reincarnation, fortune tellers or accounts of UFOs. Do I have *any* strange beliefs a reasonable philosopher may judge to be weird? Yes! I think special auras emanate from places of historical value. (I don't like the word "aura," but it is the best I can do.) The battlefields of Gettysburg and Waterloo, Dealey Plaza in Dallas, Pearl Harbor, the site of the World Trade Center in New York City, Monticello and Stonehenge are examples of places that leave me in awe. Sites at which scenes from good movies were filmed, or sites referred to in great literary works, possess an almost supernatural flavor to me. The house in Georgetown where *The Exorcist* (1973) was filmed is not an ordinary house. I have visited real landmarks in southwestern England used by Thomas Hardy in his novels. I saw the field where Tess of the D'Urbervilles danced, and the church yard where she buried her child. At any moment I expected Tess to appear. Certain real places bring fictional characters to life. There is another sense in which places possess a type of sacred aura, and *Before Sunrise* and *Before Sunset* capture that sense perfectly. At the end of *Before Sunrise,* after Celine leaves on the train, the camera shows many of the places she and Jesse have visited. The cemetery, a bench, a narrow walkway between buildings — these are no longer "ordinary" places. At the beginning of *Before Sunset* Linklater shows places the two lovers will visit in the course of the film. It is as if they are special places *waiting* for Jesse and Celine to show up!

Okay, so I have weird ideas also! But ghosts, reincarnation, prophecies and UFOs are not my bag of tea!

Movie 5: *You Can Count on Me*

Director: Kenneth Lonergan; 1 hour, 51 minutes; 2000
Watch the movie.

Questions to ponder:

1. Meursault, the main character in Albert Camus' (1913–1960) novel *The Stranger* wanders through a life that is absurd. Nothing has any deep meaning to him; everything seems empty. He is an "outsider;" he doesn't fit into any group. Near the end of the novel, a priest tries to lead Meursault to God, in order that he can find peace before he is executed. In *You Can Count on Me,* Terry (Mark Ruffalo), possesses many of the characteristics of Meursault. His sister, Sammy (Laura Linney), even calls in her preacher (played by the director of the film, Kenneth Lonergan) to try to turn Terry away from his erratic behavior and aimless wandering. Any outsider would tend to give the response Terry gives to Sammy: "I find it kinda discouraging that you seem to think I'm in need of some spiritual guidance ... I find it kinda insulting." Do you think Terry has good reason to be insulted? The preacher says, "It is [your sister's] opinion that you are not going to find what you are looking for, the way you are looking for it." Is Terry really looking for anything? Should he be? The preacher goes on to tell Terry that Sammy is helping him by being a role model and by living a good life. Terry smiles, knowing that his sister has many flaws. She is even having an affair with her boss (Matthew Broderick) whose wife is pregnant. Is Sammy a good role model for Terry? The preacher says something, which is intended to criticize Terry's beliefs. Terry responds: "I don't feel like a negligible little scrap floating around in some kind of empty void with no sense of connectedness to anything around me." At the end of *The Stranger*, Meursault, while walking to his own execution, is filled with a love of life even though that life is absurd, and even though the universe is indifferent towards him. In spite of Terry's awareness of the absurdity of all things, does he love life?

2. In one of the DVD extras, Mark Ruffalo says that the early loss of his parents had led Terry to judge that everything is meaningless. The effects of the early exit of their parents from their lives seem to be pres-

Laura Linney (as Samantha "Sammy" Prescott) and Mark Ruffalo (as Terry Prescott) as siblings who struggle with a disaster from the past in *You Can Count on Me* (2000).

ent at every moment in Terry and Sammy's lives. Can you spot instances in the film where those effects show themselves?

3. Describe Terry's relationship with Rudy (Rory Culkin). Why does Terry show up to take him fishing? Why does he take him to meet his jerk of a father, Rudy, Sr. (Josh Lucas)?

4. Several viewers commented on IMDb (Internet Movie Database) that Sammy's affair with her boss does not make sense. Early in the film, she clearly shows disgust at his absurd managing style. Can you make any sense about why she has an affair with him?

5. The first time I viewed *You Can Count on Me*, I saw a tragic film dealing with a brother and sister trying to cope with the loss of their parents. Subsequently, I discovered the film was intended to be a drama *and* a comedy. I saw that comedy during my second viewing, and thought many lines were very funny. A lot of humor can be found in Terry's reaction to things being said. Did you spot comedic elements? (Much of it is tragic-comedy. The response is like if you hit your crazy bone. You don't know whether to laugh or cry, and end up doing both.)

Movie 6: *Kinsey*

Director: Bill Condon; 1 hour, 58 minutes; 2004
Warning: Sex, sex, sex.
Watch the movie *and*—very important—watch to the end of the closing credits!

Questions to ponder:

1. I am not an advocate for promiscuity, but it is clear to me that many Americans are sexually inhibited, and are even unable to talk about sex. I have good friends in Denmark and Germany who love America, but are astounded by our attitudes about sex. They couldn't believe President Bill Clinton was in political trouble because of his tryst with Monica Lewinsky. Some years ago, I walked on a Danish beach with my friend, Erik. Up ahead I saw a bunch of swimmers in flesh-colored bathing suits. Whoops! As I got closer, I realized it was flesh — period. People can legally swim naked in Denmark. Imagine the uproar if suddenly a group of people were to show up and shed their clothing at an American beach. I have a photograph from early in the twentieth century showing a woman being arrested by a clearly disgusted policeman. A group of people looking like

Alfred Kinsey (Liam Neeson) investigates the sexual life of Americans.

a lynch mob is nearby. Why was the woman being arrested? She was illegally wearing one of the first bathing suits that showed her knees! As a good American, I gawked at the nudism on the Danish beach. My tongue was probably hanging out. In no time at all, however, the naked swimmers ceased to interest me.

Another year, I took my daughter to Spain, where almost half the women go topless on the beaches. Once again, my interest in those breasts quickly died. They ceased to be sexually provocative. (I do think beer-bellies are obscene and should be illegal.)

I'm not at all into nude bathing. However, why do so many Americans care so much about such things? *Kinsey* addresses this question fairly well. As children, many of us are lied to about sex. I was told by my mother that babies are delivered by the "stork." I don't think I really believed that explanation. *Why* was I told such a thing? Some years later, my mother informed me that people who masturbate will go blind. (When I teach a course entitled "Philosophies of Love and Sexuality" I tell my students what I was told about masturbation, and proceed to walk into a wall.) How were you introduced to topics of sexual import?

2. In the film, Kinsey (Liam Neeson), thinks that it is better to be informed about other people's sexual behavior than to be ignorant of it. Do you think it is important to have such knowledge? Why? Can some of that knowledge be dangerous, because we might erroneously be led to engage in perverse, harmful acts? Do we think that because other people do x, x must be all right? When Kinsey's older daughter says she may have intercourse with her boyfriend in a few years, his younger daughter says, "If [she] can have intercourse, I should be able to." What answer should be given to her?

3. Kinsey tells his wife, "Mac" (Laura Linney), about his sexual activities with Martin (Peter Sarsgaard). She is tremendously hurt. She asks Kinsey, "Did you ever stop to think that perhaps ... restraints are there to keep people from hurting each other?" Would it follow from what Mac said that no sexual acts are, in themselves, immoral? Is the fact that some sex acts hurt the non-participants what makes those acts immoral? Kinsey responds that the love he feels for Mac is much more important than the sexual experience he had with Martin. At that time, Mac disagrees, but later changes her mind once she enters into a sexual relationship with Martin. At that point, the view held by both Kinsey and Mac about multiple sexual relationships is like that contained in the following quote from an essay entitled "In Defense of Promiscuity" by Frederick Elliston.

Sex and eating are frequently compared, since both are appetites whose satisfaction is socially regulated. Consider a society where the following etiquette is operative. Each man is allowed to dine with only one woman. Before their first meal begins, each receives a solemn injunction: "thou shalt dine with none other so long as you both shall live." Their partnership is exclusive; no one may be invited to the meal ("three is a crowd"). Only the utensils already provided and accepted by others may be used; bringing a new gadget to the meal is an innovation attempted by many, though (curiously) condemned by all. Throughout the remaining meals the menu is fixed on the grounds that meat and potatoes are the most nourishing foods. The ways in which these meals are prepared and consumed is subject to strict regulation: one is not supposed to touch the food with one's hands; everyone must keep an upright position (it is considered an insult for one to stand while the other lies). Interaction is drastically curtailed: one is not allowed to exchange dishes; one must feed only oneself (for a man to place his spoon in his partner's mouth is a mortal sin). These rules prescribe that each person gratify his own appetite, but in the company of a select other (to eat alone is forbidden, though many do). During the meal a typical conversation consists of compliments — how good the meal is and how agreeable the company — regardless of their truthfulness.

If food and sex were only the satisfaction of appetites, these restrictions might be defensible — though the prohibitions against some changes would still be contentious. However, some innovations, at least for some people, not only could enhance the efficiency of such practices, but could add to their *meaning* as well. To "dine" with several different people can make eating not only more pleasant, but more enlightening too. To vary the "menu" is a safeguard against boredom that not only expands the topic of conversation, but also has nutritional value. To invite a guest similarly intensifies the conversation, which need not dissolve into monologues if considerateness is shown by all. People should be allowed to get their fingers sticky (sex is wet) and to eat alone (masturbation makes neither your eyesight grow dim nor your hair to fall out). Sometimes it may be more convenient to eat standing up or lying down: the exceptions of one society may elsewhere be the rule. More interaction can make the experience more significant; for example, switching dishes when the desires are different (to the dismay of many, they frequently only *look* different) provides variety, that after all, is "the spice of life."[1]

Do you think that the analogy between having sex with multiple partners and eating with various people is a good one? Why or why not?

Later in the film, Martin sees what can happen when his wife has an affair with another of Kinsey's workers, Gebhard (Timothy Hutton). Sex, Martin now sees, is not just "harmless fun," it's "the whole thing and, if you're not careful, it will cut you wide open." What does Martin mean about sex being "the whole thing"? Is he right?

Movie 7: *The Visitor*

Director: Tom McCarthy; 1 hour, 44 minutes; 2008
Watch the movie.

Questions to ponder:

1. Professor Walter Vale (Richard Jenkins) is aware that his life is empty, but can not find a way out of his emptiness. His wife has died; his occupation is unfulfilling. (I like the word "fulfilling." A person seeks to be "fully filled" as life progresses.) Piano lessons lead him nowhere. Too many people can't figure out what direction they should take in their lives. Sometimes, whole lives are lived and no fulfillment of any kind is achieved. People get into occupations that trap them. Benefits accrue and seniority is obtained, and the person fears to leave that occupation in order to seek a more rewarding career. How does a person find the path that leads to personal and professional fulfillment? Walter discovers that the beat of drums

Walter (left, played by Richard Jenkins), depressed and alone, makes an unlikely friend (Hazz Sleiman, to the right of Walter) in *The Visitor* (2008).

inspires him. Have you found anything that fulfills you to the degree that drumming inspires Walter? If not, does that mean you are living a life that lacks fulfillment? Walter also finds a "soul mate" in the unlikeliest of persons — an illegal immigrant named Tarek (Haaz Sleiman). A common stereotype of the illegal immigrant is that of a lawless person more in love with his or her own homeland than with America. Who more completely fits the ideal of what an American should be — the stereotypical American, who sits in a Lazy Boy, watches Monday Night Football, drinks beer, breaks several of the Ten Commandments, but goes faithfully to church each Sunday, and feels superior to non–Americans; or Tarek — a dynamic, peaceful illegal immigrant who helps Walter find meaning in his life? Do the former really have the right to be prejudiced against the latter?

2. *The Visitor* attempts to capture the fear of illegal immigrants felt by many Americans in the post–9/11 world. It is also true that in Los Angeles, and in other parts of the country, a huge number of crimes are committed by illegal immigrants and, thus, many feel such fear is justified. Should we be more tolerant of illegal immigrants such as Tarek and Zainab (Danai Jekesai Gurira) than of those who break other laws?

LATIN AMERICA

Movie 8: *Canoa*

Director: Felipe Cazals; 2 hours, 0 minutes; 1975
Watch the movie.

Questions to ponder:

1. *Canoa* tells the story of the lynching of four students of the University of Puebla. The students were visiting the town of San Miguel Canoa to climb a nearby mountain. Three died; one survived. The following are some of the factors that seem to have played a role in leading the townspeople to engage in such a horrible act:

   a. The students were "outsiders."
   b. The priest (Enrique Lucero) seems to be a character similar to the American Jim Jones, who formed the "People's Temple," a cult that settled in Georgetown, Guyana. Both the priest and Jim Jones controlled every facet of the lives of the people they led. In 1978, Jones organized the mass suicide of 909 Temple members. Jones' atrocious act was precipitated by the arrival of American Congressman, Leo Ryan, who was investigating Jones' activities. The priest felt threatened by incursions by "suspicious" visitors from Puebla, who might be investigating his abuse of power.
   c. Unrest by leftists in Puebla and other parts of Mexico seemed to threaten the traditional political beliefs of the citizens of Canoa. In addition, the "modern" city of Puebla, located only 7½ miles from Canoa, was viewed as a danger to the "old ways."

What other factors may have led the townspeople to do what they did? Have you ever sensed distrust of "outsiders" by any of your neighbors, or by anyone at places you have visited? Have you ever sensed that some local political leader was attempting to exert control over people beyond what was reasonable? Is there any conflict you can spot in your personal life between what you see as traditional values and "the modern way to view things"? Do some of the incidents that occurred to Muslims in America after 9/11 appear to you to be motivated by factors similar to those listed above?

ADDITIONAL RECOMMENDED DOCUDRAMAS

Canoa is a "docudrama" — a film utilizing actors to portray real people and real events, as if a camera had been actually filming those events. The following are some very realistic, powerful docudramas:

Culloden (1964). The recreation of the 1745 battle during the Jacobite Uprising. Most Jacobites were Highland Scots. Directed by Peter Watkins, whose *The War Game* (1965) depicted what it would be like to experience a nuclear attack.

JFK (1991). Directed by Oliver Stone. Jim Garrison (Kevin Costner) presents the unlikely case that *very many* people were involved in the conspiracy to assassinate John F. Kennedy. If Stone convinces you there was a vast conspiracy, do yourself a favor: read *Reclaiming History: The Assassination of President John F. Kennedy* by Vincent Bugliosi (New York: W.W. Norton, 2007). You should also check out one of the programs on the assassination produced for television by the History Channel.

Ed Wood (1994). Directed by Tim Burton. Ed Wood, played by Johnny Depp, creates trashy B movies like *Plan 9 from Outer Space, Jail Bait,* and *Bride of the Monster.*

Nixon (1995). Oliver Stone again. Anthony Hopkins does his best Richard Nixon impersonation.

Bloody Sunday (2002) and *Omagh* (2004). Paul Greengrass directs both films. The former about the killing of 27 protestors by British troops in Derry, Ireland in 1972; the latter about a bomb that detonates in an Irish market town, killing many. Paul Greengrass also directed *United 93* (2006), which is a tense, moving account of what happened during the flight of United 93 on 9/11.

Touching the Void (2003). A 1985 mountaineering accident in South America.

Good Night and Good Luck (2005). George Clooney directs and plays the newscaster Edward R. Murrow, who stood up against Senator Joseph McCarthy.

Frost/Nixon (2008). Ron Howard is the director. David Frost (Michael

Sheen) interviews Richard Nixon (Frank Langella) on the topic of Watergate.

Milk (2008). Stunning performance by Sean Penn as Harvey Milk, the famous San Francisco gay rights activist.

Movie 9: *The Official Story*

Director: Luis Puenzo; 1 hour, 52 minutes; 1985

My guess is that Argentina's "Dirty War" (1976–1983) is one of many horrible atrocities that dot the landscape of recent history, and that the majority of people today know nothing about. The historical events depicted in the film were certainly a revelation to me. After President Juan Peron died in 1976, his wife Isabel took power in Argentina. (For a fanciful depiction of her time in power, see the 1996 film *Evita*.) A military coup overthrew Isabel Peron's government. A large number of dissidents subsequently protested the military junta. The junta went on an offensive, and an estimated 30,000 Argentineans disappeared. Mass graves have been uncovered, but most of the victims were never accounted for. An interesting and disturbing side note: Publicly, United States officials voiced deep concern over civil rights abuses in Argentina. However, evidence has since been uncovered that members of the highest leadership secretly supported the crackdown on dissidents. Here, for example, is what Henry Kissinger wrote to an Argentinean official in 1976:

> We would like you to succeed ... I have an old-fashioned view that friends ought to be supported. What is not understood in the United States is that you have a civil war. We read about human rights problems but not the context. The quicker you succeed the better [reported in the December 4, 2003, *Miami Herald*].

The military junta collapsed as a result of the British attack to regain the Falkland Islands in 1982.

Watch the movie.

Questions to ponder:

1. Alicia (Norma Aleandro) tells her history class, "By understanding history, we learn to understand the world. No people can survive without memory." Do you agree with those two sentences? Do you agree that those who are ignorant of past mistakes are doomed to make those same mistakes again?

Alicia (Norma Aleandro) reacts to discovering that her husband's (Hector Alterio) official story is filled with lies in *The Official Story* (Argentina, 1985).

In every culture — it seems to me — the "official history" tends to contain false interpretations of important events. Take as an example the accepted view of the moral worth of the defenders of the Alamo. If you read high school history texts in the United States, or watch Walt Disney's *Davy Crockett at the Alamo* (1955), or John Wayne's *The Alamo* (1960), you will be stunned by the admirable qualities of William Travis, Jim Bowie and Davy Crockett. These men are presented as almost Christ-like figures. What you won't be told is that Jim Bowie had been deeply involved in a brutal and *illegal* slave trade operation in Louisiana. You won't read about a journal entry from 1833 by William Travis: "I fucked the fifty-sixth woman in my life."[1] *The Alamo* (2004) is the most historically correct film account of the events at the Alamo. The quote from Henry Kissinger above, the facts about some Alamo defenders, and Alicia's becoming aware that her own historical judgments were tainted should lead everyone to deeply question what they are told by teachers or leaders. A mature thinker will dig for the facts of a case, and will search out ethnocentric elements that cover up the facts.

2. Roberto (Hector Alterio) was an accomplice to the atrocities committed in the "Dirty War." His own father says, "It's always easier to

believe it's impossible, right? Because if it were possible, it would require complicity. Many people can't believe it, even if they see it." Roberto is not going to criticize the leaders of the Dirty War! He materially benefited from their activities.

In the early parts of the film, was Alicia covering up the truth about the war? Was it only when Ana (Chunchuna Villafañe) tells Alicia what happened to her after Ana's arrest that Alicia realizes the truth?

3. Now that Gaby (Analia Castro) has been loved and cared for by Alicia and Roberto, is the priest (Leal Rey) correct when he said, "God entrusted her to you, Alicia. That is His will. Why do you doubt His infinite wisdom? Do not offend the Lord. Do not reject what was given to you." Is the priest being dishonorable when he says this to Alicia? After all, he was with Roberto the day Roberto received Gaby. Regardless of the religious interpretation by the priest, is it the case that after years of caring for Gaby it is best for the past not to be brought up? Of course, Roberto's father is disgusted with his son. "It's not a shame to be poor ... just as it is not an honor to be rich." About whether it is better to be rich or poor, he says it "depends on what you had to do to get there ... and what you're willing to go on doing." The most important question seems to be: what would be best for Gaby, now that Alicia knows the truth?

Movie 10: *Amores Perros*

Director: Alejandro González Iñárritu; 2 hours, 34 minutes; 2000
Warning: Dog fighting; violence; sex
Watch the movie.

Questions to ponder:

1. *Amores Perros* involves three interlapping stories. Which of the three do you find most appealing? The crucial event that links all three stories is the car accident that occurs because Octavio (Gael García Bernal) seeks to get away from his pursuers. Valeria (Goya Toledo), the model, is seriously injured in the accident, and El Chivo (Emilio Echevarría) saves Octavio's dog.

2. Does Octavio come across as a mature person who authentically loves his brother's wife, Susana (Vanessa Bauche), or does he seem like an immature, naïve, unrealistic person? Given the extreme nastiness of her

Octavio's (Gael García Bernal) dog provides a link between the stories of three people in *Amores Perros* (2000).

husband, Ramiro (Marco Perez), should Susana have left town with Octavio?

3. Daniel (Alvaro Guerrero) leaves his wife for Valeria. After the car accident destroys Valeria's modeling career, and after traumatic events such as having the dog, Richie, get lost under the floor, Daniel calls his wife on the telephone, but does not speak to her. Is he tempted to reconnect with his wife because Valeria's personality has changed? Is it sexual attraction that leads him to live with Valeria, or does he truly love her? Does he still love his wife?

4. In the past, El Chivo left his wife and daughter to become a guerrilla. Eventually, he evolved into being a tramp and cold-blooded killer. As his story unfolds, however, he undergoes a character change. What factors led to that change?

5. Translated, *Amores Perros* means "Love's a Bitch." I take that to mean love contains many tragic, painful elements. Octavio loves his sister-in-law, and tries to convince her to leave with him. The concept that "love is a bitch" is shown on Octavio's face, as Valeria fails to show up at the bus station. What other instances of love being a "bitch" show up in the film?

Movie 11: *City of God*

Director: Fernando Meirelles / Kátia Lund; 2 hours, 10 minutes; 2002
Warning: Extreme violence.
Watch the movie.

Questions to ponder:

1. Many viewers have posted comments on IMDb about *City of God*, noting that Li'l Dice (Douglas Silva) may be the nastiest movie villain of all time. One person picks Alex from A *Clockwork Orange* for that honor (see movie 15). Another claims that Javier Bardem's character in *No Country for Old Men* (2007) wins hands down. Hannibal Lecter of *Silence of the Lambs* (1991) is also in the running. Heath Ledger's "Joker" in *The Dark Knight* (2008) can't be ignored. What character would you label "the worst villain" of any film you've seen?

2. There is an inevitable comparison to be drawn between the portrayal of slums in *Slumdog Millionaire* (movie 71) and in *City of God*. Which portrayal seems more realistic to you? Which film, in your judgment, contains a better plot? *City of God* jumps around from one character to another. Is *City of God* as focused as *Slumdog Millionaire*?

3. Both *City of God* and *Slumdog Millionaire* show the immensity of two of the world's largest slums. Millions of people are trapped in a world of total poverty. Do you see *any* reasonable hope that slums like those captured in these films will ever disappear? Are some people fated to be "fortunate," and others doomed to be destitute?

Movie 12: *The Motorcycle Diaries*

Director: Walter Salles; 2 hours, 6 minutes; 2004
Watch the movie.

Questions to ponder:

1. *The Motorcycle Diaries* presents a re-creation of a road trip through South America, undertaken by friends Ernesto Guevara (Gael Garcia Bernal) and Alberto Granado (Rodrigo de la Serna). Many of the sites filmed are the sites visited by Ernesto and Alberto. Ernesto later becomes the infamous "Che Guevara." Ernesto is presented as a person who merits reverence. Is that portrayal accurate? Check viewer comments posted

on IMDb. I have not found any other film to bring forth as many comments as those for this film. There are tons of admirers of Che, but even more that see him as being extremely evil. Many note that those who wear Che tee shirts have no idea what the real man was like. After Castro drove out Batista's government in Cuba, with little or no due process, Che ordered countless executions. Che personally executed several people. (Others say it is unfair to judge Che's actions if one does not equally judge the executions committed under Batista.) Che was dedicated to taking land and goods from the wealthy, and dividing them among the poor. Do you think *The Motorcycle Diaries* presents a biased view of Ernesto's character? The only indication that there is a darker side to Ernesto appears when he states that a revolution without guns is doomed to failure. (Does the American civil rights movement disprove that opinion?)

When I view a movie like *Motorcycle Diaries,* a question I repeatedly ask myself is: because I live in a capitalized society, have I become blinded to numerous, widespread, terrible injustices caused by capitalism? Are people like Che admirable, because they are rebelling against these forces

Rodrigo de la Serna (as Alberto Granado), left, and Gael García Bernal (as Ernesto Guevara) in *The Motorcycle Diaries* (2004). Two young men travel throughout South America. One of them will become the famous revolutionary Che.

of injustice? Has Che become revered by many people because of his (apparently) appealing appearance, and because of his adventurous life? Do some people tend to glorify certain historical persons without really knowing much about them? Do others often debunk historical persons without good reason?

2. The scene in which Che truthfully tells the doctor of the leper colony that the doctor's book is trite and poorly written indicates a dilemma all of us face from time to time. A friend, or loved one, asks for our truthful opinion about some personal matter. The truth would hurt, and perhaps the relationship would be damaged. Is a lie in such cases justified? Should the truth be told, regardless of the consequences?

3. Ernesto contemplates the accomplishments of the Incas while he gazes at the ruins of Machu Picchu, Peru. Because the Spanish have access to gunpowder, the Incas are destroyed, and cities such as Lima replace more natural population centers like Machu Picchu. Is Ernesto correct to be disgusted with the downfall of native populations at the hands of European invaders and, more recently, with the projects of powerful capitalists? Do you think the town, city, or countryside in which you reside has gone downhill from what it was in the past? If so, what are the factors leading to that downturn?

ADDITIONAL RECOMMENDED FILMS
FROM LATIN AMERICA

The Exterminating Angel (Mexico, 1962). Directed by the great Luis Buñuel. See also his *Los Olvidados* (1958) and *Simon of the Desert* (1965), as well as his French productions *Belle de Jour* (1967), *The Discreet Charm of the Bourgeoisie* (1972) and *That Obscure Object of Desire* (1977).

Memories of Underdevelopment (Cuba, 1968)

El Mariachi (Mexico, 1992)

Like Water for Chocolate (Mexico, 1992)

Y Tu Mamá También (Mexico, 2002)

The Year My Parents Went on Vacation (Brazil, 2006)

Great Britain and Ireland

Movie 13: *The Up Series*

Director: Michael Apted; 11 hours, 50 minutes; 2006

In 1964, cameras were turned on a group of seven-year-olds in England. Various scenes are captured from their everyday lives, and each child answers a series of questions. Every seven years, Michael Apted, the director, returns to check out how the lives of these people have gone. Eventually, a few refuse to continue to participate but most are followed to the age of 49. The result of Apted's project is unforgettable. You will find yourself laughing, sighing, gasping, and at times you will be saddened, but you will quickly become aware you are viewing one of the true miracles of film making.

Watch the entire series:

Questions to ponder:

1. The thesis of the series is expressed as "Give me a child until he is seven, and I will give you the man." It seems more exact to say that the thesis is: "Show me what a child is like at seven, and you will know what the adult will be like." Does the series verify that thesis? Do any of the twenty people followed swerve from the character they seemed destined to be?

2. In *7 Up*, the director shows that some of the children are exposed to strict discipline, while others have much more freedom. He states that "the distinction between freedom and discipline is the key to their whole future." Does the series tend to verify Apted's position? Do the children who were more disciplined turn out to be better citizens as they age, as compared to the ones exposed to more freedom?

3. In *21 Up*, Nicholas says, "It's just the limitations of such things as what the audience requires and the time, don't allow [the series] to be a real study. Maybe if we accept this — ok. I think it's probably good

entertainment.... People tend to read significance into it, that I don't think exists." Is Nicholas missing the significance of the series? What is the significance? If there is little significance, doesn't it follow that the series is merely a soap opera?

4. In *21 Up*, the three upper class friends, Charles, Andrew and John are asked if there is any truth that the series promotes the notion that upper class people who do not have to work for their wealth "have more options than others, and this is undesirable." The friends seem to agree that many people do not have the advantage of those born into wealth, but disagree about whether or not the elimination of the current system would yield better results. John says there is currently a "stability and structure in society" that hinges on there being different classes. For him, the crucial issue is how nobly a person uses the opportunities that are available. Do you agree with John?

5. Some people commented on IMDb that they find the *Up Series* to be depressing. Do you find it to be depressing? Why, or why not? Others feel many of the questions posed to the participants are rude and tasteless. Do you agree?

This is Neil. Was Neil's character set by the time he was seven years old? ***The Up Series*** **traces his life, along with the lives of numerous others his age.**

6. After "following" the lives of these participants from the age of seven to forty-nine, do we really know them?

7. A major philosophical problem involves the nature of personal identity. What is it that — in spite of all the changes that occur — remains constant over all the years of a person's life? How, for example, is *Neil* the same person at age 7 and age 28? What constitutes "Neilness"? That he possesses the same "soul" over all his years? What does the phrase "having the same soul" mean? (I can't see that it means anything.) Is Neil the same person because the cells that make up his body have the same genetic code over all his years? Does his genetic code really get to the essence of "Neilness"? Is what constitutes the essence of a person merely the sum total of experiences a person has, plus additionally the memories of the person's past experiences? David Hume (1711–1776), trying to locate his self wrote:

> When I enter more intimately into what I call *myself*, I always stumble on some particular perception or other, of heat or cold, light or shade, love or hatred, pain or pleasure. I never can catch *myself* at any time without a perception, and never can observe any thing but the perception. When my perceptions are removed for any time, as by sound sleep; so long am I insensible of *myself*, and may truly be said not to exist.[1]

Are *you* aware of something called your "self"?

8. Roger Ebert judges *The Up Series* to be one of the ten greatest films ever made. In his review of two of the episodes he raises several good questions:

> We are fascinated by the personal progressions we see on the screen. We are distracted by wonderment about the mystery of the human personality. If we can see so clearly how these children become these adults — was it just as obvious in our own cases? Do we, even now, contain within us our own destinies for the next seven years? Is change possible? Is the scenario already written? ... How do we become who we are? How is our view of ourselves and our world fashioned?[2]

How would you respond to Ebert's questions?

9. If another episode in the series is made in the future, how do you predict the various participants will have evolved?

Note: Michael Apted's name will always be linked to *The Up Series*. Amazingly, he directed several more traditional films, including two that were box office hits and critical successes: *Coal Miner's Daughter* (1980) and *Gorillas in the Mist* (1988).

Movie 14: *2001: A Space Odyssey*

Director: Stanley Kubrick; 2 hours, 21 minutes; 1968

In 1968, Andrew Sarris wrote the following in a review for *The Village Voice*: "*2001: A Space Odyssey* is a thoroughly uninteresting failure and the most damning demonstration yet of Stanley Kubrick's inability to tell a story coherently, and with a competent point of view." Two years later he changed his judgment: "*2001* is indeed a major work by a major artist."[1]

My initial reaction to *2001* was much the same as Sarris'. In 1968, I chaperoned a group of young people by train from Colorado to Chicago. My goals were to turn my charges over to their parents, and *then* to head straight to the theater that was showing the biggest movie event of the summer: *2001*. I had slept very little for two days. I remember the movie starting. There was some weird music with no images on the screen. Then the dramatic beginning shots accompanied by the main theme of Richard Strauss' "Also Sprach Zarathustra." I made it through the "Ascent of Man" segment, and then promptly fell in and out of sleep. The only other things I remember from the viewing are HAL's misbehavior, the intermission, and the psychedelic mishmash of colors in the last segment. "What the hell is going on?" I asked myself. It seemed to me Kubrick didn't know how to end the film. Now, 40 years later, I consider *2001* to be a phenomenal work of creativity.

Watch the film.

Questions to ponder:

1. Some of the most frequently asked questions about *2001* are: What are those monoliths? Where did they come from? How did they get there? How would you answer those questions? For years I thought God was involved in putting them there. It is clear to me now, however, that an alien intelligence is behind their appearance. The plot of *2001: A Space Odyssey* had its genesis in a short story called "The Sentinel" by author Arthur C. Clarke, published in 1951. From that story it is clear that the appearance of a monolith indicates that the next stage in human development is about to take place and the monoliths were placed there long ago in order to send a warning to the intelligent aliens when our conscious life has undergone a major leap forward.

2. In addition to presenting a history of human development, Kubrick also seems to be sending viewers a message about the ramifications

of our being increasingly dominated by the machines we have created to make our lives easier. The first human thought, according to *2001,* takes place when an ape realizes a bone can be used as a weapon. By the middle and last segments of the film, almost every facet of human life is controlled by machines. In controlling their spaceship, Dave (Keir Dullea) and Frank (Gary Lockwood) are pretty much reduced to being mere bystanders. HAL is in charge and turns against those he (it?) is supposed to serve. There is some evidence that in 1968 — in the midst of the cold war between the West and Russia — Kubrick was warning viewers that nuclear weapons could lead to the destruction of humankind. Only if humans "evolve" to a higher stage, beyond the machine-centered life that had been reached, would there be any hope for conscious life to endure in our solar system. That higher stage appears as the "star-child" at the end of the film. (See my comments on Nietzsche's "The Metamorphoses" in the question section of *Pather Panchali,* one of the films in *The Apu Trilogy,* movies 67, 68 and 69.) According to Nietzsche, the highest metamorphosis a human can achieve is to become like a child. Kubrick's choice of "Also Sprach Zarathustra" by Richard Strauss to be the main theme music of *2001* points to the Nietzschean influence, since the title of that composition is also the title of Nietzsche's greatest philosophic work. Strauss' theme captures the Nietzschean metamorphosis of man into a child or overman. Do you see any other messages, warnings, or prescriptions being sent by Kubrick in the film *2001?*

A philosopher who both warns us against the dangers of centering

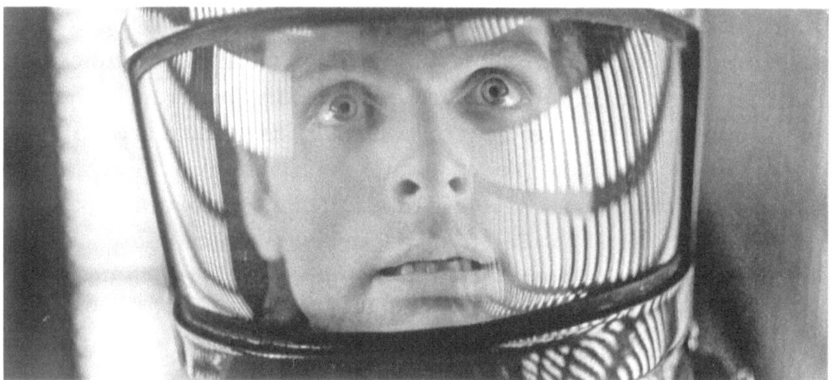

Dave (Keir Dullea) conducts a war of wits with HAL, a rebellious computer, in Stanley Kubrick's *2001: A Space Odyssey* (1968).

our lives on technology while also extolling what is valuable about technological advancement is Martin Heidegger (1889–1976). In an essay entitled "The Question Concerning Technology," Heidegger makes the following points:

a. "Technology is ... no mere means. Technology is a way of revealing.... It is the realm of revealing, i.e., of truth."[2] We learn about the nature of Being with *any* "revealing" that occurs. Coal reveals itself as something that burns. A certain herb reveals its medicinal value. For Heidegger, people should be in awe of the remarkable ability things have in being able to reveal themselves in their Being. "Whenever man opens his eyes and ears, unlocks his head and gives himself over to meditating and striving, shaping and working, entreating and thanking, he finds himself everywhere already brought into the unconcealed."[3]

b. "Enframing ... [is the] way of revealing that holds sway in the essence of modern technology."[4] Enframing means "to set aside," and "to separate from" all other beings. The construction of monstrous machines, and a way of life centered on calculation, leads humans to fall into the "the supreme danger."

A major threat for Heidegger now faces us because of the existence of nuclear weapons. But there is a greater danger: "The actual threat has already affected man in his essence. The rule of Enframing threatens man with the possibility that it could be denied to him to enter into a more original revealing and hence to experience the call of a more primordial truth."[5] Critics have noted that the characters in segments two and three of *2001* lack depth. No passion is shown. An Heideggerian interpretation of the state of mind of those characters is that they have ceased searching for the meaning of Being. Being "calls" them back to Being, back to a primordial awe of Being, but they are deaf to the call. Humans like Dave and Frank have become almost as cold as HAL. Are *we*, with our machines and technology, on the way to becoming passionless automations?

3. What is your interpretation of the psychedelic section of the last segment? Is there *really* a room in which Dave's pod lands? Dave gets progressively older. Is Kubrick saying that just as an ape-like life is no longer necessary after the ascent to humankind, humans are no longer necessary once they reach a stage we are now approaching? The "star child" replaces the human, just as the human replaced the ape.

Movie 15: *A Clockwork Orange*

Director: Stanley Kubrick; 2 hours, 16 minutes; 1971
Warning: Ultra-violent; nudity
Watch the movie.

Questions to ponder:

1. I had a very disturbing experience while viewing *A Clockwork Orange* for the first time, after its United States theatrical release in 1971. (Of course, for many viewers, just watching the film constitutes a disturbing experience.) On the screen appeared a future dystopia. I was perhaps foreseeing the world my children would live in. The thought was frightening and depressing. Then I realized the stranger sitting to my right was cheering Alex (Malcolm McDowell), as Alex engaged in violent activity. "Yeh, do it! Do it again!" Right then I realized I was possibly not watching the future, but rather being exposed to the present. Is *A Clockwork Orange* depicting the world you live in? Have some of the elements contained in the film come true: Sex promoted everywhere you turn? Lack of respect shown fellow citizens? Gross commercialization? Bureaucratic government officials?

2. An idea that is fairly common throughout the history of philosophy is that if a person delves deeply into high quality intellectual matters, that person will tend to be morally good. The argument stresses that engaging in evil is actually less fulfilling than, for example, reading great literature, or listening to Beethoven's symphonies. John Stuart Mill (1806–1873), the famous utilitarian wrote "a being of higher faculties requires more to make him happy, is capable probably of more acute suffering, and certainly accessible to it at more points, than one of an inferior type; but in spite of these liabilities, he can never really wish to sink into what he feels to be a lower grade of existence."[1]

Arthur Schopen-

Alex (Malcolm McDowell) is a gang member in the not-so-distant future (or is it the present?) in *A Clockwork Orange* (1971).

hauer (1788–1860), the greatest pessimist in the history of Philosophy, argued that intellectual endeavors involving such things as art, music and poetry can quiet what he called the Will. The Will is the blind, striving reality at the base of all things. Things are the Will objectified. All things pass — once there were dinosaurs; now there are none — but that out of which all things arise does not pass. (Many people don't seem to have a problem with the idea that things come into being due to *God's* will. There should not be any problem with seeing the possibility that things arise out of some *ungodly* universal Will.) Schopenhauer addresses the question of why we call ultimate reality "the Will."

> The word "will" which ... is to reveal to us the innermost essence of every-thing in nature, by no means expresses an unknown quantity, something reached by inferences and syllogisms, but something known absolutely and immediately, and that so well that we know and understand what will is better than anything else, be it what it may. Hitherto, the concept of *will* has been subsumed under the concept of force; I, on the other hand, do exactly the reverse, and intend every force in nature to be conceived as will.[2]

Humans, according to Schopenhauer, have no free will. A person's individual will is an offshoot of the universal Will. We are *miserable*, because we are carried along by the Will. Schopenhauer, however, held that we can find moments of peace by achieving "will-less perception" through aesthetic appreciation:

> So much is achieved simply and solely by the inner force of an artistic disposition; but that purely objective form of mind is facilitated and favoured from without by accommodating objects, by the abundance of natural beauty that invites contemplation, and even presses itself on us. Whenever it presents itself to our gaze all at once, it almost always suc-ceeds in snatching us, although only for a few moments, from subjectivity, from the thraldom of the will and transferring us into the state of pure knowledge. This is why the man tormented by passions, want, or care, is so suddenly revived, cheered, and comforted by a single, free glance into nature. The storm of passions, the pressure of desire and fear, and all the miseries of willing are then at once calmed and appeased in a marvelous way. For at the moment when, torn from the will, we have given ourselves up to pure, will-less knowing, we have stepped into another world, so to speak, where everything that moves our will, and thus violently agitates us, not longer exists.[3]

Do you find that listening to music, reading poetry, or contemplat-ing other great aesthetic works "soothes your soul"? Alex, in *A Clockwork*

Orange, loses his aggressive personality when listening to compositions by Beethoven. However, he then subsequently engages in murder and rape. Alex, thus, seems to provide a counter-example to Mill's idea that aesthetic appreciation will lead a person to be a moral person.

3. Why can't Alex bear to view film clips of violent activity at the same time Beethoven's Ninth Symphony is played?

4. At the end of the film, Alex says he is "cured." What does he mean? What cured him?

Movie 16: *Waking Ned Devine*

Director: Kirk Jones; 1 hour, 31 minutes; 1998
Watch the movie.

Questions to ponder:

1. Jackie (Ian Bannen) and Michael (David Kelly) are certainly involved in fraud. Did you cheer them on? If they had been discovered by authorities, should they have been prosecuted? If they had not been

A scene from *Waking Ned Devine* (1998). Ned Devine's friends give a toast. From left, David Kelly, James Ryland, Robert Hickey (top), Ian Bannen and Matthew Devitt.

likeable, would you have judged them differently? From his dream, Jackie is convinced he knew what Ned wanted. He will shortly say to the other townspeople, Ned "wants us to share the winnings." Can Jackie really know what Ned wants? Could he know what Ned would have wanted — or at least infer what he wanted — even if he had not had the dream?

2. To what extent is Jackie responsible for the death of Lizzie Quinn (Eileen Dromey)? Should he feel guilty? If he had given in to her demand, she would not have gone to the phone booth to call lottery officials.

Movie 17: *The End of the Affair*

Director: Neil Jordan; 1 hour, 42 minutes; 1999

In *The End of the Affair,* Bendrix (Ralph Fiennes) utters the following famous quote from the great philosopher, George Berkeley (1685–1753): "To be is to be perceived." Berkeley argued that things (mountains, trees, pens, human bodies, etc.) exist only when perceived. A thing, for Berkeley, is nothing but a bundle of qualities. Examples of those qualities are size, shape, texture, color, odor and spatial position. Most humans are "realists" who believe that such qualities exist out in the world whether perceived or not. Berkeley presents a number of amazing arguments to support his view. One argument centers on the relativity of all qualities. I once had an experience that provided substantial verification of Berkeley's "relativity argument." I was an undergraduate biology student for one semester at the University of New Mexico in Albuquerque. As I walked over an area of the campus that had not been developed, I noticed a significant number of large ant hills. I became infatuated with watching ants at their daily routines. It seemed that each ant had some project to perform. One day I spotted an amazing phenomenon. As I was watching one anthill, it started to rain. In a very short amount of time some ants clearly went to an underground morgue and brought dead ants to the main entrance at the top of the anthill. They used the dead ants to plug up that entrance — clearly to keep rainwater from entering the ant hill. Because it doesn't rain often in Albuquerque, I used to spit on ant hills to simulate rain . The ants, feeling the vibration of the spit hitting the ground clearly judged that it was raining and — lo and behold — the entrance was soon plugged with dead ants. Then one day I had my experience that seemed to verify Berkeley's relativity argument. The ants I was watching were about the size of this dash:—. Wait a minute! That is the size *I* saw.

Julianne Moore (as Sarah Miles) and Ralph Fiennes (as Maurice Bendrix) play two lovers in *The End of the Affair* (1999). One will have to make a tremendous sacrifice.

Suppose an ant would look back at its hindmost parts. Would the ant see something equal to the size I saw? Those parts would probably seem as far from its head, as my feet seem to be from my head. What is the *real* size of the ant — the size *I* see or the size the *ant* sees? To determine the size of the ant, is it enough first to measure it with a ruler? That doesn't help! How big is a ruler? If I look at a ruler, I see a size. Is the size I see the same size that an ant sees? No! If the ant were placed at the end of a ruler, the ruler would stretch out like a runway on an airport. When I look at a ruler, I don't see any size like that of a runway. That is how the "relativity argument" works on the quality of "size." Can you see how the relativity argument works on other qualities of perceived objects?

Another argument Berkeley gives to support his notion that a thing only exists when perceived utilizes the realists' beliefs that (a) qualities of things exist out in the world, whether perceived or not, and (b) that those qualities are *like* our ideas of them. Berkeley spots a serious problem. A quality out in the world is supposedly *like* our idea of that quality. Berkeley, however, says that if a quality is not an idea it cannot be *like* an idea. Nothing is like an idea, but an idea. Because an idea must be perceived in order to exist, a quality *like* an idea must also be perceived in order to exist.

Berkeley's quote, "To be is to be perceived," plays a fairly small role in *The End of the Affair*. A major part of the film's plot does, however, bear a resemblance to ideas central in the philosophy of Søren Kierkegaard (1813–1855). Kierkegaard was aware that a significant number of people who believe they are good Christians who are completely dedicated to serving God and obeying His commands, are instead motivated only by self-interest or worldly concerns. Unless a person's faith is tested, the person cannot know if he or she is a "true knight of the faith." In his work, *Fear and Trembling*, Kierkegaard retells the Abraham and Isaac story from the Old Testament. God commands Abraham to sacrifice his beloved son, Isaac, in order to test Abraham's faith. Kierkegaard's goal in this re-telling is to provide readers with an example of someone who is tested by God, passes the test, and thus, is a "true knight of the faith." I remember as a child admiring Abraham, but did not think the Abraham/Isaac story was such a big deal. God says, "Do x." Abraham marches Isaac to the hill and proceeds to do x. God is pleased by Abraham's obedience, and stops Abraham at the last moment. Good man, Abraham. Kierkegaard asks, however, what was it like to be Abraham on that day? Put yourself in Abraham's place. Suppose a voice comes to you and says, "This is God. I want you to kill your son." You had better ask yourself whether you are sane or insane! Suppose you decide you are sane, what then? You, then, better ask whether it is God, or the devil speaking to you! Doesn't it sound like something the devil would say: "Hey — this is God. I want you to kill your son"? Suppose you decide that it is God speaking and not the devil. You must then decide whether you are going to obey or not! Abraham decides to obey. Now you realize you will be making your decision out of faith, not knowledge; but you start out for the mountain, holding the hand of your child. Your hand is shaking, your head is bowed. You feel crushed. You walk with "fear and trembling." However, in the end, you pass this extreme test.

If I see someone who is clearly distraught, holding the hand of a child, and who says — when I ask if I can be of any assistance — "No, God has commanded me to kill this child and that is what I am going to do," I will rush to call 911. If the knife is going up, and the only way to stop him is to shoot him, then I'll shoot him. And I should!

Kierkegaard was aware of the difficulty of justifying Abraham's decision. God commands Abraham to kill his son, yet it was God who commanded "Thou shalt not kill." No objective explanation can possibly be adequate in explaining an act committed out of faith. In a section of *Fear and Trembling*, Kierkegaard presents a concept called "the teleological suspension of the ethical": since it is God who gives us ethical rules to obey, He can suspend His own rules.

The Abraham story was important to Kierkegaard because it mirrored a "sacrifice" he believed God commanded Kierkegaard, himself, to make. Kierkegaard was engaged to Regina Olsen. Various reasons have been given for why Kierkegaard caused the engagement to be broken. Some speculate that it may have been because he suffered from either depression, or a deep sense of sin that arose from an earlier sexual transgression. Perhaps he was aware that he was an "outsider," who did not perform well in social situations. Also, he was much older than the teenage Regina and may have felt he could not give her a happy life. However, there are clues that Kierkegaard believed he was asked by God to sacrifice his love for Regina, in order to dedicate his life to obeying God's commands. For example, Kierkegaard eventually became aware that the Danish Lutheran Church — the spiritual, political and economic center of Danish life — was not as God-centered as it should be — it was too materialistic. Subsequently, Kierkegaard waged a war of words with the leading bishop of the church. The written material from that debate can be found in a book entitled *Attack Upon Christendom*.[1]

Kierkegaard sacrificed his love for Regina, and apparently regretted his decision for the rest of his life. He may even have thought he would eventually get her back. The problem: Regina married someone else.

Watch the movie.

Questions to ponder:

1. Sarah Miles (Julianne Moore) promises to "sacrifice" her love for Bendrix as she prays to God to bring him back to life. If God will do that, she will break off her affair with him. Do you think that Sarah later has good reasons for believing that God had a hand in Bendrix surviving the explosion of the bomb? An instant after Bendrix types the message that he hates God, Sarah dies. Is there any connection between those two events? Sarah kisses the birthmark on the cheek of Lance Parkis (Samuel Bould). Subsequently, the mark goes away. Has God performed a miracle through Sarah's act? At the end of the film is Bendrix wavering in his unbelief?

2. Why does Henry Miles (Stephen Rea) invite Bendrix to live at his house during Sarah's last days? Is it an act of love for Sarah, or is there some other motivation?

Movie 18: *The Reader*

Director: Stephen Daldry; 2 hours, 4 minutes; 2008
Watch the movie.

Questions to ponder:

1. Is Hanna Schmitz (Kate Winslet) more ashamed of being illiterate than of being involved in Nazi atrocities?

2. From what we see of Hanna, is there any way to tell what she was like as a guard of Jewish persons?

3. Young Michael (David Kross) knew that Hanna was illiterate. Thus, Hanna could not have written the report that led to her being given a life sentence. (The other guards receive a mere sentence of four years.) Why did Michael remain silent?

4. Does Hanna know older Michael (Ralph Fiennes) is in the courtroom?

Hanna (Kate Winslet) keeps a secret from her past from young Michael (David Kross) in *The Reader* (2008).

5. Why does Hanna commit suicide, knowing that Michael arranged for her to have a life outside prison?

ADDITIONAL RECOMMENDED FILMS
FROM GREAT BRITAIN AND IRELAND

Goodbye, Mr. Chips (1939)

Great Expectations (1946)

Kind Hearts and Coronets (1949)

The Third Man (1949)

Lawrence of Arabia (1962)

This Sporting Life (1967)

The Wicker Man (1973)

The Remains of the Day (1985) and *A Room with a View* (1993). Two films directed by James Ivory.

My Left Foot (1989)

The Crying Game (1992)

The English Patient (1996)

Jude (1996)

Trainspotting (1996)

Secrets and Lies (1996)

The Full Monty (1997)

The Boxer (1997)

Hilary and Jackie (1998). The relationship between the great cellist Jacqueline du Pré and her sister.

The War Zone (1999)

Iris (2001). The life of the novelist Iris Murdock.

The Wind That Shakes the Barley (2006). Check out director Ken Loach's other works, including *Kes* (1970), *Raining Stones* (1993), *Ladybird Ladybird* (1994), *My Name Is Joe* (1998), *Bread and Roses* (2000) and *The Navigators* (2001).

SPAIN

Movie 19: *The Spirit of the Beehive*

Director: Victor Erice; 1 hour, 37 minutes; 1973
Watch the movie.

Questions to ponder:

1. Almost all critics proclaim *The Spirit of the Beehive* to be a wonderful film that captures the inner life of a child. The fascination and terror experienced by Ana (Ana Torent) as she watches *Frankenstein* is evident. The landscape, as seen by Ana, is captured by a master cinematographer,

Ana, played by Ana Torent, left, watches the movie *Frankenstein* and enters a world of imagination in *The Spirit of the Beehive* (1973).

Luis Curdrado, who, a few years after his work in the film, tragically lost his eyesight and committed suicide. The deserted shed and nearby well are every bit present to the viewers as to Ana. For Ana, the soldier in the deserted farmhouse is the spirit of the Frankenstein monster. Are there any other scenes that seem to capture Ana's youthful experience?

2. What is the significance of the title of the film? Does it mean anything that windows on the house look like beehives? The father (Fernando Gomez) tells of someone who recoiled in horror after being shown "the constant agitation of the honeycomb" and "the mysterious commotion of the nurse bees over the nests." What conclusions are we to draw from this "horror"?

3. There is much debate over how much of *The Spirit of the Beehive* is an allegory about Franco's stranglehold on Spain, and the loss of a cherished traditional way of life. Does life in the village and in Ana's house seem to exist in a fallen state? Are there scenes in the film that provide evidence that it is political allegory? (One thing is clear — the injured man in the shed is an anti–Franco Republican.)

Movie 20: *El Bola*

Director: Achero Mañas; 1 hour, 28 minutes; 2000
Warning: Crude language and a scene showing abusive behavior.
Watch the movie.

Questions to ponder:

1. Was life easier for you when you were a child? Pablo (Juan José Ballesta) certainly has one of the most difficult problems many children face — having an abusive father (Manuel Morón). Many adults probably think like the customer at Pablo's father's store: "If we were Pablo's age, we wouldn't have problems. I bet nothing bothers you (Pablo). You're fine." Alfredo (Pablo Galán) has a loving family life, but he also shows that he is deeply bothered by elements of his life. What is disturbing Alfredo?

2. Achero Mañas, the director of *El Bola,* describes Pablo's father as one "who's capable of scarring his son for life and who brings pain to that boy through his hatred, frustration and problems in an almost pathological manner." Do you think everything parents do to, or for, their children will have a major impact on the child's future character?

3. What is the significance of having Pablo's ball bearing run over by the train? Does that mean he has been saved by Alfredo's father (Alberto Jiménez) and no longer needs his good luck charm?

Movie 21: *The Sea Inside*

Director: Alejandro Amenábar; 2 hours, 5 minutes; 2004

I included the 1981 film *Whose Life Is It Anyway?* in *Plato and Popcorn* (pages 92–94). In that film, Richard Dreyfuss gives one of his best performances. He plays a man who has lost the will to live after becoming a paraplegic. *The Sea Inside* is very similar in plot to *Whose Life Is It Anyway?* Here the story told is a true one, based on the life of Ramón Sampedro. Javier Bardem captures the essence of Ramón. After watching the film, check any video of the real-life Ramón Sampedro on Google. You will realize that the person in the video is indistinguishable from the person in the film. (The last time I had such a realization was when I compared Ben Kingsley's portrayal of Gandhi in the film of that name to actual footage of the great leader.)

In the history of philosophy there appears a stunning rebuttal by David Hume (1711–1776) to arguments given by Thomas Aquinas (1225–

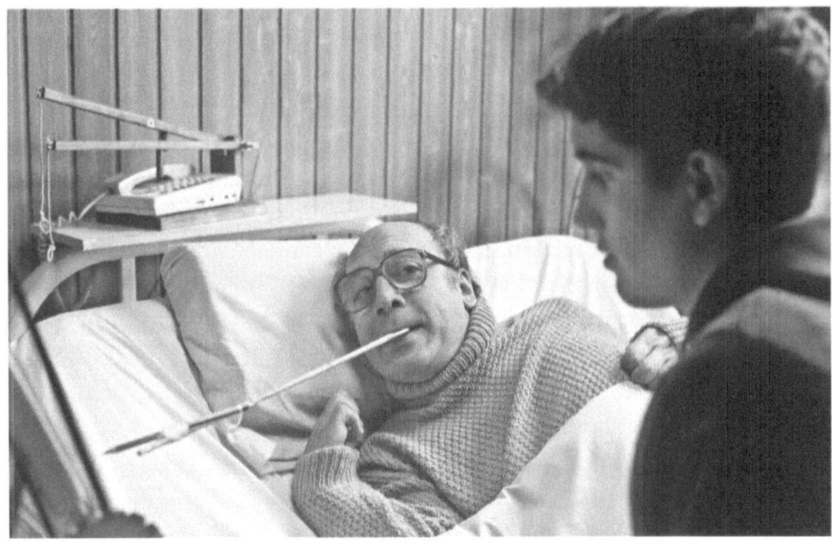

Javier Bardem as Ramón Sampedro, a real-life poet who fought for the right to die in *The Sea Inside* (2004). Tamar Novas, as Javi, appears at right.

1274) that suicide was one of the greatest of all sins. Basically, Aquinas' position is that suicide is a sin because it:

> a. goes against the natural law that stresses "everything naturally loves itself, the result being that everything naturally keeps itself in being and resists corruption so far as it can."
>
> b. does harm to one's community because each person is part of that whole.
>
> c. involves a rebellion against God's will because it is God who will "pronounce sentence of death and life."

So, according to Aquinas, suicide does harm to oneself and one's community, and also goes against God's will.

Aquinas' arguments are generally well formulated. However, in support for his notion that one who commits suicide "sins against God," he makes an appalling, disgusting assertion: "Hence, whoever takes his own life sins against God, even as he who kills another's slave sins against that slave's master...."[1] There is no indication that Aquinas believed that owning slaves is a sin. Killing a slave, according to Aquinas, is a sin because the property of another person is being taken away from that person.

In an essay published posthumously, David Hume—without mentioning Aquinas by name—attempts to show that Aquinas' three arguments are flawed. In one sentence, Hume makes it clear that he is responding to Aquinas: "If suicide be criminal, it must be a transgression of our duty, either to God, our neighbor or ourselves."[2]

For Hume:

> a. Suicide is not necessarily a transgression of our duty to God because God clearly gave us reasoning powers, so that just as we can "divert the Nile or Danube from its course," we can divert blood from our own veins. "Where then is the crime of turning a few ounces of blood from their natural channels?"[3]
>
> b. Suicide is not necessarily a transgression of our duties to our neighbor or community because, Hume writes:
>
>> A man who retires from life does no harm to society. He only ceases to do good, which, if it be an injury, is of the lowest kind ... I am not obliged to do a small good to society, at the expense of a great harm to myself. Why then should I prolong a miserable existence, because of some frivolous advantage which the public may, perhaps, receive from me?[4]

    c. We do not necessarily transgress our duty to ourselves. In fact, suicide might — in certain circumstances — be an act done out of rational self-interest. Hume believes "that no man ever threw away life while it was worth keeping." It is not in one's self-interest to keep that which is not worth keeping.[5]

As you view *The Sea Inside*, you will be exposed to Ramon Sampedro's arguments that he should be allowed to end his life. His arguments are very similar to those of David Hume. A priest appears in a few scenes. It is clear the priest would accept Thomas Aquinas' arguments.

Watch the movie.

Questions to ponder:

1. Do you think Ramón Sampedro makes a convincing case in behalf of his wish to die? Is he correct in his assertion that if someone truly loves him, he/she would support him in his wish?

2. Why does Ramón make the fateful dive that results in injuries, leaving him a paraplegic? I believe everyone at one time or another chooses to do something out of the ordinary, and in so choosing, could very possibly end up like Ramón. It is very frightening to think about such possibilities. Can you think of any past choices that could have changed your life in tragic ways? (Just one example from my life: As a teenager, I jumped off a high platform into a large pile of hay. I barely missed a pitchfork that was hidden in the pile and was pointing upward.) Do you think *every* choice we make involves a calculated risk? What factors differentiate (a) going for a walk and perhaps getting hit by a car, and (b) diving off a cliff into what seems to be deep water and hitting a submerged rock? Is one a "reasonable" choice, and the other one an "irrational" choice?

Additional Recommended Films from Spain

Belle Epoque (1992)

Open Your Eyes (1997)

Lovers of the Arctic Circle (1998)

Talk to Her (2002). If you like this Pedro Almodovar film, also try his *Women on the Verge of a Nervous Breakdown* (1988), *Tie Me Up, Tie Me Down* (1990), and *All About My Mother* (1999).

FRANCE

Movies 22 and 23: *Jean de Florette* and *Manon of the Spring*

Director: Claude Berri; 2 hours / 1 hour, 53 minutes, 1986

Manon of the Spring is not a sequel to, but rather a continuation of the plot begun in *Jean de Florette*. It is difficult to believe that Daniel Auteuil, who plays Ugolin, is the same actor who appears both as the debonair captain in *The Widow of St. Pierre* (movie 24) and as the contemporary European of *Caché* (movie 39). Gérard Depardieu is always Gérard Depardieu, whether in *Jean de Florette, Cyrano de Bergerac* (1990), or *A Pure Formality* (movie 56), but he is regularly a scene stealer. Yves Montand rounds out the cast of male actors by capturing the nasty character of Papet. The child Manon (Ernestine Mazurowna) of *Jean de Florette* and the adult Manon (Emmanuelle Béart) of *Manon of the Spring* completely come across as one and the same person.

Watch the movie.

Questions to ponder:

1. There is never any doubt Papet and Ugolin will be successful in destroying Jean. However, Jean did not help his cause by using several bits of bad logic in his plans to become self-sufficient in Provence. For example, he commits what is known as the "gambler's fallacy" when he concludes that "It'll rain tonight." His reasoning: "In May, we only had three days of rain instead of the [average] six." It hasn't rained in June, so we're owed five days of rain." A gambler who has lost several times straight may conclude that winning must be just around the corner. The problem is, that the chance of winning or losing is always the same, regardless of whether there has been a winning or losing streak.

A "false cause fallacy" is committed when Jean concludes that a dowser with a "divining rod" could locate water on his land. Such a fallacy involves an assertion that x is the cause of y, when there is no good reason to believe that x is indeed the cause. Here are some examples of false cause fallacies: (a) If a black cat walks in front of you, bad luck will come your way. (b) As historically reported, President Abraham Lincoln was asked by a congressional delegation to remove General Ulysses S. Grant from power. Although Grant was winning battles, he was an alcoholic. Lincoln replied that he wished he had a keg of the whiskey Grant drank, in order to give some to his other generals who were losing battles. Of course, Lincoln was not serious, but his remarks suggested that he believed Grant won battles because he was drunk on whiskey. (c) The day after moving back to my hometown — after spending years in the Southwest — I got a terrible sore throat. My grandmother told me how to get rid of the sore throat. "Tonight, when you go to bed, tie the left sock you have been wearing all day around your neck. The crud in the sock will draw out the crud in your throat. Like likes like." I told my grandmother I would do it, even though I was not about to. Goodness! Why wouldn't the crud in my throat draw in the crud from my socks? I could get athlete's throat! The next morning I called my grandmother and said, "Nanna, I still have the sore throat. Are you sure it was supposed to be

Jean (Gérard Depardieu) struggling to bring water to his farm in *Jean de Florette* (1986), directed by Claude Berri.

my left sock tied around my neck, and not the right sock?" She said, "You know ... I worried about that all night, and couldn't sleep. Maybe it should have been the right one!"

Can *you* think of any other examples of false cause fallacies?

2. I hope none of the questions I raise about films in this book are judged by readers to involve "nit-picking." If there is one, it might be the following: The first time I viewed *Manon of the Spring*, I was stunned at the moment I realized Jean was Papet's son. That moment stands out as one of the most memorable of any of the countless number of films I have viewed. However, while viewing the film once again for this book, I kept feeling that Papet should have put two and two together. After he was told Jean had inherited the farm, Papet could have easily deduced Jean's age. That age would indicate that he, Papet, might be Jean's father, because it was the same number of years since Papet had been sexually intimate with Jean's mother. Am I missing something?

Movie 24: *The Widow of Saint-Pierre*

Director: Patrice Laconte; 1 hour, 48 minutes; 2000

Do you think capital punishment is a desirable practice because (a) it deters people from committing heinous crimes, or (b) "an eye for an eye" is a reasonable rule for all to follow? Would there be any way to *prove* that capital punishment acts as a deterrent? Have you ever heard of anyone saying "I was going to kill someone, but I didn't because I might be caught and executed"? How could anyone ever know that a crime was not committed because of the threat of execution?

If you think "an eye for an eye" is a reasonable rule, should a rapist be raped? What crimes should be punished with the same type of violence utilized in the committing of a crime? If a murder is committed out of an act of rage, should the executioner perform his duty in a state of rage? Why not? The rage probably terrified the victim.

It seems to me most rational people would view the executioner with repugnance. Do you agree? If capital punishment is performed as an act of justice, shouldn't we hold the executioner in high esteem?

Does it bother you that even in murder cases where the evidence is overwhelming that person x is guilty, mistakes have been made? Does it bother you that a guilty man may be accused, but by the time the execution is to take place, person x is a radically different person — a good per-

Madame La (Juliette Binoche) showing compassion to the prisoner, Neel (Emir Kusturica), in *The Widow of St. Pierre* (2000).

son? Does it bother you that poor people often have less chance of getting lighter sentences than do wealthy people who can afford the best lawyers?

Watch the movie.

Questions to ponder:

1. Why does Madame La (Juliette Binoche) want to relate to the murderer, Neel Auguste (Emir Kusturica) who is waiting for his execution? She clearly loves her husband, the Captain (Daniel Auteuil). Why does the Captain support his wife and her projects with Neel? In the DVD extras, Juliette Binoche says that Neel is like the child Madame La never had. When I see the movie, I see something other than a parental type of love developing between Madame La and Neel. What kind of relationship do you see? Madame La asks Neel why he does everything she asks. What do you think the reason is?

2. Why do the town leaders demand Neel be executed? Their wives and all the townsfolk have learned to admire and respect Neel. The leaders continually stress that the law has spoken, and the law requires Neel's death. Is this a case where they should find a way to circumvent the law? Would the town leaders have been more lenient if the Captain had not shown such a haughty attitude toward them?

Movie 25: *A Very Long Engagement*

Director: Jean-Pierre Jeunet; 2 hours, 13 minutes; 2004

In *Plato and Popcorn,* I included movies I called "puzzlers"—movies that contained plots that for one reason or another were, from beginning to end, difficult to figure out. *A Very Long Engagement* is a puzzler. I saw the movie when it was released in 2004. I was impressed with both Jean-Pierre Jeunet's direction and, from my long-term interest in the military history of World War I, the scenes of trench warfare. However, I could not have given an account of exactly what happened to whom. In 2008, I decided to read the critically-reviewed original novel by Sebastian Japrisot. As I read, I kept a list of characters' names and recorded facts about them that probably would be of significance. It was like finding jigsaw puzzle pieces that eventually fit with other pieces until a full picture appears. It wasn't easy to reach the awareness of the whole picture, but it was well worth the effort. Though it is not necessary, I recommend reading the novel before viewing the film. The novel is indeed captured well by the film.

Rather than have you watch the movie, and then immediately answer questions, I have provided a list of the names of crucial characters. Try to figure out who does what, when, who lives, who dies. It is a fascinating mystery that you can solve if you make the effort. *After* watching the movie, read what I present below as an outline of facts about the characters. Beware—there are "spoilers" in that outline.

Watch the movie.

The characters:

A. THE FIVE CONDEMNED SOLDIERS

1. Kleber Bouquet (Jérôme Kircher)—nickname "Bastoche." His best friend is Benjamin Gordes (Jean-Pierre Darroussin). His girlfriend is Véronique Passavant (Julie Depardieu). At the front, Bastoche wears German boots. If the Germans capture him and see him wearing those boots, they will surely kill him. Gordes, who wears the same size boots, trades boots with him before Bastoche is forced into no man's land. In the months before the affair at Bingo Crepuscule, Gordes and Kleber have a fight. Gordes' spirit is being destroyed by the war. He is married to a widow with four children. The widow dies. He then marries Elodie (Jodie Foster) who is the mother of another child. Thus, Kleber is stepfather to

five children. If a sixth child is born, Klaber will be released from military service. The problem — he is sterile. He convinces Bastoche and Elodie to engage in sex to get Elodie pregnant so he can be discharged. After initial embarrassment, Bastoche and Elodie perform beautifully, though Elodie does not get pregnant. Unexpectedly, Gordes becomes extremely jealous of his friend's time with his wife, and they come to blows. They don't reconnect until meeting at Bingo just before Bastouche is forced out of the trench.

2. Francis Langonnet (Denis Lavant) — nickname "Six-Soux." Pacifist. He is a welder, married with two daughters. Celestin Poux (Albert Dupontel) sees him die in no man's land.

3. Benoît Notre-Dame (Clovis Cornillac) — Bravest of the five, married with a son named Titou. Celestin Poux thinks he saw a bomb pulverize Benoit, but as will be noted below, Benoit survives.

4. Ange Bassignano (Dominique Bettenfeld) — nickname "Common Law." He is from Corsica and is a deceitful person. He was in jail for murder, but was released to fight in the war. He was a pimp. One of his whores, Tina Lombardi (Marion Cotillard), loves him. Celestin Poux sees him killed by Corporal Thouvenel (François Levantal). Tina Lombardi kills Thouvenel in revenge.

5. Manech Longonnet (Gaspard Ulliel), 19 years old — nickname "Cornflower." He is deeply in love with his fiancée, Mathilde (Audrey Tatou), the main character of the film. Various terrible experiences in the war, including being splattered with the remains of a comrade hit by a bomb near him, lead him to completely lose touch with reality. After years of trying to get 100 percent proof that Manech died in no man's land — otherwise she will not believe he is dead — Mathilde makes several discoveries that guide her to find him — alive. For example, Celestin Poux had given Manech a bright red glove with white dots that was "tightly knitted and tightly fitted," and probably would not have fallen off. None of the dead men found in no man's land was wearing such a glove. Also, Tina Lombardi tells Mathilde she met a male nurse named Phillipot (Stéphane Butet) who cared for the five condemned men, and who was sure he saw a wounded soldier from Bingo who was wearing German boots, carrying another wounded soldier who was "thin-built." Because Benjamin Gordes had traded boots with his friend, Kleber Bouquet, it may seem Gordes is the soldier seen by Phillipot. But he isn't. Gordes goes into no man's land to search for his friend Kleber, who is dead. Gordes is

then gravely wounded and crawls into the remains of a cellar where he finds Benoît Notre-Dame, also wounded. Additionally, Manech is in the cellar. Gordes dies and Benoît exchanges some of his clothing, including the German boots, for that worn by Gordes. Benoît then carries Manech away from the battlefield. Mathilde also decodes the last letter Benoît Notre-Dame sent to his wife. In that letter, he tells her to sell everything and meet him in Bernay. Had he survived, he would have gone there. Who was the thin-built, young soldier carried by Benoît? Yes. Mathilde finds him. Benoît had passed Manech off as Jean Desrochelles, another soldier who died in no man's land. Manech, having amnesia, was sent to live with Jean Desrochelle's mother who, having lost her real son, receives Manech as her adopted son, knowing him only by the name of Jean.

B. OTHER CHARACTERS

1. Daniel Esperanza (Jean-Pierre Becker) survived the war, but is dying of the Spanish flu when he contacts Mathilde with copies of the last letter written by the condemned men. He also gives her a copy of a photograph taken of the five prisoners at Bingo.

Manech (Gaspard Ulliel) carves his lover's initials into a tree in no man's land in the Somme during World War I in *A Very Long Engagement* (2004), directed by Jean-Pierre Jeunet.

2. Sylvain (Dominique Pinon) and Bénédicte (Chantal Neuwirth) look after Mathilde at their house in the country.

3. Captain Favourier (Tchéky Karyo) receives the five prisoners at Bingo and is ordered to force them into no man's land.

4. Celestin Poux is a soldier at Bingo who feels great sorrow, particularly for Manech. Manech desires cocoa and honey. Celestin, the "smartest thief" who can get anything in the worst conditions, goes off and obtains cocoa and honey. He gives Manech a glove for his uninjured hand. See more about Celestin Poux above in the comments about Manech.

5. Germain Pire (Ticky Holgado) is a private detective hired by Mathilde to try to track down Celestin Poux and Tina Lombardi, because Mathilde is convinced they have important information about the events at Bingo.

Questions to ponder:

1. In *Paths of Glory* (1957), a movie covered in *Plato and Popcorn* (pages 106–108), as in *A Very Long Engagement*, soldiers are executed as an example of what happens if they do not do their duty. Do you think that in war, commanders are in the right to order such executions? They judge that such executions will deter others from failing in their duty, and thus, victory is more probable with executions, than without.

2. At the end of the film, as in the novel, Manech knows himself only as Jean Desrochelles. In the novel, Mathilde is persuaded not to try to take "Jean" away from the only mother he knows, his adopted mother. In the film, the adopted mother died two months before Mathilde finds Manech. So, it is assumed she is free to take him home with her. Which ending do you like best? Why?

Movie 26: *13 Tzameti*

Director: Géla Babluani; 1 hour, 35 minutes; 2005
Warning: Extreme Violence
Is there such a thing as luck in the universe? If a list of causes were drawn up that would explain why two automobiles come together in a collision, would one of the causes be bad luck? What does a person mean by the word "lucky," as in the assertion "I was lucky — I won the lottery"?
In his *Physics*, Aristotle (384–322 B.C.) presents an analysis of

the concept of "chance" concluding that chance "is not the *cause*— without qualification — of anything." An example he gives shows the main points of his analysis:

> A man is engaged in collecting subscriptions for a feast. He would have gone to such and such a place for the purpose of getting the money if he had known (he could get the money there). He actually went there for another purpose, and it was only incidentally that he got his money by going there.... If he had gone with deliberate purpose and for the sake of this — if he always or normally went there when he was collecting payments — he could not be said to have gone by chance.[1]

The man, based on his knowledge of the causes, could not have predicted with any confidence that he would get the money by going to that place. You can imagine him saying, "That was just a chance meeting" or "I got lucky."

Causes led both the man who was collecting the subscriptions, and the man who was met "by chance," to that place. For Aristotle, one of the causes involved in any event is the "final cause"— the purpose that, for example, leads one to travel to someplace. Perhaps the men in Aristotle's example were drawn to the stall of a food seller. Each man went there for the purpose of buying food. The man collecting subscriptions got "lucky."

If I am driving my car to a movie theater, and a huge tree branch crashes on my car as I wait at a red light, I will say that I was "unlucky," or I had "bad luck." If I find a winning lottery ticket lying in the grass

A frightening game of Russian roulette highlights *13 Tzameti* (2005).

next to a trail on which I am hiking, then I will call myself "lucky." If something happens that could not be predicted, and it brings pleasure, I will call it "good luck;" if it brings pain, I will call it "bad luck."

Since "chance" or "luck" occurs only as a result of goal-directed deliberation, Aristotle held that it would be inappropriate to consider any "inanimate thing or a lower animal or a child" to be lucky or unlucky "except metaphorically, as Protarchus, for example, said that the stones of which altars are made are fortunate because they are held in honour, while their fellows are trodden underfoot."[2] A human adult can be lucky in meeting someone unexpectedly at a marketplace; but, for Aristotle, inanimate things, lower animals, and children cannot be goal-directed as a result of deliberation. Thus, they "cannot do anything by chance." In response to Aristotle, I would say he is correct about inanimate things. Is it as certain that lower animals, such as ants or worms should not be judged as lucky or unlucky? If a worm, seeking a moist area, slithers across a mousetrap and springs it, isn't that an unlucky worm? If a lost dog — against all odds — happens to be at a spot where he comes upon his master, then that dog is lucky. Do you think a young child can be lucky or unlucky? Does it make sense to say that a child is lucky, or unlucky, to have the parents he has? In determining the answer to that question, is it a significant fact that the child was never going to have any other parents but these parents? Does it make sense to say the child that has good parents could have been unlucky and have had rotten parents? (What do you think of the judgment: "There but for the grace of God, go I"?)

The word "luck" is mentioned several times in *13 Tzameti*. If you like this film, compare it to the Spanish movie *Intacto* (2001). In that film, you will have to accept a far-fetched premise that some people possess an extraordinary, mystical ability to be lucky. Accept that premise, and *Intacto* is a fun thriller. For a film that contains scenes of contests like the one depicted in *13 Tzameti*, see *The Deer Hunter* (1978).

Watch the movie.

Questions to ponder:

1. In an extra on the DVD of *13 Tzameti*, a person who has actually engaged in the type of gamble portrayed in the film, claims he enjoys life, but has been willing to gamble it for the money that can be won. The money enables him to do many things he would not otherwise be able to do. He also seems to appreciate the *thrill* of the contest. What is your reac-

tion to such a person? Do you think he is insane? He thinks some people are genetically programmed to take tremendous risks. Is he correct? When asked if there is ever any cheating in such contests he answers that cheating would be "terrible." According to him, the contest is a game governed by rules. Do you find it strange that he thinks breaking the rules of the contest is terrible, but does not seem to think that the contest itself is terrible?

2. The person interviewed on the DVD extra is asked if the participants in the contest "have the right to kill because [they have] already agreed to die." What punishment do you think participants who have killed in such a contest deserve? Suppose a contest is raided just as the first round was about to start. What punishment should be given to those who were about to pull the trigger?

3. One person places a bet on Sébastien (George Babluani) even though Sébastien is an inexperienced competitor. The rationale for the bet is that the bettor has always done well when he has gone against logic. Is there any way that a bet on inexperienced Sébastien is a wise bet? What does experience have to do with having a better or worse chance of winning this type of contest?

Movie 27: *March of the Penguins*

Director: Luc Jacquet; 1 hour, 25 minutes; 2005

One of the most common "proofs" for the existence of God is called "The Teleological Proof." This proof provides the main substance behind the arguments of those in the "intelligent design" movement.

The most famous proponent of the Teleological Proof is William Paley (1743–1805). To prove God's existence, Paley presented what is called his "watch example." Here is Paley's argument:

> In crossing a heath, suppose I pitched my foot against a *stone* and were asked how the stone came to be there, I might possibly answer that for anything I knew to the contrary it had lain there forever ... but suppose I had found a *watch* upon the ground, and it should be inquired how the watch happened to be in that place? I should hardly think of the answer which I had before given, that for anything I knew the watch might have always been there.[1]

If while hiking we find a watch, we would rationally assume someone accidentally dropped it. Where did that person get the watch? Probably from some store. From what source did the store get the watch? From some manufacturing firm. Where did the firm get the watch? *It didn't.* The watch was made by the firm. Some designer designed the watch, and employees used tools and machines to make the watch from raw materials. Besides the fact that we know about watch factories from experience, the conclusion that the watch was designed and manufactured follows from the type of thing the watch is. The watch *shows* design. If someone were to theorize that the leather, gold, glass, and other materials that make up the watch had come together by chance and just happened to become connected to each other, listeners would justly wonder about that person's reasoning abilities. Suppose there were hills outside Tulsa, Oklahoma, that had white rocks at the top and dark rocks at the lower points. If a few white rocks were found to be among the lower rocks, we would reasonably infer that the white rocks fell there due to erosion and gravity. However, if there were a hundred white rocks in the dark rock area, and the white rocks spelled out "Welcome to Tulsa," then we would not conclude that those rocks fell there by chance. The message "Welcome to Tulsa" would have been designed. Though it is possible hundreds of rocks just happened to stop in those positions, the odds are so great against such a happening, it is not reasonable to believe that they got there by chance.

The faces on Mount Rushmore could have come into existence by chance, but it wouldn't be reasonable to believe that either. (Can you name the four presidents carved on Mount Rushmore?)

March of the Penguins (2005): Do these penguins show evidence of a designer god?

Paley's watch, the "Welcome to Tulsa" sign, and the faces on Mount Rushmore all show signs of design. Whenever you see things like these, you rationally infer that those things did not happen by chance. Now, if you consider it, the universe and everything in it show such harmony; the universe can be compared to a watch. Think of Halley's Comet returning to the same points much like the second hand of a watch. The "Welcome to Tulsa" sign was made by a designer who wanted to welcome visitors to Tulsa. An eye has a purpose — to see. A heart has a purpose of pumping blood to various parts of the body. If the purpose of a watch was given to it by a designer, then the purposes of an eye and of a heart must have been given to them by a designer. The orderliness of the working of the universe and the purposes that things have, rationally lead to the conclusion that there is a God — the intelligent designer of things.

There is something about the Teleological Proof that convinces many people that a Supreme Being exists. You can hear people pointing to the sky, to flowers, and to babies, and saying, "These things couldn't happen by chance." A close loved one recently viewed the exhibit "Our Bodies, the Universe Within," and was so amazed at the tremendous complexity and organization of human body parts she exclaimed, "This couldn't be an accident." If such things can't come into existence by "chance" or "accident," it would seem that they must come into existence by some plan. Thus, there must be a "planner."

Unfortunately, the Teleological Proof does not stand up well to deeper scrutiny. Here are some problems with the proof.

1. It *is* difficult for ordinary people to conceive that things of great complexity come into being by natural means. Let us assume it is impossible to understand how nature might contain, in itself, the causes that could explain things. How is that problem eliminated by postulating the existence of a God, who created the complex things of the complex world? *How* did He do it? The problematic postulate that Nature is responsible for the existence of all things is now replaced with an even more problematic postulate — that by an act of will, a Supreme Spirit caused those things, in all their complexity, to come into existence. How is *that* a better postulate?

2. A fallacy may be hidden in the poof. Whenever one argues that a whole thing must have characteristic x because parts of that thing have characteristic x, one is committing what is called a "composition fallacy." If I say that the cake I am holding is the best possible cake because I used

the "best ingredients," then I have committed a composition fallacy. Perhaps it is true I used the best ingredients (parts), but it does not follow this is the best cake (whole). I may have used too much of one ingredient, or burnt the cake, or dropped it in the john.[2] The Teleological Proof may likewise commit a composition fallacy. It may be true that certain particular things (watches, signs, the Mount Rushmore figures) might require designers. It does not follow the *whole* universe requires a designer.

3. David Hume (1771–1776), in his great work *Dialogues Concerning Natural Religion,* presents a large number of arguments against the Teleological Proof. One centers on the fact that the proof depends on an analogy, and, according to Hume, one should never trust a philosophic argument that rests on an analogy. The following example will make Hume's point: There is a serial killer who calls himself "Zero." At every full moon, Zero seeks out some new victim and that victim is always approximately 55 years old, is about 5'5" tall, and is a balding, white male. Zero stabs the victim in the back, and carves a "Z" on the chest ("Z" for "Zero"—not "Zorro"). After 14 murders over a period of 14 months, Zero is captured. Zero confesses, and gives the police information only the murderer would know. A knife in Zero's house is recovered and proven to be the murder weapon. Zero is guilty and his guilt is established at a subsequent trial. He is sentenced to be executed, but prior to his execution he escapes. On the next evening there is a full moon, and a 55-year-old, 5'5" balding white male is murdered by a stab wound in his back and a "Z" is carved on his chest. Zero is again captured, once more confesses, and once more gives information only the murderer would know. He awaits execution, but again escapes. This time, however, something unexplainable happens to Zero. Suddenly he becomes aware of the wrongness of the crimes he has committed, and a deep sense of guilt hits him. He now wants to make only moral decisions that will benefit society. For a while, he thinks it would be best to turn himself in. Then, however, he decides it would bring about the greatest amount of happiness to the greatest number of people if he were to dedicate his life to doing good things. By means of cosmetic surgery he disguises his identity. He becomes a model citizen. He becomes a school crossing guard, volunteers to teach immigrants English, and joins crews that pick up litter on the side of major roadways. One evening after a full day of doing good deeds, he decides to relax and go for a walk. There is a full

moon. A white man — about 55 years old, 5'5" tall, balding — comes towards him, and as that man passes by, he and Zero wish each other a nice evening. The 55-year-old continues walking away from Zero. Unknown to either the 55-year-old, or Zero, there is a third person lurking in the shadows, waiting for the 55-year-old to pass. This mysterious third person knows all about the Zero murders, and knows that Zero has escaped from police custody. As the 55-year-old man passes, this stranger jumps out of the shadows, stabs the man in the back and carves a "Z" on his chest. He then disappears into the darkness. Who will the police, and everyone who reads about the murder, say was the murderer? Zero! And that would be false. Here is a case in which every victim was very similar, all were killed when there was a full moon, and all of the wounds were of the same type. If, as in the Zero example, a false conclusion can be deduced from similar events, how can an analogy be trustworthy when such dissimilar things as watches and the universe are being compared? If a good analogy can lead to a falsehood, what faith should we have in a bad analogy? Don't trust the analogy in the Teleological Proof.

4. Hume, however, does not stop with his notion that philosophic arguments based on analogies should not be trusted. *Even if* you trust the analogy at the base of the Teleological Proof, the proof does not establish the type of God its adherents suppose it establishes. Let us take the analogy in the proof seriously. We must, then, not only compare the universe to a watch; but we must also compare God to a watch maker. Ask yourself the following questions:

>   a. How many people are involved in making a watch? Perhaps one person, but probably many persons.
>   b. What is the sex of the watchmaker? Some watchmakers are male; some are female.
>   c. I have a watch that was made in the 1930s. Is the watchmaker who made that watch alive or dead? Probably dead.
>   d. Is the watchmaker a good person or a bad person? Some watchmakers are good people; some are evil.
>   e. Is the watchmaker a master watchmaker or an apprentice (student) watchmaker?

By comparing God to a watchmaker, the above questions lead us to the conclusion that the maker of a certain watch might be:

(a) One person   or   many people
(b) Male   or   female
(c) Alive   or   dead
(d) Good   or   evil
(e) A master god   or   an apprentice god

If I tell you I have a friend, but I can't tell you if my friend is one person or many people, nor whether my friend is male or female, alive or dead, good or evil, a master or student of anything, have I told you anything about my friend? No! Nor does the Teleological Proof tell you anything about the designer God(s). Adherents of the Teleological Proof often seem to indicate that they think the intelligent design argument proves God has the characteristics on the left of the above list. God is one, male, living, good master. However, the Teleological Proof is also compatible with the idea that the design of the universe was due to many dead, evil, female gods who were students who received Fs on their project — the creation of this universe. The Teleological Proof does not work.

Watch the movie.

Questions to ponder:

1. As I viewed *March of the Penguins* for the first time, the idea came to me that the documentary provides strong evidence against the theory of "intelligent design." Subsequently, I was shocked at the numbers of viewers who judged that the film provided *support* for creationism, as well as support for traditional family values. In a *New York Times* article written by Jonathan Miller, several quotes by film critics and Christian intellectuals were given:

> Of *March of the Penguins*, conservative film critic and radio host Michael Medved said in an interview, *Penguins* is "the motion picture this summer that most passionately affirms traditional norms like monogamy, sacrifice and child rearing." Speaking of audiences who feel movies ignore or belittle such themes, he added: "This is the first movie [conservatives have] enjoyed since *The Passion of the Christ*. This is the passion of the Penguins...."
>
> To Andrew Coffin, writing in the widely circulated Christian publication *World* magazine, [the documentary provides] a winning argument for the theory that life is too complex to have arisen through random selection. "That any one of [the penguin's] eggs survives is a remarkable feat — and some might suppose, a strong case for intelligent design...."
>
> Other religious conservatives have seized on the movie as a parable of

steadfast faith. In Sidney, Ohio, Ben Hunt, a minister at the 153 House Churches Network, has coordinated trips to the local theater to see the film…. "Some of the circumstances [the penguins] experience seemed to parallel those of Christians," he said of the penguins. "The penguin in falling behind, is like some Christians falling behind.[3]

Are these commentators reading too much into the penguins' behavior? Does *March of the Penguins* provide evidence for intelligent design? (It seems to me a Creator could have attached jet packs to the backs of the penguins to help them get to their destinations. Making penguins waddle the 70 miles between the feeding area and the breeding ground does not seem too intelligent to me.) Does the film support monogamy? The penguins are amazingly loyal during the long mating routine, but they have different mates the next year! Doesn't that indicate that too many people read too much into the film?

ADDITIONAL RECOMMENDED DOCUMENTARIES

The Up Series (movie 13) and *March of the Penguins* are the only documentaries discussed in this book. Every one of the following documentaries is well worth viewing:

Nanook of the North (United States, 1922) and *Man of Aran* (United States, 1934). Silent masterpieces by the pioneer documentarian, Robert J. Flaherty.

Triumph of the Will (Germany, 1935). Leni Riefenstahl does everything she can to make Hitler's Germany look appealing. For a balanced documentary on Riefenstahl, herself, see Ray Müller's *The Wonderful, Horrible Life of Leni Riefenstahl* (1933).

The Sorrow and the Pity (France, 1972). Life in Clermont-Ferrand, France, under the Nazi occupation.

Marjoe (United States, 1972). A fake evangelist tells his story and shows how he dupes his audiences.

Harlan County USA (United States, 1976). An account of a labor strike by coal miners.

Burden of Dreams (United States, 1982). This is a documentary on the making of Werner Herzog's film *Fitzcarraldo* (1982). Watch *Fitzcarraldo* first, and then the documentary. It is a miracle the entire crew did not die on the set of the film.

Roger and Me / Bowling for Columbine / Fahrenheit 9/11 / Sicko / Capitalism: A Love Story (United States: 1989/2002/2004/2007/2009). Four documentaries by the controversial Michael Moore. The first film investigates the car industry; The second goes after the gun industry; the third exposes the Bush Administration's response to 9/11, and the fourth is critical of the American health-care system. *Capitalism: A Love Story* (2009) is Moore's take on abuses caused by capitalism.

Shoah (France, 1985). Over eight hours in length, unforgettable documentary on the Holocaust. The director interviews townspeople who lived near concentration camps but "didn't know what was going on inside the camps." Survivors are interviewed; some return to the site of the camp for the first time since their terrible experiences there.

Brother's Keeper (United States, 1992) and *Paradise Lost: The Child Murders at Robin Hood Hills* (United States, 1996). Two crime thrillers from co-directors Joe Berlinger and Bruce Sinofsky. For an update on the former film, see *Paradise Lost 2: Revelations* (2000).

Hoop Dreams / The Heart of the Game (United States: 1994/2005). Documentaries on high school basketball teams. The director is Ward Serrill. *Hoop Dreams* centers on a boys' team; *The Heart of the Game* on a girls' team.

When We Were Kings (United States, 1996). The 1974 championship boxing match between Muhammad Ali and George Foreman.

4 Little Girls (United States, 1997). Spike Lee directs a documentary on the bombing of the Sixteenth Street Baptist Church in Birmingham, Alabama in 1963. In this racial attack, four African-American girls were killed.

The Last Days (United States, 1998). Interviews with Holocaust survivors.

One Day in September (Switzerland, 1999). The attack on Israeli athletes during the Munich Olympics.

Buena Vista Social Club (Germany, 1999). Great Cuban musicians brought together out of retirement.

Mr. Death: The Rise and Fall of Fred A. Leuchter, Jr. (United States, 2000). An in-depth look at a "scientist" who "proved" no one was gassed at Auschwitz.

The Eyes of Tammy Faye (United States, 2000). A sympathetic look at the former wife of tele-evangelist, Jim Bakker.

Sound and the Fury (United States, 2000). Not to be confused with William Faulkner's novel, this documentary is a moving presentation about the decision some parents face about whether or not their deaf children should get cochlear implants, enabling them to hear.

The Gleaners and I (France, 2000)

The Endurance (Great Britain, 2001). "The Endurance" is the name of explorer Sir Ernest Shackleton's ship, used on his attempt to reach the South Pole in 1913. Great adventure story.

Winged Migration (France, 2001). You will migrate with birds. Be sure to check out the extra on the DVD to see how portions of the film were made.

Stevie (United States, 2002). The story of a bad ass. Directed by Steve James (not the "Stevie" of the title), who also directed *Hoop Dreams* and *The Heart of the Game* (see above).

Spellbound (United States, 2002). Follows several contestants of the National Spelling Bee. (Compare the fictional 2006 *Akeelah and the Bee* with *Spellbound*.)

Bus 174 (Brazil, 2002). An armed young man takes over a bus filled with passengers.

The Parrots of Telegraph Hill (United States, 2003)

The Fog of War (United States, 2003). Eleven lessons from the life of Robert S. McNamara.

Born into Brothels: Calcutta's Red Light Kids (United States, 2004)

Control Room (United States, 2004). The Iraq War according to Al Jazeera, an Arab news organization.

Why We Fight (United States, 2005). Why America tends to rush into war.

Enron: The Smartest Guys in the Room (United States, 2005)

No Direction Home: Bob Dylan (United States, 2005). Directed by Martin Scorsese.

Grizzly Man (Germany, 2005)

Jesus Camp (United States, 2006). A camp for children, run by Christian fundamentalists.

In the Shadow of the Moon (United States, 2007). About the Apollo journeys to the moon.

Young @ Heart (United States, 2007). Elderly inhabitants of a nursing home find meaning in their lives by banding together to sing hard rock songs in public.

Enlighten Up (United States, 2009). A skeptic enters the world of yoga.

Food, Inc. (United States, 2009). A glance at how our food is processed. Not a pretty sight.

The Cove (United States, 2009). An investigation into the slaughter of porpoises.

Movie 28: *I've Loved You So Long*

Director: Philippe Claudel; 1 hour, 57 minutes; 2008

The title *I've Loved You So Long* seems appropriate for a romantic film. Don't be fooled. This film is not a traditional love story. It deals with a woman's attempt to adjust to reality while having to live with something traumatic from her past.

Watch the movie.

Questions to ponder:

1. Critics generally praised the originality of *I've Loved You So Long* and raved about the acting. A significant number, however, felt the ending is a cop-out. A friend agreed with those critics by saying he was disappointed when he discovered the motive that drove Juliette (Kristin Scott Thomas) to kill her son was "mercy killing." Were you disappointed by the ending? My concern is the improbability that Juliette's parents and friends would abandon her after the killing of her child. Wouldn't they know from an autopsy that the child had a terminal illness? Wouldn't Lea (Elsa Zylberstein) learn the truth? Wouldn't Juliette's husband know she

Lea (Elsa Zylberstein, left) and Juliette (Kristin Scott Thomas) in *I've Loved You So Long* (2008). What motive drove Juliette to do something terrible?

acted out of love? He also deserted her. Knowing the facts of the case, would a judge really give Juliette such a long sentence?

2. Are there any clues to why Captain Faure (Frédéric Pierrot) commits suicide? He was so excited about perhaps taking a trip to see the Orinoco Pines.

ADDITIONAL RECOMMENDED FILMS FROM FRANCE

L'Atalante (1934)
Grand Illusion (1937)
The Rules of the Game (1939)
Jules and Jim (1962)
The Umbrellas of Cherbourg (1964)
Au Revoir, les Enfants (1988)
Colonel Chabert (1994)
Ridicule (1996)
The Girl on the Bridge (1999)
With a Friend Like Harry (2000)
Amélie (2001)
8 Women (2002)
He Loves Me, He Loves Me Not (2003)
L'Enfant (2006)

SCANDINAVIA

Movies 29 and 30: *Scenes from a Marriage* and *Saraband*

Director: Ingmar Bergman

Television miniseries of *Scenes from a Marriage* (1966)—4 hours, 55 minutes

Theatrical version of *Scenes from a Marriage* (1973)—2 hours, 47 minutes

Saraband: (2003)—1 hour, 52 minutes

This entry is the third that centers on two people talking to each other. Talking, talking, talking. The other two are *Before Sunrise/Before Sunset* (movies 3 and 4) and *Oleanna* (movie 92). The characters in Bergman's *Scenes from a Marriage* and *Saraband* are very different from those in the latter films. Those differences, plus the unique styles of the directors make each film distinctive. In *Before Sunrise/Before Sunset*, the two characters are soul mates; in *Oleanna* each character is portrayed as being a victim of the other. In *Scenes from a Marriage*, you will follow the ups and down of a marital relationship. Years later, Bergman returned to the couple featured in *Scenes* for his last theatrically released work, *Saraband.*

You must make a choice of whether to watch the five hour uncut television version of *Scenes from a Marriage*, or the shorter theatrical release. I highly recommend the uncut version; you can never get enough of Bergman. The list of questions below will be appropriate for either version.

Watch *Scenes from a Marriage.*

Questions to ponder:

1. In the last episode, Marianne (Liv Ullmann) tells Johan (Erland Josephson) that she has never loved or been loved. Johan responds, "I love

you in my selfish way.... We love each other." Do they love each other? At every moment of every episode? Does Johan love Marianne *when* he tells her he is leaving for Paris with Paula? Does it seem to you that Marianne's love for Johan is more constant than Johan's love for her? In Episode Six, she admits to having had an affair early in their marriage. Did that surprise you? How would you describe the characters of Johan and Marianne? Would you have nastier words to describe Johan than Marianne? In Episode Three, Johan says, "I don't imagine for one minute that I've touched on the truth about us. I don't think there is such a thing as truth." Is Johan correct that words cannot adequately describe the truth of their marriage? One scene in Episode Four caused me to gasp, and convinced me Johan is just a self-centered slob who does *not* truly love Marianne. Marianne is baring her soul, by reading from her diary. The camera pans over to Johan. He is asleep. I imagine he would do the same thing in the company of his second wife, or with any of his lovers. How did you react to that scene?

2. In Episode Two, Marianne admits whatever she senses seems

Liv Ullmann (as Marianne) and Erland Josephson (as Johan) try to communicate in a tumultuous marriage in Ingmar Bergman's *Scenes from a Marriage* (1973).

"deadened and dry." She includes "music, scents, faces, voices." Everything seems empty. Nothing matters. She is in a state described by Jean-Paul Sartre (1905–1980) in his novel *Nausea*. For most of the novel, Roquentin, the main character, is unable to relate to anything he encounters. People who speak to him seem to be merely babbling. He has been writing a biography of a historical personage but drops that project, because the facts he has written about seem non-essential. He really cannot know this person whose life he is investigating. He goes to a museum. He experiences only emptiness. He looks at himself in a mirror, but sees only a lump of unfamiliar clay. Have you ever experienced this state which Sartre calls "nausea"? Nausea (or "angst") appears to be a totally negative state of mind. However, several existentialists — including Sartre — also find nausea to be a necessary component of the human being. People, they say, tend to live shallow lives. Only if the emptiness of those lives is shown to be nothing, can the door to a more authentic life be opened. Are there any signs that Marianne has more self-esteem in later episodes than she does before nausea strikes?

3. At one point, Johan asks, "Do you think people who live together can ever be completely honest? ... Is it even necessary?" How would you answer these questions?

4. Episode One mentions Saint Paul's remarks in Corinthians 13:4–8 on the nature of love. Here are Paul's words:

> Love is patient and kind. Love envies no one, is never boastful, never conceited, never rude; love is never selfish, never quick to take offense. Love keeps no score of wrongs, takes no pleasure in the sins of others, but delights in the truth. There is nothing love cannot face; there is no limit to its faith, its hope, its endurance.[1]

Go through each of the characteristics of love listed above, and decide whether or not Johan or Marianne abide by them.

5. When Marianne first finds out about Johan's affair with Paula, she turns to a friend for comfort and advice. She is crushed to discover that all of her friends have been aware of the affair, but none have told her. Should those friends have told her? Why or why not?

Watch *Saraband*

Warning: Brief nudity

Questions to ponder:

1. Karin (Julia Dufvenius) has the opportunity of a lifetime. She can leave home and receive top-notch instruction on cello, followed by a career

in an orchestra. The problem: her presence is the only meaningful element in the life of Henrik (Börje Ahlstedt), her father. She reasonably believes that he will be suicidal if she leaves. What should she do? Don't children have a duty to stand by their parents? Don't parents, however, also have a duty to free their adult children?

I have had several students who were forced to make a decision that involved a dilemma similar to the one faced by Karin. One was a female from an impoverished background. She was in her third year of college, and dedicated to her studies. She had plans that would probably have led to a stable job following graduation. However, she received a jolt when a letter arrived from her single mother. The letter informed her that the mother had terminal cancer, and wanted the student to return home. If she goes home she can help her mother, but she will have to drop out of school and possibly never return. What should she do? Oh yes — there is a tidbit I failed to tell you — her mother had not gone to any doctor and, thus, had never had tests that diagnosed her with cancer. Given that information, what would you tell her? She asked for my advice. I couldn't give any. Suppose I tell her to stay in school? Clearly, however, her mother has *some* problems, and needs her. Suppose she stays in school, and her mother commits suicide because she is in a mind set much like that of Henrik?

2. Karin shares with Marianne the letter Karin's dying mother has written. In the letter the mother pleads with her father to free Karin. Marianne says the letter "is what love is." What does Marianne mean?

3. In the last scene, Marianne says she feels a deep kinship with Anna, someone she has never met. She also connects her feelings about Anna with her own recent meeting with her daughter, Martha (Gunnel Fred). What is it that Marianne sees in the story of Anna's life that means so much to her?

Movie 31: *My Life as a Dog*

Director: Lasse Hallström, 1 hour, 41 minutes, 1985
Watch the movie.

Questions to ponder:

1. There is a short essay by Kurt Vonnegut included in the Criterion edition of *My Life as a Dog*. Vonnegut pinpoints something that makes me realize why I have cherished this film through numerous viewings:

"This movie, directed and largely written by Lasse Hallström and released in 1985, when he was thirty-nine and I was sixty-three, made me like life and human beings much more than I had ever done before." If you respond to the film in the same way as Kurt Vonnegut, what is it about almost every character that touches a chord, and gives you a hopeful feeling about human nature? Is it that, as Vonnegut says, "in this village, at least, dogs and orphans alike encounter such kindness and love from simple people, and partake with everyone else in sports, and in misadventures so odd and human and hilarious and endearing, that life anywhere else could not be more marvelous." Do you think your neighborhood, or the town where you live, has an atmosphere like the one found in *My Life as a Dog*?

In general, I would have to say my childhood life in Lititz, Pennsylvania very much mirrored the communal lifestyle of the Swedish village in the plot of *My Life as a Dog*. Do you think it is now more difficult to have a healthy community like the one in that village? What factors have been involved in making community life less communal?

2. Ingemar (Anton Glanzelius) possesses an amazing coping mechanism by comparing his situation with the situations of others. He thinks

Anton Glanzelius as Ingemar, right, a boy who imagines what it is like to be a dog shot into space in *My Life as a Dog* (1985). On the receiving end is Melinda Kinnaman.

"it's important to have something like (what happened to Laika, the space dog) to compare things to." Why might it make some people who have troubles feel better if they compare themselves to others who are worse off? Ingemar says, "I've been kind of lucky ... compared to others. You have to compare. So you can get a little distance on things." What would be the effect if we compared our misfortunes with people who are more fortunate than us?

3. Ingemar smiles many times during the film. He often smiles after clearly pondering about something terrible that has just happened. He seems to achieve some understanding that pulls him away from his morbid thoughts. His smile at these times is unforgettable. What does he understand that makes him smile? Is it that in spite of the hardships he experiences, there is still so much about life that can give joy? Is his smile an attempt to cover up the pain he feels?

Movie 32: *Hamsun*

Director: Jan Troell, 2 hours, 40 minutes, 1996
Watch the movie.

Questions to ponder:

1. No one can doubt that Hamsun (Max von Sydow) is sincere in his belief that (a) England is a danger to Norwegian independence, and (b) Nazi Germany will lead Norway to be a free state. He feels he is promoting what is good for Norway. Does the label "traitor" accurately describe Hamsun? What types of actions make one a traitor? Various German civilians were

Max von Sydow as Knut Hamsun, winner of the Nobel Prize in literature and an admirer of Adolf Hitler in *Hamsun* (1996).

involved in attempts to assassinate Hitler. Should those Germans be judged "heroes" or "traitors"? Is one person's hero another person's traitor, so that judgments about whether someone is a hero or a traitor are mere opinions, or subjective judgments?

2. For years I have been deeply impressed with a statement found in Immanuel Kant's great ethical work *Foundations of the Metaphysics of Morals*: "...the sight of a being adorned with no feature of a pure and good will, yet enjoying uninterrupted prosperity, can never give pleasure to a rational impartial observer."[1] Kant argues that the good will is the only thing absolutely good, no matter what the situation. Even God is good, not because he has knowledge and power, but because he has a good will. Person A who is intelligent, powerful, wealthy, honored, and healthy, but who lacks a good will, will cause another person B pleasure if A is beneficial to B. B is not an "impartial" judge of the goodness of A. Because B benefits from A, B will tend to label A "good." An impartial observer C will not judge A to be good. Also, B may judge A to be good if B is an irrational person. Hamsun and his wife admire Hitler. Are they "impartial, rational observers"? Why or why not? Hitler certainly lacks "a good will." Thus, it would seem to follow that since Hamsun and his wife seem to think Hitler is "good," they must either lack impartiality, or be irrational.

3. Obtain a copy of Plato's *Apology*— Plato's account of Socrates' self-defense at his trial. Compare Socrates' speech at his trial with Hamsun's defense as portrayed in the film. Both Socrates and Hamsun feel strongly about the rightness of their past activities. Both claim they are driven by their sense of right and wrong. Do you agree that Socrates' defense is stunning, whereas that of Hamsun — though presented from the heart — falls flat? List and evaluate the points made by these two geniuses at their trials.

Movie 33: *Elling*

Director: Petter Naess, 1 hour, 29 minutes, 2001

A substantial number of films covered in this book involve tragedies, and may be judged by some viewers as "downers." *Elling* is not one of them. You are about to be exposed to an "odd couple." If there is any depth to the plot, it has to do with the difficulties faced by people who had a far-from-normal childhood. The film also captures how two friends can help each other grow into mature people. *Autumn Spring* (movie 49) will also capture that latter theme. The opposite, showing how a friend can lead one down the wrong path, can be found in *4 Months, 3 Weeks, 2 Days* (movie 53).

Watch the movie.

Questions to ponder:

1. Plato was a polytheist. Each of Plato's gods had a certain function. Eros, the god of love, had the function of leading persons from ignorance and shallowness to knowledge of the Good. The true lover or friend acts in the same manner as Eros. The true lover leads the loved one to a wiser, better, more fulfilling state of being than the loved one would have achieved without the lover. Elling (Per Christian Ellefsen) and Kjell Bjarne (Sven Nordin) are two friends because they struggle to raise each other up. As stated above, a main character in *4 Months, 3 Weeks, 2 Days* causes her friend to fall into a state of emptiness and despair. A friend who does that is not truly a friend — he/she is an enemy. An important question all people should ask is "Are my friends truly friends? Are they helping me become more knowledgeable, more caring, and more dynamic? Or, are they stifling me and using me? Are they really my enemies?" Do you think Elling is a true friend to Kjell? The person in charge of Elling and Kjell

Elling (Per Christian Ellefsen) isn't always alone — he makes his way through his adult life with a little help from his friends in *Elling* (2003).

is a social worker named Frank Asli (Jørgen Langhelle). Is he a true friend, or is he merely doing a job?

2. If there were a sequel, Elling and Kjell would certainly still be kooky characters. In what direction do you think Elling's life will go? Can you picture what life is like for Kjell, Reidun (Marit Pia Jacobsen) and their baby?

Movie 34: *Lilya 4-Ever*

Director: Lukas Moodysson; 1 hour, 49 minutes; 2002

Warning: Very disturbing plot; very disturbing scenes. One critic commented that *Lilya 4-Ever* is "just about the grimmest, most despairing thing I've ever seen. When it was over, I wanted to hang myself."[1] Don't say I didn't warn you!

Lilya 4-Ever is reminiscent of two other movies I highly recommend: *Kids* (1995) and *Maria Full of Grace* (2004). Catalina Sandino Moreno particularly excelled in *Maria Full of Grace*. Oksana Akinshina is unforgettable as Lilya.

Watch the movie.

Questions to ponder:

1. Moodysson dedicated his film to the huge number of exploited girls trapped in the sex trade. The most important question the viewer should ask is, "What can be done to eliminate the abuse of girls like Lilya?"

2. Andrei (Pavel Ponomaryov) is so convincing that he authentically cares for Lilya. Given her hopeless situation, does Lilya have any choice but to trust Andrei? Is there *anything* in the whole story she should have done differently?

3. Lilya clearly becomes a mother figure to Volodya (Artyom Bogucharsky). Should she stay with Volodya, whether Andrei is a fake or not? Volodya depends on her every bit as much as Lilya had depended on her mother.

4. Lilya states her birthday is the same as that of Britney Spears, though Lilya is four years older than Britney. She then states that it would have been "cool to have been mixed up in the hospital." If Lilya had been switched with Britney, she would have been a pop star, and Britney would have turned out to be a lost soul in Russia. Is there an element of injustice in the universe that hands one person a prosperous life, and another

Oksana Akinshina as Lilya, a young girl trapped in a hopeless situation in *Lilya 4-Ever* **(2002).**

a life of unspeakable horror? Is the word "injustice" inappropriately used in that question?

Movie 35: *After the Wedding*

Director: Susanne Bier; 2 hours, 0 minutes; 2006
Watch the movie.

Questions to ponder:

1. In the film, Jørgen (Rolf Lassgard) says, "I am just a good person." Is he a good person? In an extra on the DVD, director Susanne Bier asks, "Does anyone have any right to want to control other people's lives?" Jørgen clearly connives to have Jacob (Mads Mikkelsen) stay in Denmark, and become intimately involved with his family after Jørgen's death. Does Jørgen know Jacob was the father of Anna (Stine Fischer Christensen) when he has Jacob travel from the Mumbai orphanage to Denmark to discuss charitable donations? Bier also asks: "Can anyone who manipulates other people to benefit them ever really know what is good for them?"

Helene (Sidse Babett Knudsen) and Jacob (Mads Mikkelsen) in a scene from *After the Wedding* (2006). Why were Helene and Jacob brought together by her husband?

Bier says Jørgen's plans are successful, but asks if they are "morally responsible." Does the end justify the means? Jørgen does not tell Anna he is dying. Anna is clearly hurt that Jørgen kept such a secret from her. Bier asks: "Does anyone have a right to be secretive towards loved ones?" Jørgen wants everyone in his family to live a normal, happy life as long as possible. What, if any, kinds of things do you think you should keep from loved ones?

2. Jørgen says: "Every acquaintance, every friend, every person who has a place in your heart — it is the time with them that really means something. Nothing else matters." Do you agree with Jørgen? If we suddenly face death, will we realize the truth of what he says?

ADDITIONAL RECOMMENDED FILMS FROM SCANDINAVIA

The Emigrants (1971)
Pelle the Conqueror (1987)
The Celebration (1998)
Mifune (1999)
Italian for Beginners (2000)
The Inheritance (2003)

GERMANY

Movie 36: *Ali: Fear Eats the Soul*

Director: Rainer Werner Fassbinder; 1 hour, 34 minutes; 1974
Watch the movie.

Questions to ponder:

1. Ali (El Hedi ben Salem) feels alienated because he is treated like a "foreigner" in his chosen country, Germany. Some Germans see "foreigners" like Ali to be "swine." Emmi (Brigitte Mira) feels that life is passing her by. Her children are grown and do not have close regular contact with her. Her husband has died. Here are two lonely people who find each other, and — though different in age and background — fall in love. As the plot unfolds, it seems their relationship is doomed — not because of their differences, but because of the overwhelming pressure from prejudiced neighbors and workmates. Shouldn't people be *happy* for Ali and Emmi? Why is so much hate directed towards them? One character says the relationship between Ali and Emmi is "unnatural." Is it "unnatural" in any way?

ADDITIONAL RECOMMENDATIONS

It appears that *Ali: Fear Eats the Soul* is a German remake of Douglas Sirk's *All that Heaven Allows* (1955). Sirk's movie was also remade in 2002 by Todd Haynes. The title of Haynes' excellent film is *Far from Heaven*.

Rainer Werner Fassbinder directed a number of other films that are included in most lists of all-time great German films. See, for example, his *BRD Trilogy: The Marriage of Maria Braun* (1979); *Veronica Voss* (1982); and *Lola* (1981). This trilogy tells the stories of three remarkable women. Fassbinder died from a drug overdose at the age of 36, before his epic *Berlin Alexanderplatz* was given its American theatrical release. The running time

Ali (El Hedi ben Salem) is treated as a foreigner in his chosen country and is involved in a forbidden relationship in *Ali: Fear Eats the Soul* (1974).

for *Berlin Alexanderplatz* is 15 hours, 41 minutes. It first appeared on German television in 1980.

Movie 37: *Run Lola Run*

Director: Tom Tywker; 1 hour, 21 minutes; 1998

In Chapter 5 on "Fate and Determinism" in *Plato and Popcorn*, I presented two movies, Roman Polanski's *Tess* (1980), and a Gwyneth Paltrow vehicle entitled *Sliding Doors* (1998). Both films contain what I term "flukes" in their plots. A fluke is some small event in a person's life that leads the person down a path that could not have been predicted. If that small event had not happened, then a radically different path would have been taken by the person. In *Sliding Doors*, two stories are told. One story is of what happens to Helen (Paltrow's character) if she makes it on time to a subway train. The other shows the path taken if a little girl slows her down on the subway steps, and the doors shut just before Helen can enter the subway. Being delayed by the girl would be a fluke. *Tess* also contains a large number of flukes. In one instance, it is extremely important to Tess to get a note to someone who is in a room behind a door. She slips the note under the door, and all seems well. The problem is that Tess does not know there is a rug on the other side of the door. The note goes under the rug and does not get to the intended recipient.

I presented *Run Lola Run* as a "recommendation" following my *Plato and Popcorn* comments on *Tess* and *Sliding Doors*. I categorized it as a "roller coaster of a movie." It is indeed that. Like *Tess*, *Run Lola Run* captures one fluke after another.

Watch the movie.

Questions to ponder:

1. List as many "flukes" as you can from *Run Lola Run*. Do you think it is reasonable to show, in quick flashes, possible future paths of the people Lola (Franka Potente) encounters in her three alternate journeys?

2. Is there any significance to Lola's piercing scream in the casino? Does the scream cause the ball to stop at the right number?

3. Though I see the paths Lola takes as being caused, is it possible that elements of free will enter the picture at various times? Does she freely start the journey over when it does not end in a desired way? Does such a starting over make any sense? Only one path is really possible.

Lola (Franka Potente) runs to do what is almost impossible in *Run Lola Run* (1998).

4. Does the third alternative depict what actually happens? Lola, though apparently disgusted with what has transpired, walks off with Manni (Moritz Bleibtreu), who is unexpectedly safe.

Movie 38: *Downfall*

Director: Oliver Hirschbiegel; 2 hours, 36 minutes; 2004
Watch the movie.

Questions to ponder:

1. Hitler (Bruno Ganz), after claiming that all his efforts were for the German people, makes several comments in *Downfall* that indicate that when the chips are down he cares only for himself. In one scene, he responds to concerns that civilians will unnecessarily suffer if the decimated German forces do not surrender. He says: "In a war like this, there are no civilians." Hitler has clearly never cared about the fate of enemy civilians. Now he is even indifferent to the suffering of his own people. Later he says, "If the war is lost, it's immaterial if the people perish too. It is not necessary to consider the German people's primitive survival needs." Goebbels (Ulrich Matthes) expresses a similar view: "The strongest can only be victorious by eradicating the weak." (A contrary view is expressed in the 1956 film *Abandon Ship*— see *Plato and Popcorn*, pages 23–25 — in which one character says, "The whole point of civilization is for the strong to protect the weak.") Clearly, Hitler is merely an egomaniac, and his cause is based on racist principles. Is there *any* cause, so important that the protection of civilians should be ignored, and for which it would be "immaterial if the people perish"? Is there *any* cause that, if lost, would justify the killing of one's own children? Magda Goebbels (Corinna Harfouch) clearly thinks National Socialism is such a cause. Is this act of infanticide just one more example of Goebbels' selfishness?

2. Albert Speer (played by Heino Ferch in the film) has often been called "the good Nazi." At the Nuremberg Tribunal, he accepted responsibility for the unfathomable abuses of Hitler's regime. Late in the war, he disobeyed several of Hitler's orders, and later even claimed that he had planned to assassinate Hitler. However, to fulfill his duties as "Hitler's architect"—and as minister of armaments and war production—Speer utilized millions of slave laborers, many of whom were prisoners of war and concentration camp inmates. It seems impossible that being in con-

The last days of Hitler's Germany are captured in *Downfall* (2004): Juliane Kohler as Eva Braun, Bruno Ganz as Adolf Hitler and Heino Ferch as Albert Speer.

stant communication with other high-ranking Nazi officials, Speer did not know about the "final solution." It may well be that he was the ideal technocrat who was so concerned with proficiently fulfilling his duties that he turned a blind eye to the victims of Nazi brutality. Even so, isn't such indifference inconsistent with "being good"? Is it possible to be both "good" and a Nazi? Are any of the other main characters in *Downfall* "good people"? What about Professor Dr. Ernst-Günter Schenck (Christian Berkel) and Traudl Junge (Alexandra Maria Lara), Hitler's secretary? (For more on Traudl Junge, see the 2002 documentary *Blindspot: Hitler's Secretary,* where she portrays herself as someone who was young, impressionable and uninterested in politics. Only after the war, according to her, did she become aware of the Nazi abuses.)

3. *Downfall* centers on the fall of Berlin as Russian troops attack from the west. War always forces the people involved to make numerous moral decisions. One dilemma involving the Russian advance has stood out for me since I was exposed to it in the 1960s by reading *Situation Ethics,* a bestseller by Joseph Fletcher (1905–1991). That book caused a controversy by seeming to undermine some of the absolute moral rules many

people think have been given to us by God. Fletcher argues that, in some situations, love dictates that certain cherished laws must be broken. After discussing the Ten Commandments, Fletcher says, "situation ethics has good reason to hold it as *duty* in some situations to break them, *any or all of them*. We would be better advised, and better off to drop the legalist's love of law and accept the law of love."[1] One of the examples Fletcher gives to support his general principle deals with the result of the Russian advance. A German mother of three children was picked up by Russian troops, and shipped to a prison camp deep in Russia. Her husband had previously been captured and was a prisoner of war in Wales. Shortly after the mother was placed in the prison camp, the Russians take Berlin and meet the Allies at the Elbe and World War II ends in Europe. You would think that the Russians would release German civilians after the conclusion of the war, but with the Cold War commencing and the arbitrariness of Stalin's rule, the woman is forced to remain in the prison camp. Her husband is freed, and reunited with his children. The German woman eventually discovers a way to be released. There is a rule at the camp that pregnant prisoners would be set free. As Fletcher put it: "She turned things over in her mind and finally asked a friendly Volga German camp guard to impregnate her, which he did. Her condition being medically verified, she was sent back to Berlin and her family."[2] Her husband accepts her pregnancy. Eventually, the baby is born, and becomes part of the family. The husband and wife move on with their lives. Did the woman act immorally? Remember: "Thou shalt not commit adultery" is a moral rule that millions of people believe is handed down by God. Fletcher held that love trumps any rule. Do you agree with Fletcher?

Movie 39: *Caché*

> Director: Michael Haneke; 1 hour, 58 minutes; 2005
> Warning: Violence
> Watch the movie.

Questions to ponder:

1. In an interview for one of the extras on the DVD of *Caché*, Michael Haneke says: "the movie is a tale of morality ... dealing with how one lives with guilt." Clearly, after it becomes obvious to Georges (Daniel Auteuil) that the video and pictures are being sent by someone who knows

what Georges did to Majid (Maurice Benichou) when they were young, Georges shows concern. His job may be in jeopardy if the truth gets out. His son, Pierrot (Lester Makedonsky), may turn against him. Is there any evidence in what is presented that Georges is filled with guilt before the videos and pictures show up? Haneke also says the film is about "coldness." He says Georges is not able to communicate with his wife, Anne (Juliette Binoche). Haneke asks, "Does this coldness come from everything that was swept under the rug?" Haneke clearly thinks that is probably the cause. He also thinks many people have cold personalities, as a result of the repression of guilt. Do you think Haneke is correct? My view is that lots of people are cold merely because they are cold, and not because they are repressing memories of previous deeds. In fact, it is possible that Georges was a cold child, and that is why he treated Majid the way he did. If that is the case, his coldness as a youth was not the result of repressed guilt. I think Haneke's view, that a lot of people are cold because of repressed guilt, commits a false cause fallacy. (See my comments on the nature of false cause fallacies in movies 22 and 23: *Jean de Florette* and *Manon of the Spring*.) Do you think Haneke is indeed committing such a fallacy in his judgment about the cause of coldness?

2. A *very* important sub-plot is at work in *Caché*. Majid's parents were killed by police in Paris, along with scores of other Algerian-born protesters, as they demonstrated against the French involvement in Algeria. All

In *Caché* (2005), an evil act in the past catches up with the evildoer.

evidence suggests that the police over-reacted against the protest. Racist beliefs held by the police probably fueled the attacks. Haneke was not aware of that historical event for years. It was a secret, "hidden" by the French — a truth repressed by the French psyche. Thus, countries will repress guilt just as individuals do. Haneke says *Caché* could take place in *any* country. If *Caché* were situated in the United States, what might be the repressed event?

3. Does Anne also have a secret? Is Pierrot right in his suspicion that his mother is having an affair with the family friend (Daniel Duval)? Is there any evidence that such an affair is taking place?

4. Now for the big question: Who is doing the video taping? Majid? His son (Walid Afkir)? Haneke is a perspectivist. He would accept Friedrich Nietzsche's (1844–1900) judgment that all there are are interpretations. For Haneke, "the truth is always hidden.... We never ever know what the truth is. There are 1,000 truths. It's a matter of perspective." Many people believe that truth is relative, i.e., that what one believes is true, depends on one's cultural conditioning. In my view, a majority of academicians are relativists. The same is true of the majority of my students. Time after time, students will write the following on philosophy tests: "Who knows what is right or wrong? No one can tell. There are only opinions." They are perspectivists and relativists. Are you a perspectivist?

ADDITIONAL RECOMMENDATIONS

Michael Haneke's also directed: *The Seventh Continent* (1989) and *Benny's Video* (1992). I recommend them, but be aware that they contain numerous extremely disturbing scenes and themes. The films may seem exploitative and contain little redeeming social value. However, interviews with Haneke found in "Special Features" of the DVDs of those films readily show that he is dealing with significant questions. The plot of *The Seventh Continent* is loosely based on an actual event. The big question to be raised in that film is, "Why does the family in the story do what it does?" In *Benny's Video*, Benny (Arno Frisch) is asked by his father why he did x. Benny answers he wanted to see what it was like to do x. In the DVD interview, Haneke claims there have been numerous cases in which people, after committing atrocities, explain they just wanted to see what it felt like to do what they did. Haneke thinks many people are so captivated by images on movie, television, or computer screens, that they do questionable things in order to experience what those things are "really like." They feel the need to know whether, or not, the real thing is different from the screen image. The answer, of course, is that the real thing is *always* different from the image, because faced with the image, one is not *really* challenged. Haneke raises another very tough question about a portion of *Benny's Video:* If you are a parent, and your child discloses something to you similar to what Benny did, what would you do?

Haneke's most famous film is *Funny Games* (1997). He remade that film with English-speaking actors in 2007. In 2009, he won the Golden Palm at the Cannes Film Festival for *The White Ribbon.* At the end of 2009, *The Times of London* chose *Caché* as the best movie of the decade.

ADDITIONAL RECOMMENDED FILMS
FROM GERMANY

Nosferatu (1922)
Metropolis (1927)
The Tin Drum (1979)
Das Boot (1981). A harrowing account of life on a German submarine in World War II.
Wings of Desire (1987)
Stalingrad (1993)
The Promise (1995)
Aimée and Jaguar (2000)
Nowhere in Africa (2003)
Good Bye, Lenin (2003)
Sophie Scholl: The Final Days (2005)

Eastern Europe

Movies 40, 41 and 42: *The War Trilogy* (*A Generation, Kanal, Ashes and Diamonds*)

Director: Andrzej Wajda; 1 hour 23 minutes (1954) / 1 hour 31 minutes (1957) / 1 hour 43 minutes (1958)

Why is there war? Why is there institutionalized violence that has led to the deaths of millions of people over the centuries? One reason resides in the fact that some leaders and some groups of people just seem innately aggressive, and attempt to take by force what others have. It is also the case that when any group determines that idea x is of great value, members of that group will tend to look askance at those who reject x. Under certain conditions, "looking askance" can accelerate to aggressive behavior toward one's "enemies." Or maybe one group just *wants* what another group has. Ethnocentric and racist values often motivate violent invasions.

The reasons for war are generally the same as reasons behind any individual behaving violently against others. In cases of road rage, one driver is angered that someone is traveling too slowly, and is depriving them of their access to the roadway. A racist, prejudiced against members of a minority group, assaults a person met randomly from that group. A person lacks a car, and breaks into a garage to steal one.

Ordinarily, when individuals assault others for reasons like those above, the full force of the law will be utilized to apprehend them. Such perpetrators of criminal acts are reviled. However, when the same types of acts occur in a war between nations, people hesitate to express reprobation against those involved. There are, of course, major exceptions. The Holocaust involved institutionalized violence in which orders came down from the top to eliminate millions of people. Those who obeyed the orders are judged to deserve punishment. Under what conditions should an individual soldier who has been ordered to do x, refuse to do x? Should only those who gave the orders be punished?

Is there something noble about war? Every Sunday during football season, two groups of men meet in battle on the football field. It is a contest of strength, stamina and judgment, and the goal is to come out ahead. Isn't war somewhat similar? War is a game of the highest stakes. Just as there is a parade for the Super Bowl champions, there are Victory Day celebrations. For the former, however, there is only one parade; for the latter, each anniversary of the Victory Day is celebrated. Instead of a mere trophy, the winning side gets the land desired, or the wrong righted, or victory over the "enemy."

Millions of people are fascinated by the spectacle of football. Many more are fascinated by the spectacle of war — particularly if they are not victims of it. Many rush off to war because they see it as the adventure of a lifetime. Those who fight together — like the Home Guard in *The War Trilogy* or the "Band of Brothers" from World War II — often develop the strongest human bond imaginable, and that bond is one of the most important elements of their lives.

In *Kanal* (1957), Tadeusz Janczar and Teresa Izewska play partisans traveling through the sewers of Warsaw, Poland, in World War II.

The War Trilogy captures the Polish people's struggle for self-preservation during the period 1943–1945. *A Generation* centers on the Ghetto Uprising in Warsaw in 1943; *Kanal* on the uprising of the entire population of Warsaw in 1945, and *Ashes and Diamonds* on the assault on democracy in Poland by communist forces, as Russia drives the Germans out of Polish territory.

Here are some things to look for and appreciate in the films of *The War Trilogy:* (a) the long opening 360° shot of the ghetto in A *Generation* is brilliant, (b) the visual presentation of the attempt to make it through the sewers of Warsaw in *Kanal,* and (c) the artistic creativity of many scenes directed by Wajda. Wajda was influenced by the American movies *Citizen Kane* (1941), *The Asphalt Jungle* (1950) and *Rebel Without a Cause* (1955). If you know those movies, it is worth while looking for scenes in *The War Trilogy* that somehow seem familiar. Most clearly, Zbigniew Cybulski in *Ashes and Diamonds* seems to be copying James Dean's style from *Rebel Without a Cause.* In the Criterion Collection DVD of *Ashes and Diamonds,* Wajda discusses his initial concern that Cybulski was not right for the lead in the film — he did not look, or dress like members of the Home Guard. As time went on, however, Wajda realized Cybulski was perfect for the role because he created a new type of cinematic character for Poland. Likewise, I remember when *Rebel Without a Cause* came out. James Dean was brilliant as a rebellious teenager even though no teenager looked or acted like him.

Watch *A Generation.*

Questions to ponder:

1. Wajda had to include socialist values in his film in order to guarantee that the authorities would not reject it. (Even so, certain scenes were censored to Wajda's dissatisfaction.) In the film, Mr. Sekula (Janusz Paluszkiewicz) gives a lecture to Stach (Tadeusz Łomnicki) on how capitalism works, by making money on the employees' efforts. What justifications would you give to support capitalism? Is it fair for owners of companies to reap more from the work of the employees than the employees themselves? Here is the exchange between Mr. Sekula and Stach.

> Mr. Sekula: "It's simple arithmetic. How long did it take you to fit those doors?"
> Stach: "Two hours."
> Mr. Sekula: "And what's your weekly pay?"

STACH: "36 zlotys."

MR. SEKULA: "That's six zlotys a day. And Berg charges 12 zlotys for fitting one door. It takes you two hours to do the job, so your day's pay is covered in one hour. You do four a day. Berg gets 48 zlotys for them and pays you 6. So he makes 42 zlotys off you, day in and day out."

Is there anything wrong with this picture? (No mention, for example, is made of the cost of raw materials, or of bills for such things as electricity.)

2. Wajda is known for the realistic images in his films. He lived through the events he depicts and tries to capture them. To what extent do you think he succeeds, and to what extent does he fail? (The same question can be asked of *Kanal.*)

3. Wajda has been criticized for downplaying the uprising in the Jewish Ghetto. It is certainly the case that the world has been exposed to innumerable accounts of the Jewish uprising, but little has been written about the courage shown by the Polish Guard. Can Wajda be excused for centering on the struggles he was a part of, or should he be criticized for not acknowledging the Jewish sacrifices?

Watch *Kanal.*

Questions to ponder:

1. *Kanal* has been praised for the long sequence in the sewers. Numerous critics compared the descent into the sewers to the descent into Dante's inferno. Do you think the praise, and the comparison is justified? (One character in the film quotes from Dante: "Thither we come, and thence down in the moat I saw a people smothered in a filth that out of human privies seemed to flow.")

2. A major goal of the People's Guard was to halt the Nazi drive to the east. The Poles expected help from the Russian forces that were moving on Warsaw from the east. Of course, the Russians wanted to stop the Nazis, but the Russian leader Stalin held back aid to the Polish fighters, and even convinced Britain and the United States to do the minimum to help the Poles. (Stalin apparently foresaw that Russia would enter Poland after the war, and he saw that fighters of the Polish Guard — fighters who sought Polish independence — would rebel against Russian domination.) In *A Generation,* Dorota (Urszula Modrzyńska) proclaimed, "The Red Army is with us." In *Kanal,* however, as Polish fighters slowly lose their

struggle against the Nazis, they also begin to realize the Red Army will not provide them aid. The feeling of total hopelessness sets in. Do you think *Kanal* captures their sense of hopelessness?

Watch *Ashes and Diamonds*

Questions to ponder:

1. Are you amazed that the Communist authorities allowed *Ashes and Diamonds* to be released? They saw Szczuka (Waclaw Zastrzezynski) as the hero of the film. He was the wonderful communist who is going to lead his people forward to better and better times. Maciek (Zbigniew Cybulski) was seen as a villain, who dies where he belongs — on a garbage heap. The vast number of Polish viewers saw the opposite. They judged Szczuka got what he deserved, and Maciek was a hero who died like many of their war heroes — in rubble. Which of the two — Szczuka or Maciek — do you see as the hero of the film? Why?

2. Critics are divided over which of the films in *The War Trilogy* is the greatest. *Kanal* and Ingmar Bergman's *The Seventh Seal* (1957) were co-winners of the Jury Prize at Cannes. *Ashes and Diamonds* attracted more international viewership, probably in part because of the popular appeal of actor Zbigniew Cybulski, the Polish James Dean, and also because of the obvious influence of other popular elements from American cinema. Which of the three films in *The War Trilogy* do you think is the greatest? Why?

Additional Recommendation

Almost fifty years after the completion of *The War Trilogy*, Wajda has given us *Katyn* (2007), another powerful film on the Polish experience during World War II.

Movie 43: *The Cranes Are Flying*

Director: Mikhail Kalatozov; 1 hour, 34 minutes; 1957
Watch the movie.

Questions to Ponder:

1. Is there any way to understand why Veronika (Tatyana Samojlova) succumbs to the advances of Mark (Aleksandr Shvorin)? Is the film sending a sexist message that women are the "weaker sex"?

2. After making her grand mistake, Veronika is so despondent she

In *The Cranes Are Flying* (1957), Vasily Merkuryev (top, as Byodor Ivanovich) and Aleksey Batalov (as Boris) portray two Russian comrades struggling to survive in World War II.

doubts there is any meaning to her life. What could possibly be the meaning of life for Veronika, given her deep love for Boris (Aleksey Batalov)? If Boris had returned alive, should he have forgiven Veronika? Will Veronika now dedicate her life to the child named Boris, who was separated from his parents? How would you answer the question: "What is the meaning of life?" Is it easy for you to answer that question? A lot of the meaning of my life seemed to go out the door, when my children left for college. I set up a series of goals in order to try to establish a meaningful life: to take up golf and break 90 (I did); to achieve a greater appreciation of classical music and reach a point where I could even enjoy opera; and to travel. I since have had a number of great experiences with classical music, including attending a concert by the great pianist Evgny Kissin that concluded with nine standing ovations. I have attended powerful performances at the Metropolitan Opera and traveled to places as diverse as Ireland, New Zealand, and Kauai. Is that what constitutes the meaning of life — to set up a series of goals and work towards them? Does the meaning of life center on worshipping God? On serving other people?

Movie 44: *The Sacrifice*

Director: Andrei Tarkovsky; 2 hours, 29 minutes; 1986
Watch the movie.

Questions to ponder:

1. Do you think the world would change for the better if, as Alexander (Erland Josephson) asserts, "every single day at exactly the same stroke of the clock one were to perform the same single act, like an unchanging, systematic ritual, every day at the same time"? Why, or why not? Alexander gives the example of waking up in the morning and, always at the same time, flushing a glass of water down the toilet. What act would you do every day? Are there already acts you perform every day at the same time? If so, does that show that Alexander's idea is an empty one?

2. Otto (Allen Edwall) says Alexander should not "grieve" so much, and that he "shouldn't yearn so for something." In fact, Otto says *we all* yearn for something, wait for something. Do you think Otto is correct? If so, what are you waiting for? Do all humans wait for the same thing? Will we never know what we are waiting for?

3. Otto refers to a major theme of Nietzsche's (1844–1900) philosophy—the idea that all things eternally recur. The "dwarf" that Otto mentions appears in the following quote from Nietzsche's *Thus Spoke Zarathustra*:

> Not long ago I walked gloomily through the deadly pallor of dusk—gloomy and hard, with lips pressed together. Not only one sun had set for me. A path that ascended defiantly through stones, malicious, lonely, not cheered by herb or shrub—a mountain path crunched under the defiance of my foot. Striding silently over the mocking clatter of pebbles, crushing the rock that makes it slip, my foot forced its way upward. Upward—defying the spirit that drew it downward, toward the abyss, the spirit of gravity, my devil and archenemy. Upward—although he sat on me, half dwarf, half mole, lame, making lame, dripping lead into my ear, leaden thoughts into my brain.

•   •   •

> Then something happened that made me lighter, for the dwarf jumped from my shoulder, being curious; and he crouched on a stone before me. But there was a gateway just where we had stopped.
> "Behold this gateway, dwarf!" I continued. "It has two faces. Two paths meet here; no one has yet followed either to its end. This long lane stretches back for an eternity. And the long lane out there, that is another

In Andrei Tarkovsky's *The Sacrifice* (1986), the Earth is about to face devastation. What will one person be willing to sacrifice for the Earth to be spared?

eternity. They contradict each other, these paths; they offend each other face to face; and it is here at this gateway that they come together. The name of the gateway is inscribed above: 'Moment.' But whoever would follow one of them, on and on, farther and farther — do you believe, dwarf, that these paths contradict each other eternally?"

• • •

"Behold," I continued, "this moment! From this gateway, Moment, a long, eternal lane leads *backward*: behind us lies an eternity. Must not whatever *can* walk have walked on this lane before? Must not whatever *can* happen have happened, have been done, have passed by before? And if everything has been there before — what do you think, dwarf, of this moment? Must not this gateway too have been there before? And are not all things knotted together so firmly that this moment draws after it *all* that is to come? Therefore — itself too? For whatever can walk — in this long lane out *there* too, it *must* walk once more.[1]

Do you think things eternally recur? The concept of eternal recurrence is a very strange one. John F. Kennedy has been assassinated an infinite number of times? You have read these words an infinite number of times? In the future, all events will occur again an infinite number of times? I wrote my master's thesis on Nietzsche's doctrine of eternal recurrence. I asked why he included such a strange notion in his works. He constantly attacks metaphysical theories, and yet eternal recurrence is a metaphysical theory. He even presents a logical argument to support eternal recurrence: The amount of matter in the universe is finite. Therefore, the amount of possible combinations of matter is finite. Time is infinite. Therefore, in infinite time, what *can* happen will have happened, and will happen again and again.

I have concluded that what is important to Nietzsche about the idea of eternal recurrence is that it provides a test to determine whether a person is a "thisworldly," or an "otherworldly" thinker. An "otherworldly" thinker *needs* some future life after death, a life in which there is no pain or suffering. Nietzsche, a "thisworldly" thinker, has no time for other worlds. Life necessarily involves pain and suffering. In spite of the fact that he continually had migraine headaches, couldn't sleep, and probably knew he was going insane, Nietzsche was not willing to turn against this life by becoming an "otherworldly" thinker. He was willing to will that this life eternally recurs.

One question I had was: why was Nietzsche *so* critical of "otherworldly" thought? I think I have found an explanation. Suppose I tell you

I am very happy that I will be leaving my home in Lancaster County, Pennsylvania, to live in San Francisco. I explain I am disgusted with Lancaster County because I consider its inhabitants to be stupid, intolerant, religious fanatics. San Franciscans, I say, are intelligent, morale agents with balanced views on religion. In Lancaster, movie goers talk nonstop; San Franciscans are silent in movie theaters. The books in yard sales in Lancaster are Harlequin romances; out there you can find unbelievably exciting, original books in yard sales. Summers in Pennsylvania are yucky — the humidity is unbearable; San Francisco is the "air-conditioned" city, cooled by the Bay. Now — if I talk like that — do I have a healthy attitude about the people and environment of Lancaster County? No! "Otherworldly" thinkers regularly speak about this world in terms that — for Nietzsche — indicate they do not have a healthy regard for this world. They say things like, "This world is filled with sin and unbearable suffering, but the 'other world' will be wonderful!" Read the works of "otherworldly" philosophers such as Plato and St. Augustine. Look for the disgust they express about this world, and about their bodies. For Nietzsche, any element of "otherworldliness" will show such disgust for this world. Do you agree with Nietzsche that any "otherworldly" thought involves some element of harm to this world?

4. A central theme in Plato's philosophy is that certain elements of our soul (mind) are closely connected to our material bodies, but one element — the rational part — will, in a wise person, control those two elements. Plato compares the two irrational elements to two wild horses, and the rational element to a charioteer. If the charioteer controls the two wild horses, harmony arises in the soul. If the souls of the citizens of the state show harmony, the state will be just and rational. Alexander accepts a very similar view of the nature of the human individual, and the state of society when he says "we have acquired a dreadful disharmony, and imbalance, if you will, between our material and our spiritual development. Our culture is defective." Does your culture show such disharmony? How? Is it too late to bring harmony about?

5. In giving the gift of the map of Europe, Otto claims that every gift is a "sacrifice." Later, after World War III begins — or seems to begin — Alexander prays to God and offers to sacrifice himself if only God will return the lives of his loved ones and of all other humans back to normal. Do you think *that* is the sacrifice referred to in the title? Is the burning of his house Alexander's fulfillment to his promise to God to sacrifice everything?

6. When nuclear war breaks out, it is clear to all in the house that the end of a comfortable life has abruptly taken place. Alexander declares that he has been waiting for this terrible event all his life. Is that what Alexander was "waiting for" in question 2 above? After our recent history from Hiroshima to 9/11, are we all waiting for that? What should our day-to-day attitude be towards that looming threat?

7. On the advice of Otto, Alexander goes to see Julia (Valérie Mairesse). In order for Alexander to be "saved," Otto suggests he should "lie with her." What do you make of that?

OTHER RECOMMENDED TARKOVSKY FILMS

Ivan's Childhood (1962)

Andrei Rublev (1966)

Solaris (1971). It is fun to first read the novel *Solaris* by Stanisław Lem, watch the Tarkovsky film (be sure you have the full 169 minute version), and then watch the American remake starring George Clooney (2002).

Stalker (1979)

Movies 45, 46 and 47: *The Three Colors Trilogy* (*Blue, White, Red*)

Director: Krzysztof Kieślowski; 1 hour, 38 minutes (1993) / 1 hour, 32 minutes (1994) / 1 hour, 39 minutes (1994)

I included Krzysztof Kieślowski's masterpiece *The Decalogue* (1988) in *Plato and Popcorn* (pages 59–65). That film consists of ten one-hour movies made for Polish television. Each episode centers on one of the Ten Commandments. There are different actors, actresses, and even cinematographers for each episode, though here and there characters from earlier episodes fleetingly appear in later segments. The setting for all ten films is a Polish ghetto.

Each of the films of *The Three Colors Trilogy* centers not only on colors — the color blue is highlighted in *Blue*, as are white and red in the other films — but also on the concepts symbolized by each color. *Blue* in the French flag symbolizes *liberty*, white *equality*, and red *fraternity*. Figuring out how the plots center on those themes is much like figuring out how the plots of the ten films in *The Decalogue* center on the biblical commandments. Once again, as in *The Decalogue,* Kieslowski uses different cameramen for each film.

Watch *Blue*.

Questions to ponder:

1. In what way is the theme of liberty central to the plot of *Blue*? Kieslowski was not interested in political themes, and so was not going to stress political liberty in his film. My interpretation is that because Julie (Juliette Binoche) is so devastated by the death of her husband and daughter, she loses all interest in keeping up connections with people from her life before the accident, people who would remind her of her husband and daughter. She is trapped in a void; she is having what existentialists call "an existential crisis" in which nothing (no-thing) matters. She attempts to destroy the fragments of her late husband's composition which honors the unification of Europe. She moves to an area where no one knows her. She concentrates in an absent-minded way on meaningless little things like sugar cubes soaking up coffee. She is more dead than alive. By the end of the film, however, she has regained her ability to establish new relationships, and renew old ones. She is even able to complete the musical composition left unfinished by her husband's death. Thus, she experiences more

Irène Jacob stars in Krzysztof Kieslowski's *Red* (1994), a story about parallel lives.

freedom in living, than she had while being in a state of withdrawal from life. Clearly, Julie's road back to living a more productive life begins when she discovers that her husband, Patrice (Hugues Quester), had been having an affair. Subsequently, Julie even finds out that Sandrine (Florence Pernel), Patrice's mistress, is pregnant. Why does the knowledge that her husband had been unfaithful act as a trigger leading Julie back to living more fully?

There is another way in which *Blue* may capture the theme of liberty. When her husband and child are killed in the accident, Julie's organized comfortable life is totally destroyed. Nothing is left. What is she to do now with her life? It is totally up to her — she is free to choose from a large number of possible paths. Suicide? Stay in the house that she and Patrice had established? Run away from the past?

2. Why does Julie give the house she and Patrice had occupied to Sandrine?

3. Interpret the last scene in which the following characters encountered in the course of the film are pictured:

> a. Antoine (Jann Tregoet), the hitchhiker who tried to return Julie's necklace to her;
> b. Julie's mother (Emmanuelle Riva);
> c. Lucille, the prostitute (Charlotte Very);
> d. Sandrine, her husband's mistress;
> e. Olivier (Benoît Régent), seen reflected in Julie's eyes.

These are the people who enter Julie's consciousness as she begins again to live. What effect does each one have on her? How does she affect each of them? Is there any significance that Olivier, as seen in the reflection, is naked with his back to Julie, and appears to be in a pensive position?

4. The way the musical score meshes with the various scenes is stunning. Another Kieślowski film, *The Double Life of Veronique* (1991), is also noteworthy in regard. Two other films that are unforgettable because the music is inseparable from their various scenes are *2001: A Space Odyssey* (movie 14) and *Apocalypse Now* (1979). Are there any other films that, for you, brilliantly mesh music and content?

Watch *White*.

Questions to ponder:

1. Of the three films of *The Three Colors Trilogy*, *White* seems to me to be the weakest. Sure, Kieślowski's direction is excellent, but I expected more whites in the film just as there are many blues in *Blue*. Kieślowski

always leaves gaps in his plots to make viewers think about how those gaps can be filled, but reasonable interpretations are usually relatively easy to come by. In *White*, however, a number of gaps just seem to depend on a weak plot. What follows is a list of problematic plot elements. What sense, if any, can you make out of them?

a. Is it reasonable that all of the authorities involved fail to use scientific tests to verify that the corpse to be buried is indeed that of Karol Karol (Zbigniew Zamachowski)?

b. Karol watches the funeral from behind a nearby tree. Of course, no one sees him.

c. Karol shows Dominique (Julie Delpy) love throughout the film, but then sets her up so that she is accused of his murder. Does the shift in Karol's character make sense? Then she falls in love with him. Why? Because he made a lot of money? Because he finally gave her great sex? Very mysterious. Also, how can Karol get away with showing up at prison? He's supposed to be dead. Wouldn't it be more realistic for Dominique to start screaming, "There's the bastard who framed me!"

d. Even when Kieslowski does a comedy, it is usually "realistic." (See *Decalogue X*, for example.) However, who can believe Karol could survive in a suitcase for such a length of time as seen in *White*. That's just stupid.

In an interview given while *White* was still in production, Kieslowski made the following comments which provide some solutions to questions I have about the theme of equality in the film:

> *White* is about equality understood as a contradiction. We understand the concept of "equality," that we all want to be equal. But I think this is absolutely not true. I don't think anybody really wants to be equal. Everybody wants to be more equal. There's a saying in Polish: There are those who are equal and those who are more equal.... This is what the film is about. At the beginning, Karol is humiliated, trampled into the ground.... Everything he ever had is taken away from him and his love is rejected. Consequently, he wants to show that not just is he not as low as he has fallen, not just is he on a level with everybody else, but that he is higher, that he is better. So he does everything he can to prove to himself and to the woman who, to put it mildly, has spurned him, that he's better

than she thinks. And he does. Therefore he becomes more equal. Except that, while becoming more equal, he falls into the trap which he's set for his wife because it turns out that he loves her. His aim was to get even with her. Whereas with this revenge it suddenly appears that love has returned. Both to him and to her.[1]

White symbolizes equality. Thus, after Dominique gets Karol in trouble by accusing him of torching her salon, Karol gets even by getting her accused of his murder. Karol equals the sexual performance of the person who serviced Dominique while Karol had been listening on the phone. By the way, what accounts for Karol becoming a better lover?

e. Why does Mikolaj (Janusz Gajos) decide he does not want to be killed? Is it because, by using a blank instead of a real bullet, Karol has led Mikolaj to realize what it is like to die? Is it because by his shooting the blank, Karol showed such humanity to Mikolaj that life, for Mikolaj, took on new meaning?

Watch *Red*.

Questions to ponder:

1. After hitting Rita, the dog, Valentine (Irène Jacob) returns Rita to her owner, the reclusive Judge (Jean-Louis Trintignant). He asks her whether she saved Rita for his sake. He doubts it. Kieślowski, himself, said:

> Valentine wants to think of others but she keeps thinking about others from her own point of view. She simply can't have any other (point of view). The same way as you or I don't have any other way of looking at things. That's how it is. Now the question arises: even when we give of ourselves, aren't we doing so because we want to have a better opinion of ourselves: It's something to which we'll never know the answer. Philosophers haven't found it in 2000 years and nobody will."[2]

Do you agree that when a person does something good, a bit of self-interest is involved? Does that mean that people are never perfectly good? Or does Kieślowski possibly miss something: Is it admirable for a person to do good because they feel good doing it? Shouldn't a person have a pleasing self-image when they do something admirable? Wouldn't it be much worse if a person does something evil because it gives them pride? Kieślowski seems to be saying that if self-interest enters the picture, then a person can't be perfectly good. What, however, is questionable about acting out of self-interest if we feel better doing good? A person can be both an egoist *and* an altruist. Here, roughly, is the logic: I want to act in my own self-interest. It is not in my self-interest to have a low regard for myself. I will have a higher regard for myself if I do good, rather than evil. Altruistic acts are good. Therefore, it is in my self-interest to engage in altruistic acts.

What do you think of that argument? Using that argument I can interpret the scenes in *Red, White* and *Blue* where an elderly person is seen trying to put a bottle in a recycling bin. What is going on here? Why does Kieślowski include the same type of scene in the three films? Only one person — Valentine, in *Red* — goes to help the elderly person? That is the clue that she is, in some respect, a more moral person than those who failed to help the elderly person in the earlier films. So what if she did what she did out of self-interest? (Of course, if she would help someone in order to get a monetary reward, she would not be judged as good.)

2. Why is Valentine's winning at the slot machine called a "bad sign"? Why is she happy when she loses?

3. The Judge seems to have special powers. There is evidence that the Judge is a fictionalized version of Kieślowski himself. Kieślowski once said, "Of course, I peep and eavesdrop on my characters."[3] A director knows what will happen to the characters of his films. Before I came across the above interpretation, it seemed to me that the Judge was analogous to God or a god. God is a judge. God would be disgusted with many of the actions of people. God hears what people say, and sees what people do. God knows the future. Which interpretation do you favor: that the Judge is a fictionalized Kieślowski or that he is a god?

4. What do you make of the fact that the Judge and Auguste (Jean-Pierre Lorit) experience strikingly similar events? Both dropped books that opened to a page containing information that helps them in their exams. The Judge says he saw his fiancée in a reflection in a mirror. She is having sex with another man. Auguste climbs up to the window of his fiancée's bedroom, and sees her being unfaithful. At the end of the film, we are led to assume that Valentine and Auguste will fall in love with each other, and that their relationship will be a good one. Does that mean that if the Judge were forty years younger, then he and Valentine would have been perfect for each other? Had they been the same age, according to Kieślowski, Valentine and the Judge:

would probably have been very happy together. They probably suit each other very well. That's the theory of the two halves of an apple. If you cut one apple in half and cut another identical one, the half of the one apple will never fit with the half of the other. You have to put together the halves of the same apple to make the apple whole. The whole apple is comprised of a matching pair and it's the same with people. The question is: has a mistake been committed somewhere? And if it has, then is there anybody in a position to rectify it?[4]

Valentine and the Judge would have "fit together" well if they had been born at approximately the same time. Now, however, life has embittered the Judge. Valentine does not have a good relationship with the boyfriend who is never seen. The apple pieces don't fit. What "rectifies" the situation turns out to be the fact that Auguste is almost a mirror image of the Judge when he was younger. Just as the Judge, years before would have been perfectly compatible with Valentine, Auguste now can fit that role.

The idea that love occurs when one person finds his or her "other half" can be found in Plato's (427–347 B.C.) great dialogue *The Symposium*. In that dialogue, different speakers present their views on the nature of love. By the end of *The Symposium*, Plato will have combined parts of the views that have been expressed, and will then add his own final touches. One of the earlier speeches is made by Aristophanes (ca. 446–ca. 386 B.C.), the great writer of comedies: In the far distant past, claims Aristophanes:

> Each person's shape was complete: they were round, with their backs and sides forming a circle. They had four hands and the same number of legs, and two absolutely identical faces on a cylindrical neck. They had a single head for their two faces (which were on opposite sides), four ears, two sets of genitals, and every other part of their bodies was how you'd imagine it on the basis of what I've said. They moved around in an upright position, as we do today, in either of their two forward directions; and when it came to running, they supported themselves on all eight of their limbs and moved rapidly round and round, just like when acrobats perform that circular manoeuvre where they stick their legs out straight and wheel over and over.

However, a problem arose. The round humans maliciously bumped into the gods, and made them very angry. The gods considered destroying all humans, but, according to Aristophanes, Zeus came up with a better idea:

> Zeus said ... "What I'm going to do is split every single one of them into two halves; then they'll be weaker, and at the same time there'll be more

in it for us because there'll be more of them. They'll walk about upright on two legs."

Now there were no longer round humans who would bump into the gods. Each human became like half a human missing its other half. They would find another half human and embrace, hoping to be made whole again. However, they really didn't mesh well and so they began to "die out."

> Zeus took pity on them, however, and came up with another ingenious idea: he changed the position of their genitals round to their fronts. Up until then, their genitals too had been on the far side of their bodies.... So Zeus moved their genitals round to the front of their bodies and thus introduced intercourse between two humans beings, with the man as the agent of the generation taking place within the woman. His reasons for doing this were to ensure that, when couples embraced, as well as male-female relationships would at least involve sexual satisfaction, so that people would relax, get on with their work and take care of other aspects of life.[5]

Movie 48: *The Ascent*

Director: Larisa Shepitko; 1 hour, 51 minutes; 1977
Watch the movie.

Questions to Ponder:

1. Judging by the few films she completed, Larisa Shepitko showed promise of being one of the greatest directors of all time. Tragically, she and four co-workers died in an automobile accident in 1979. She was only 39 years old. *The Ascent* is her greatest work. Some critics praised the feminine touch shown in this powerful war film. Would you have been able to tell *The Ascent* had a woman director if you did not know it? What elements would lead you to that conclusion? Shepitko made only one film in color. Does the fact that *The Ascent* is black and white better enable the viewer to experience the cold landscape, and realize the horrors of war?

2. A major theme of the film is that some things are more important than life. The "hero" is Sotnikov (Boris Plotnikov). What is more important than life to him? Did you notice how "Christ-like" Sotnikov was? Tortured, tempted by the Germans to give information about the partisans, and executed in a public place as a warning to others, Sotnikov does not buckle. Rybak (Vladimir Gostyukhin), on the other hand, plays

the role of Judas — a bystander even calls him "Judas." There is a real question whether, or not, the children of Demchikha (Lyudmila Polyakdova) can survive if their mother is executed. Should Sotnikov give the Germans enough information to have the mother (possibly) released? Is "coward" a word that fits Rybak? After all, before he was captured he bravely fought side by side with Sotnikov, suffering a great deal, and endangering himself by not abandoning his comrade, Sotnikov. In fact, in the first half of the film Rybak seems to be the "hero."

3. In *The Ascent*, the demonic Portnov (Anatoli Solonitsyn) forces Sotnikov and Rybak into making a decision. They are damned no matter what they choose. They must either give crucial information about the

Boris Plotnikov, left, stars as Sotnikov, a Christ-like person who is a victim of the Nazis in *The Ascent* (1977). The others are unidentified.

partisans, or Demchikha's children will perish. In *Sophie's Choice* (1982), the main character (played by Meryl Streep) is forced to choose which of her children is to be handed over for execution by her German captors. If she does not decide, both children die. In *The Ascent*, the choice forced on Sotnikov and Rybak is motivated by the Germans' desire for information. What possibly could motivate the German who forces Sophie to make her decision?

Movie 49: *Autumn Spring*

Director: Vladimir Michálek; 1 hour, 35 minutes; 2001

I recommended *Autumn Spring* in *Plato and Popcorn*, in my chapter on films about death. As it turns out, however, I see this film centering much more on life and living fully, rather than on death. Though *Autumn Spring* is about elderly people, there is a youthful spirit about it that should also appeal to much younger viewers.

In *Plato and Popcorn*, I wrote the following:

> There is something perhaps you should not know before viewing this film. Maybe it would be best not to know it *after* viewing it! But — now that I mentioned it, if you must know — watch the movie and *then* read the following sentence, the letters of which are written in reverse order: 2002 NI EDICIUS DETTIMMOC (ADNAF) YKSDORB LIMITSALV. Though admittedly hokey, I simply don't want your reaction to the movie to be colored by this information.

I'm repeating the above because after viewing the film, I was tremendously stunned when I found out the fact that is expressed in the backwards sentence above. "How could that be?" I asked myself. Were there signs in the film that provided clues about what would happen?

Watch the movie.

Questions to ponder:

1. Fanda (Vlastimil Brodsky) does not want to give up living, merely because he has aged. His wife, Emílie (Stella Zázvorková) is a "stick-at-home," addicted to thoughts about death and making preparations for that event. Is her change of character near the end of the film believable? She takes on the role of imposter to fill a void left in Fanda's life by the downfall of his friend, Eda (Stanislav Zindulka).

2. You probably admired Fanda's hoaxes. Should you have? Realtors

and owners of houses being sold give up a significant amount of time and money to show this imposter their real estate. Does the pleasure Fanda gets from his misadventures justify the deceit he engages in?

3. Fanda says, "Good deeds pave the way to heaven." Eda asks, "But is there an afterlife?" Fanda jokingly answers, "Who knows? Just in case ... be good." Shouldn't you do good deeds because you should do good deeds — not because good deeds may get you to heaven? If a person does something because a reward may be received, is that person good? If I jump into a river to save someone drowning, and I know that the person is very wealthy and will probably reward me, am I a good person?

Movie 50: *The Death of Mr. Lazarescu*

Director: Cristi Puiu; 2 hours, 30 minutes; 2005
Watch the movie.

Questions to ponder:

1. *The Death of Mr. Lazarescu* is judged by many critics to be a "black comedy." The first time I viewed it I judged it to be a tragic exposé of a

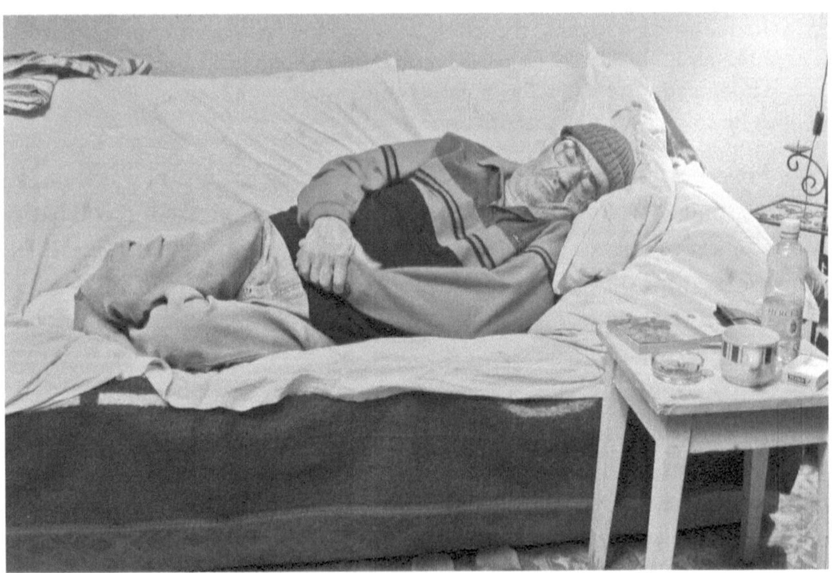

Ion Fiscuteanu, who becomes a pawn in Romania's health system, is the title character in *The Death of Mr. Lazarescu* (2005).

medical system that was bureaucratic, and unable to handle a huge number of patients. On other viewings, I saw the comedy. What, if any, comic elements did you spot?

2. Is Mr. Lazarescu (Ion Fiscuteanu) mistreated by the hospital staff because he is economically deprived? Because he is an alcoholic? If medical staffs are overburdened, should they care first for people who take responsible care of themselves?

3. Should those who do not take responsible care of themselves (i.e., smokers, alcoholics, drug addicts, people who ride motorcycles without helmets, etc.) be treated last?

4. Does Mr. Lazarcscu die at the end of the film?

Movie 51: *Grbavica: The Land of My Dreams*

Director: Jasmila Zbanic; 1 hour, 31 minutes; 2006
Watch the movie.

Questions to ponder:

1. The following are some of the questions raised in *A Natural History of Rape*, a controversial book published in 2001 by Randy Thornhill and Craig T. Palmer. I don't have answers to these questions, but they are important to ponder.

> Why are males the rapists and females (usually) the victims?
> Why is rape a horrendous experience for the victim?
> Why is rape more frequent in some situations, such as war, than in others?
> Why does rape exist in many, if not all, species?
> How can rape be prevented?[1]

Given that biologists will probably find the answers to these questions, how would you now answer them?

2. In his *Leviathan*, Thomas Hobbes (1588–1679) presents explanations as to why humans bond together to form societies, and why wars are natural occurrences. These explanations can also provide some insight into why rape was so prevalent in the Bosnian War, and more recently in wars in such places as Ghana and Sudan.

Most social and political philosophers in the past argued that people band together because they love one another. Hobbes disagreed. According to him, societies form because people are *afraid* of one another.

In a "state of nature" every person would have to depend totally on their own resources to survive.

> In such condition, there is no place for Industry; because the fruit thereof is uncertain: and consequently no Culture of the Earth; no Navigation, nor use of the commodities that may be imported by sea; no commodious Building; no Instruments of moving and removing such things as require much force; no Knowledge of the face of the Earth; no account of Time; no Arts; no Letters; no Society; and which is worst of all, continuall feare, and dangers of violent death; and the life of man, solitary, poore, nasty, brutish and short.[2]

Hobbes was an egoist who argued that all people always act only in their own self-interest. A problem arises, however, when people realize it is not in their self-interest for their lives to be "solitary, poore, nasty, brutish and short." So, humans make agreements with one another to work together for mutual support. Each person must sacrifice certain things they would not naturally be willing to sacrifice: taxes must be paid, property belonging to other people must be respected, and time serving on police forces or in the military might be required. People are kept in line by the fear of punishment resulting from breaking the contract with the establishment.

A "state of nature" is actually a state of war, according to Hobbes. Every human is against every human. In such a state, physically weak people can use their intellect to plan to take what they want from others. A rock dropped off a cliff unto the head of someone carrying food is enough to gain the food for the assailant. In *Quest for Fire* (1981), a prehistoric man assaults a woman who is bending over a creek, collecting water. People in a state of nature take what they want. Once humans band together, war is still going to occur. Now, instead of persons warring against persons, it is one's group warring against the other's group. Civilians caught in war's path experience the horrors found in the state of nature — their lives tend to be "solitary, poore, nasty, brutish and short." The amount of civilian casualties, property damage, and atrocities committed is incalculable in any sizeable war. The treatment of prisoners can be ghastly. Think of Andersonville in the American Civil War, the "killing fields" in Cambodia, the ethnic cleansing of the Armenians, and the countless other examples of horror on a grand scale that have occurred in just the last two hundred years.

Do you think Hobbes' analysis of the natural human is correct? Is

Mirjana Karanović stars as a victim of the Bosnian War in *Grbavica* (2006).

there a connection between the natural character of humans, and the atrocities that occur in war?

Movie 52: *The Island*

Director: Pavel Lungin; 1 hour, 52 minutes; 2006
Watch the movie.

Questions to ponder:

1. Is *The Island* a film of deep spiritual significance, or is it merely the account of a religious quack? Does Father Antoli (Pyotr Mamanov) give good advice to those who come to him for help, or is the advice groundless and irrational? (He tells one woman to sell all her possessions, and go to France to look for her missing husband who can be found there. The high probability is that the husband was killed in the war. Father Antoli throws away the crutches of the young boy who was, clearly, seriously injured. He requires the child's mother to stay at the monastery and pray for some days, even though in doing so, she would lose her job and have no income.) Admiral Tikhon Petrovich (Yuri Kuznetsov) brings his insane daughter to Father Antoli. Were you bothered that it was such a

coincidence that the admiral turns out to be the same Tikhon Father Antoli shot during the war? Did the admiral *know* Father Antoli is the one who shot him? After all, it seems the coal that Father Antoli regularly shovels from a sunken barge is the same coal and the same barge from the first scenes. Wouldn't the admiral know this is the area in which he was shot? If he didn't know, how improbable is it that he will travel to meet a miracle worker who just happens to be the person who shot him?

2. For what reason does Father Antoli raise the question to Father Job (Dmitriy Dyuzhev): "Why did Cain kill Abel?" Do you know the answer to Father Job's question? If you don't, the answer is provided in Genesis 40:

> [Adam] lay with his wife Eve, and she conceived and gave birth to Cain.... Afterward she had another child, Abel. He tended the flock, and Cain worked the land. In due season Cain brought some of the fruits of the earth as an offering to the Lord, while Abel brought the choicest of the firstborn of his flock. The Lord regarded Abel and his offering with favour, but not Cain and his offering. Cain was furious, and he glowered. The Lord said to Cain, "Why are you angry? Why are you scowling? If

The Island **(2006): Does God speak to a member of a religious community in an isolated area of Russia?**

you do well, you hold your head up. If not, sin is a demon crouching at your door; it will desire you, and you will be mastered by it.

Cain said to his brother Abel, "Let us go into the country." Once there, Cain attacked and murdered his brother.[1]

Is Father Antoli implying Father Job is jealous of him?

3. Given the scenario that opens the film, should Father Antoli feel such deep, continued guilt in his later life? He is terrified as his German captors hold his life in their hands. As it turns out, the man he shoots does not die — though Father Antoli could not know that. The issue I am raising deals with the difference between warranted and unwarranted guilt. I am not saying Father Antoli should not feel guilt over his actions. However, I suspect many people are wracked by guilt that is unwarranted. I write from experience. When I was a child, I was very inquisitive. One day I went to a field near the edge of my hometown and engaged in a scientific experiment. I held a paper bag upside down, and struck a match setting the edges of the open bag on fire. I wanted to see if the bag would rise up like a hot air balloon. Just then a wind gust blew away the burning bag, starting the field on fire. I ran home, and told my mother about the burning field. She called the fire company, and the firemen doused the fire. The firemen probably found my matches in the field, and probably put two and two together. They talked to my mother and my mother confronted me in my bedroom. "Billy," she said, "I want you to tell me the truth — Cub Scout's honor: Did you start that fire in the field?" Well — what do you think? Did I answer truthfully? After all, I was a Cub Scout and took the Cub Scout oath very seriously. Plus, the commandment "Thou shalt not bear false witness" was drummed into me.... I said, "No, I didn't." For *years*, I felt guilty, and was deeply ashamed that I had lied to my mother about that fire. Of course, eventually I grew up and realized that such a small lie on such a small matter is fairly insignificant in the scheme of things, but that was after a great deal of suffering.

There is an interesting addition to the above story. After telling one of my classes about the lie and the guilt I felt, a student asked me if I *ever* told my mother the truth. I said I hadn't, but I would the next time I was with her. When I next met my mother, the following conversation took place:

> ME: "Mother — do you remember when there was a field fire at the edge of town when I was about six years old? You asked me — Cub Scout's honor — if I started the fire, and I said 'no.'"

> MOTHER (looking puzzled): "I don't remember that!"

I think I gasped. I was amazed that something that caused me so much grief was not important enough to be remembered by a person directly involved. But, the conversation went on:

> MOTHER: "However, now that you made that confession, I want to make one myself. Do you remember when you were about that same age, and I asked you to go to the bank to deposit a small amount of money. You came back to me and told me you lost the money. I yelled and yelled at you. Right then you went to get your Cub Scout picture taken. I still have that picture, and ever since I feel so bad about my yelling. You look so sad in your Cub Scout picture!"
>
> MY RESPONSE: "I don't remember that!" Both my mother and I experienced long-term guilt over matters that were of next to no import. The feeling of guilt was not warranted.

Do you have any unwarranted feelings of guilt?

Movie 53: *4 Months, 3 Weeks and 2 Days*

Director: Christian Mungiu; 1 hour, 53 minutes; 2007

Warning: This film contains several scenes that will be extremely disturbing to many viewers.

In the past decade, no moral issue has so divided Americans as has the abortion issue. Prior to *4 Months, 3 Weeks and 2 Days,* I found the most thought-provoking film on abortion to be the HBO production *If These Walls Could Talk* (1996) covered in *Plato and Popcorn* (pages 142–143).

Until the second part of the 20th century, philosophers generally ignored topics that now fall under the label of "Contemporary Moral Issues." Topics such as capital punishment, sexual harassment, racism, sexism and abortion are not found in great philosophic works except perhaps to condemn such "immoral practices." A landmark essay entitled "A Defense of Abortion" by Judith Jarvis Thomson (born 1929) was published in 1971. At present, it is still the essay on abortion that regularly gets republished in introductory philosophy texts, and in texts on contemporary moral issues. In addition, it has constantly been very controversial. The main thrust of Thomson's support for abortion centers on a scenario she presents. This scenario does not involve an abortion, but Thomson sees it as dealing with a case that is perfectly analogous to the abortion issue. Here is the scenario:

You wake up in the morning and find yourself back to back in bed with an unconscious famous violinist. He has been found to have a fatal kidney ailment, and the Society of Music Lovers has canvassed all the available medical records and found that you alone have the right blood type to help. They have therefore kidnapped you, and last night the violinist's circulatory system was plugged into yours so that your kidneys could be used to extract poisons from his blood as well as your own. The director of the hospital now tells you: "Look, we're sorry the Society of Music Lovers did this to you — we would never have permitted it if we had known. But still, they did it and the violinist now is plugged into you. To unplug you would be to kill him. But never mind, it's only for nine months. By then he will have recovered from his ailment and can safely be unplugged from you." Is it morally incumbent on you to accede to this situation? No doubt it would be very nice of you if you did, a great kindness. But do you *have* to accede to it? What if it were not nine months but nine years? Or longer still? What if the director of the hospital said: "Tough luck, I agree, but you've now got to stay in bed, with the violinist plugged into you, for the rest of your life. Because remember this: All persons have a right to life, and violinists are persons. Granted you have a right to decide what happens in and to your body, but a person's right to life outweighs your right to decide what happens in and to your body. So you cannot ever be unplugged from him.[1]

Otilia (Anamaria Marinca) and Gabita (Laura Vasiliu) are about to make a very bad decision in *4 Months, 3 Weeks and 2 Days* (2007). The actor at left is Vlad Ivanov.

You are hooked up to the violinist against your will. If the violinist were part of the plot leading you to be hooked up, then you would probably say you have a right to pull the plug. If a rape victim becomes pregnant, she has the right to abort the fetus. (Those who argue that abortion is wrong because it deprives the fetus of the right to life will be inconsistent if they claim that abortion is immoral *except* in the case of rape. If the fetus has a right to life, it has that right no matter how conception came about.)

Suppose, however, that the violinist was unconscious, and had nothing to do with the plan to hook him up with your body. Would you be doing anything immoral if you unhooked yourself? To address that question, Thomson came up with a different scenario. Suppose your house is stuffy, so you open a window. A burglar then comes through the window. Should you be blamed for the invasion? Get it? The window is a vagina and the burglar is an unwanted fetus. Of course, Thomson is assuming that the desire to engage in sex is every bit as rational as the desire to open the window. Opponents would accuse Thomson of committing a weak analogy fallacy. Fulfilling the desire to have sex is radically different from fulfilling the desire to get fresh air into your room.

Thomson presents a number of other scenarios in an attempt to show that the arguments of pro-life advocates fail to establish the notion that abortion is always immoral.

It is one thing to present cold arguments in support of abortion; it is another to see scenes like those in *4 Months, 3 Weeks and 2 Days*. There is no evidence that Thomson would support certain decisions made by characters in the film.

Watch the movie.

Questions to ponder:

1. Pro-choice proponents often argue that if abortion were made illegal, then abortions like those shown in the film would become common. Is that a good reason for legalizing abortion?

2. Compile a list of things Gabita (Laura Vasiliu) is supposed to do, but doesn't. It is a stunningly long list. Why does she "do the wrong thing" time after time? In the last scene, Otilia (Anamaria Marinca) just sits, looking at the camera. What is she thinking? Could it be: "How could I have such a friend as this?"

3. Cristian Mungiu, the director of *4 Months, 3 Weeks and 2 Days*, feels

that the "dinner scene" that included relatives and acquaintances of Adi (Alexandru Potocean) was the most difficult scene to film. With Otilia in the center, various shots tend to look like the Last Supper. I find myself entranced by the scene because I know what Otilia is going through. Do you think the scene is also significant because of what the people who are speaking are saying? Is the scene showing what Otilia's future life would be like if she were to marry Adi? A number of viewers commented on IMDb that the dinner scene is a seven-minute bore. What do you think?

Movie 54: *12*

Director: Nikita Mikhalkov; 2 hours, 39 minutes; 2007

12 is a remake of the great American film, *12 Angry Men* (1957). Sidney Lumet directed the latter film with an all-star cast, and there is barely a second that seems out of place. Mikhalkov, who also directed the excellent *Burnt by the Sun* (1994), clearly admires the plot of the American version. (The 1957 film was itself a remake of a 1954 television broadcast of the teleplay written by Reginald Rose.) The spirit of *12 Angry Men* can often be spotted in *12*, but too many segments feel a bit out of place. I recommend you watch the Sidney Lumet version first. A scene involving a knife is especially powerful in Lumet's film. Do you think the same scene

Sergey Gazarov as one of 12 angry men in *12* (2007).

provides an equal punch in the Russian version? Is *12* more, or less, powerful than *12 Angry Men,* because the former contains scenes of events that took place outside the courthouse whereas the latter, for the most part, is filmed only in the jury room? Does *12 Angry Men* suffer in comparison because it is in black and white?

Watch the movie.

Questions to ponder:

1. *12 Angry Men* was the first film covered in *Plato and Popcorn* (pages 9–10). That film well captures major themes from the skeptical philosophy of David Hume (1711–1776.) Hume argued that any sentence that purportedly conveys a fact about the world, or reality, could indeed be false. In *12,* one of the jurors states coincidences don't happen in real life. The Jewish juror (Valentin Gaft) says, "Anything can happen. Anything." That quote indicates the main Humean idea at work in both versions of the story. It is *possible* the Chechen boy (Apti Magamayev) was not the murderer of his uncle. Does the fact that it is *possible* Umar did not kill his uncle, give any reason to think there is reasonable doubt he is guilty?

2. Several jurors tell stories that supposedly undermine some of the testimony given during the trial. The Jew, to support the idea that "anything can happen"— tells of his father who fell in love with the wife of a Nazi officer. The nasty cab driver (Sergey Garmash) gets the Harvard-educated juror (Yuri Stoyanov) to act out a scenario in which he finds his wife and daughter have been killed by someone like the Chechen boy. The cabby finally changes his vote when told a story about how, perhaps, female jealousy convinced a witness she saw the boy kill his uncle. (The cabby's lover lied about his son who subsequently tried to hang himself.) Do any of these stories suggest reason to doubt the boy's guilt?

3. Near the end of the film, the jury foreman (played by the director, Nikita Mikhalkov) argues that the boy should be judged guilty because he would live longer in jail than out of jail. The boy, according to the foreman, would look for the real killer who would, in the end, murder the boy. Did the foreman's argument make any sense to you?

ADDITIONAL RECOMMENDED FILMS
FROM EASTERN EUROPE

Battleship Potemkin (Russia, 1925)
War and Peace (Russia, 1969). An almost 7-hour epic.

Come and See (Russia, 1985)

Tito and Me (Yugoslavia, 1993)

Prisoner of the Mountains (Russia, 1996)

Kolya (Czech Republic, 1996)

Russian Ark (Russia, 2002). A presentation of Russian history as the camera glides through the Hermitage, the great museum in Saint Petersburg. There are no edited scenes; rather this film is recorded in one unbroken sequence.

The Return (Russia, 2003)

Movie 55: *The Tree of the Wooden Clogs*

Director: Ermanno Olmi; 3 hours, 6 minutes; 1978
Warning: Scenes of animal slaughter.
Watch the movie.

Questions to ponder:

1. *The Tree of the Wooden Clogs* won the Grand Prize at Cannes in 1978. Given the fact that there is little in the film that constitutes a developed plot, do you think it deserved such a prestigious award? Why? Olmi did not use professional actors in the film. Do you think that approach may have contributed to the film's air of authenticity? Did you sense the omnipresence of the landlords hovering over the lives of the peasants? Is the landlord within his rights for forcing the family off his land, after the father cuts down the tree?

2. Does *The Tree of the Wooden Clogs* glorify the life of the peasants? In various essays, Martin Heidegger (1889–1976) argued that peasants were closer to "authentic being" than those people living in areas of large population, and surrounded by technology and the machines of industrialized society. In his essay "The Origin of the Work of Art," Heidegger searches for an explanation as to why several of Vincent Van Gogh's paintings feature shoes owned by peasants. Most people would look at those paintings, and think that it was absurd of Van Gogh to paint such mundane objects as peasants' shoes. Heidegger says:

> But what is there to see here? Everyone knows what shoes consist of. If they are not wooden or bast shoes, there will be leather soles and uppers, joined together by thread and nails. Such gear serves to clothe the feet. Depending on the use to which shoes are to be put, whether for work in the field or for dancing, matter and form will differ.[1]

Shoes, to most people, seem to be unimportant disposable *things*. Heidegger, however, sees more than mere *things*, and is convinced Van Gogh was trying to capture the essence of peasants' shoes — the essence missed by people who live in a society that readily throws out things, and replaces them with other things.

Heidegger sees: (1) that the peasants' shoes show a healthy closeness to the "earth:"

> From the dark opening of the worn insides of the shoes the toilsome tread of the worker stares forth. In the stiffly rugged heaviness of the shoes there is the accumulated tenacity of her slow trudge through the far-spreading and ever-uniform furrows of the field swept by a raw wind. On the leather lie the dampness and richness of the soil. Under the soles stretches the loneliness of the field-path as evening falls. In the shoes vibrates the silent call of the earth, its quiet gift of the ripening grain and its unexplained self-refusal in the fallow desolation of the wintry field. This equipment is pervaded by uncomplaining anxiety as to the certainty of bread, the wordless joy of having once more withstood want, the trembling before the impending childbed and shivering at the surrounding menace of death. This equipment belongs to the *earth*....[2]

(2) The peasants' shoes are examples of equipment that show their users a phenomenal trait: they show "reliability."[3] A piece of equipment shows users that they can count on it because it shows its "essential Being." Most people will probably ask, "What does it matter that we depend on our shoes performing as shoes for a period of time?" Heidegger, however, is in awe of the fact that useful things show their usefulness to us. This notion, that a central characteristic of Being is the showing of essential traits, constitutes a mystical element in Heidegger's world view. If a reader sees the world the way Heidegger sees it, then the world is no longer a world of mere things. Things in the world open themselves to us so we can dis-cover, or un-cover their being. (Philosophers have debated the nature of "truth" for centuries. For Heidegger, truth is "uncovering" or "dis-covering" — the taking away of covers so a thing can show itself.)

Are the peasants in *The Tree of the Wooden Clogs* in a more authentic relationship with their environment than are the landlord or the city folk? Do peasants have a healthier respect for things than people "who have it all"? Do programs that take underprivileged children out of the city to spend time with families in rural areas provide evidence that country life is, in some ways, more fulfilling than city life? (Heidegger would rejuvenate himself by periodically leaving the university, in order to spend time with peasants.) Given that we tend to live in a "throw

A scene from *The Tree of the Wooden Clogs* (1978) showing peasants at the mercy of their landlord.

away society," would it be better if we had a greater respect for the things that serve us?

Movie 56: *A Pure Formality*

Director: Giuseppe Tornatore; 1 hour, 48 minutes; 1994
Warning: Two brief scenes of Gérard Depardieu nude. Not a pretty sight.

Giuseppe Tornatore's *Cinema Paradiso* (see *Plato and Popcorn*, page 189) is a wonderful feel-good film. Tornatore shows amazing range with his very different *A Pure Formality*. There may be a problem tracking down this film. No DVD edition is currently available.

Watch the movie.

Questions to ponder:

1. Mick LaSalle, film critic of the *San Francisco Chronicle* wrote the following about *A Pure Formality* on June 30, 1995:

The ending of *A Pure Formality* actually reverberates backward, trivializing most of what had gone before. You walk out feeling cheated, and it's easy to forget that the picture is 98 minutes of a very good movie.... All this artfulness, plus two superb performances — and in the end Tornatore takes a tense crime drama and turns it into an episode of *The Twilight Zone.* Why, oh why?

Did you have the same reaction as LaSalle about the end of the film? If most of it was good, but you did not like the conclusion, how would you have finished the story?

2. Is there any significance to the name of Gérard Depardieu's character, Onoff (On-off)?

3. Many viewers reported on IMDb that they think the name of the inspector (Roman Polanski) is *really* Leonardo da Vinci. They hold that the inspector is like a St. Peter checking out the credentials of newly dead arrivals at his gate. Leonardo, they say, is a genius, whose job is to evaluate other geniuses. The name Leonardo da Vinci comes up when Onoff identifies himself. The inspector doesn't believe him. (Wouldn't the inspector *know* who he is interrogating?) He says, "If you are Onoff, then I am Leonardo da Vinci." It seems to me that the inspector is merely being facetious. Later, when Onoff asks the inspector's name, he answers that he can be called Leonardo. What is your response to this debate?

4. Are there any clues early in the film that would indicate Onoff is

Gérard Depardieu, left, is being interrogated by Roman Polanski in *A Pure Formality* (1994).

dead? For example, Paula (Maria Rosa Spagnolo) can't hear his voice when Onoff calls her on the telephone.

ADDITIONAL RECOMMENDATIONS

Read Jean-Paul Sartre's play *No Exit*. Three people die and go to hell. Suicide is one of the topics involved in the plot of this play. Also, interesting is Roman Polanski's *Death and the Maiden* (1994). A lot of the feel of that film — as well as its plot — is similar to *A Pure Formality*.

Movie 57: *The Best of Youth*

Director: Marco Tullio Giordana; 6 hours, 6 minutes; 2003
Watch the movie.

Questions to ponder:

1. The one big puzzle about the plot centers on the morbidity of Matteo (Alessio Boni). Do you think he is morbid in the beginning of the film? Does he undergo a major transformation on the trip towards Norway when Georgia (Jasmine Trinca) is picked up by the two policemen as she buys ice cream? He refuses to continue the trip with Nicola (Luigi Lo Cascio), and joins the army instead.

2. After Matteo's suicide, Nicola feels guilty that he didn't do more to divert Matteo from the path he was on. He also feels that he should have stopped Giulia (Sonia Bergamasco) from becoming ever more involved with the radical Red Brigade. Here's what he says:

> I should've been the one to understand, but I didn't understand a thing. Maybe that's not true, maybe I understood but — life with Giulia. I could have stopped her ... [Matteo] turned around, looked at me. And I closed the door and erased everything. Now there's nothing left ... I should have stopped them both, but I wasn't capable of imprisoning them with this love. It was my idea of freedom. I thought everyone had a right to live as they pleased. But what freedom is death?

Could Nicola have done anything to keep Matteo from committing suicide? Should he have done anything to dissuade Giulia from taking a path that would lead to greater and greater violence? Is there anything to his idea that he should not interfere with Matteo's and Giulia's freedom, even though their choices could well lead to their destruction?

3. Most critics raved about *The Best of Youth*. Roger Ebert wrote:

Alessio Boni (as Matteo Carati), left, and Luigi Lo Cascio (as Nicola Carati) star as two unforgettable brothers in *The Best of Youth* **(2003).**

Every review of *The Best of Youth* begins with the information that it is six hours long. No good movie is too long, just as no bad movie is short enough. I dropped outside of time and was carried along by the narrative flow; when the film was over, I had no particular desire to leave the theater, and would happily have stayed another three hours. The two-hour limit on most films makes them essentially short stories. *The Best of Youth* is a novel.[1]

A few critics judged the film to be merely a long soap opera. What was the film to you: an epic tale capturing the ups and downs of a real family over a 35-year period, or a soap opera? I was truly interested in each character, and entranced with the mystery of what the future would hold for each of them. Did you feel the same about those characters?

Movie 58: *Elsa and Fred*

Director: Marcos Carnevale; 1 hour, 46 minutes; 2005
Watch the movie.

Questions to ponder:

1. In my questions for *You Can Count on Me* (movie 5), I referenced Albert Camus' novel *The Stranger*. Here, I turn again to that novel. Camus began the work with the following:

> Mother died today. Or, maybe, yesterday; I can't be sure. The telegram says: YOUR MOTHER PASSED AWAY. FUNERAL TOMORROW. DEEP SYMPATHY which leaves the matter doubtful, it could have been yesterday.[1]

The reader immediately gets the impression that Meursault, whose mother just died, is indifferent to that tragic event. As it turns out, Meursault is indifferent to just about everything. Nothing seems important. Everything seems empty.

Meursault is informed that his mother had a boyfriend at the nursing home. The warden of the nursing home says to him:

> I've given permission to an old friend to your mother to come with us. His name is Thomas Perez.... It's a rather touching little story in its way. He and your mother had become almost inseparable. The other old people used to tease Perez about having a fiancée. "When are you going to marry her?"[2]

The children of Elsa (China Zorrilla) and Fred (Manuel Alexandre) are disgusted that such elderly people are starting a relationship, and are involved in a "revolution." They sound like Meursault at the beginning of *The Stranger*. (A similar scenario will also be found in *Innocence*, movie

Elsa (China Zorrilla) brings laughter and love into the life of Fred (Manuel Alexandre) (2005).

84). Why is it that a significant number of people will look askance at elderly people falling in love? Isn't it possible that older people may be more certain that love is actually involved in their relationship than inexperienced young people may be?

At the end of *The Stranger*, Meursault understands "why at her life's end, [my mother] had taken on a fiancé...."[3] Life is about beginning anew — about living with passion. Why should anyone expect people *of any age* to cease to live, love, and grow?

2. Elsa early becomes aware that Fred has not had much laughter in his life. He and his wife had seldom laughed. Elsa proceeds to get Fred into situations where he is led to laugh with her. Does the film provide evidence that a relationship between lovers will be healthier than common if laughter is a key component in it? Can a married couple truly love one another, if laughter is absent from their relationship? Why is laughter so important?

Most chronic liars tend to be repulsive. Elsa is a chronic liar, but even her husband deeply loves her. Why does Elsa lie so much? Are most of her lies self-serving? Would she be as loveable, if she doesn't lie so much? In spite of her lies, can Fred trust that Elsa will always be there for him?

ADDITIONAL RECOMMENDED
FILMS FROM ITALY

The Bicycle Thief (1948)
La Dolce Vita (1959), *8½* (1963), and *Amarcord* (1973). Three Fellini greats.
The Gospel According to St. Matthew (1967)
The Garden of the Finzi-Continis (1970)
Seven Beauties (1976)
Malena (2000). Directed by Giuseppe Tornatore who also directed *A Pure Formality* (Movie 56).

Movie 59: *The Gods Must Be Crazy*

Director: Jamie Uys; 1 hour, 49 minutes; 1980
Watch the movie.

Questions to ponder:

1. When *The Gods Must Be Crazy* was released, quite a bit of discussion was generated over whether the film contains racist elements. Bushmen aren't that dumb, are they? Clearly, the great slapstick comedy lampoons the behavior of whites more than the behavior of Bushmen, doesn't it? Do you think there is unfair stereotyping of Bushmen in the film?

2. On the IMDb message board for *The Gods Must Be Crazy*, "agentdc7" posts an hilarious list of "things we learned" from the film. "agentdc7" listed over 40 things he learned. Can you add anything to the following partial list from the message board:

- Coke bottles are evil things.
- When you see a plane's smoke, it's flatulence from the gods.
- A bazooka's scope is not very accurate.
- When sitting on a moving jeep, you will fall off if it stops abruptly.
- Bottles make "whoop, whoop, whoop" noises when you throw them in the air.
- If you have nervous trouble around women, it's an interesting psychological phenomenon.
- Rocks make good parking brakes.
- People need cars to get to a mailbox 20 feet away.
- If you have a bad experience, you don't want to talk about it.
- Jumping and screaming will scare lions away.
- To stop an armored vehicle, stand in front of it, and let it crash into your booth.
- Telescopes have little people in them.[1]

A Coke bottle stars in *The Gods Must Be Crazy* (1980), a comedy about the clash of cultures.

RECOMMENDATION

Don't waste your time on *The Gods Must Be Crazy II* (1989).

Movie 60: *Moolaade*

Director: Ousmane Sembène; 2 hours, 4 minutes; 2004
Warning: Brief nudity. The topic: female circumcision
Watch the movie.

Questions to ponder:

1. One of the themes that dominates *Moolaade* is the distrust of the outside world by many of the members of the village. The men are particularly disturbed by the influence of the radio and television on their women. Ibrahima (Théophile Sowié), who has returned from Paris, states that the whole world is available to those who have access to radio or TV. How-

ever, he does not take a strong stand on that issue, or on female circumcision. Though Amasatou (Salimata Traoré) would probably be a good match for him, he rejects her at his father's bidding, because she has not been "cut." Is he thus less admirable than the Mercenaire (Dominique Zeida), who at least tries to protect Colle (Fatoumata Coulibaly) as she is being whipped? Ibrahima is shocked at the high prices of Mercenaire's goods, but remains silent because he will not jeopardize his standing with his father and the other men of the village.

2. Why would so many of the men demand that young girls be circumcised? Is it because as the girls mature they will not lust for men other than their husbands? Sex, for them, will probably be painful. Why would the husbands want that? Why would many of the women support circumcision knowing how painful and dangerous it is, and knowing its after effects?

In *Moolaade* (2004), young girls face a terrible fate as a result of tribal customs.

OTHER RECOMMENDATIONS

Ousmane Sembène was 81 years old when he made *Moolaade,* his last film. He died in 2007. If you appreciated *Moolaade,* check out his earlier *Blade Girl* (1966), *Xala* (1975) and *Faat Kine* (2000).

Movie 61: *Tsotsi*

Director: Gavin Hood; 1 hour, 35 minutes; 2005
Watch the movie.

Questions to ponder:

1. What motive would Tsotsi (Presley Chweneyagae) have for taking the baby with him, after discovering it in the back seat of the car?

2. By the end of the film, Tsotsi's character has changed dramatically. From being a thug, Tsotsi morphs into a person with a sense of responsibility. That he has developed so much, is the reason the ending is moving and tragic. Do such character changes only happen in movies? Why don't more real people undergo major character changes? My view is that a person's character is pretty much set by an early age. After that point, the character will change only if events occur that modify it. It seems to me that "free will" has nothing to do with a change of character. What led Tsotsi to become more responsible? Would the film have been as good as it is, if Tsotsi had merely — on a whim — chosen to be more responsible? Suppose there were a scene where he kills someone, and then — out of mere free choice — decides to be a much better person. Would that make sense?

In *Plato and Popcorn* (pages 119–120), I covered the film *American History X* (1998). Derek (Edward Norton), the main character of that film, changes from being a violent racist to being non-violent, and being one who appreciates members of other ethnic groups. Does Derek freely choose to make such a change? Not at all. While in prison, he is raped by other white toughs, and then is protected by an African-American prisoner. Those factors lead him to drop his racist views.

Jean-Paul Sartre (1905–1980), on the other hand, would support the view that both Tsotsi and Derek are free agents before their character changes, and that these changes are the result of free choice. As previously referenced in *Now, Voyager* (movie 2), Sartre held that "existence precedes essence," which means no human is given their essence or purpose in life. Humans come into existence — they do not choose to be born.

Because most people believe that they have "free will," they would tend to agree with Sartre's idea that "existence precedes existence." They would reject the philosophy of determinism, which denies human choices are the result of free will. So, determinists face a serious problem. They say there is no free will, while a large majority of people say there is. How could so many people be wrong? Here are three reasons determinists give as to why people (mistakenly) believe in free will:

   a. We *feel* we are free. We know what it is like to make decisions, and we feel we are the ones responsible for the decisions we make. When we make a "bad choice" we feel guilty, and say things like "I wish I hadn't chosen that!" Such a sentence presupposes we believe we could have made a better choice. Determinists would respond that indeed we do make decisions, but these decisions are caused. Feeling that we are free is not proof that we are free.

   b. People are ignorant of the causes of their decisions. I am convinced most people think they use reason prior to making a decision to vote for A (a Republican), or B (a Democrat) in an election. The following seems to weigh against that belief. I was raised in a conservative Protestant, Republican area of Pennsylvania. When I was a child, you couldn't find a Democrat to spit on — there were none. I remember the Kennedy/Nixon campaign. Propaganda was widespread in my area stating that if you voted for Kennedy you would be voting to be ruled by the Pope. Well — I saw Nixon as a person who would save us from that fate. Years later, I moved to northern New Mexico. There everyone was liberal, Catholic, and Democratic. You couldn't find a Republican to spit on. As time went on, I asked myself why everyone was conservative, Protestant and Republican in my home area of Pennsylvania. The obvious answer: because everyone else was. The programming to support certain principles along with the peer pressure against wandering to a different set of beliefs, was overwhelming. The people of northern New Mexico were liberal, Catholic and Democrat, because everyone else was.

   c. People are programmed to think they have free will. From earliest childhood, children are told they have free will. Our religious leaders tell us such things as "God created us in His image.

Tsotsi (played by Presley Chweneyagae) is a hoodlum faced with a moral dilemma.

He has free will, so He gave us free will. We can freely choose to follow God, or go against Him." If a child has difficulty making decisions, parents say "You can do it — it's up to you." Well — if it is up to *you*, then you have free will. Although I have taken a stand on the free will/determinism debate, it is clear to me that — in a very important respect — the issue lacks practical significance. Whether I freely choose to enjoy reading, or I am programmed to enjoy reading, I like to read. Whether John Wilkes Booth freely chose to assassinate Abraham Lincoln, or was caused to assassinate Lincoln, he assassinated Lincoln. For most of my life I believed I had free will; now I do not. However, whether I am freely deciding to be a determinist or I have been caused to be a determinist, I am now a determinist.

3. The DVD of *Tsotsi* contains two alternate endings. In the film, as released, he is last seen with his hands up in surrender. In the first alternative ending, the scene continues: Tsotsi raises his hands, but the baby then cries, and Tsotsi reaches for his pocket. The police assume he is pulling out a gun, and thus they shoot him. Tsotsi was reaching for a bottle of milk to give to the baby. The director decided such an ending was "a cheap shot," but admitted that some viewers thought this ending brought a "closure" to the movie. The second alternate ending extends beyond the first alternate ending. Tsotsi reaches for the milk bottle, the police shoot. Tsotsi is wounded, but the police are shocked when they realize Tsotsi was reaching for a bottle, not a gun. As they hesitate from that shock, wounded Tsotsi runs away and escapes. The director decided this ending was also "contrived." What are your views of these three endings?

Note: Many viewers were disturbed by two scenes in *Tsotsi:* the one in which Tsotsi's father kicks the dog, and the one showing the baby covered with ants. Feel at ease. The former scene shows a dog trained to crawl as if injured, and the ants in the bottle scene were not real — they were digitally generated.

ADDITIONAL RECOMMENDED FILMS FROM AFRICA

Yeelen (Mali, 1987)
Yesterday (South Africa, 2004)

Movie 62: *Walk on Water*

Director: Eytan Fox; 1 hour, 43 minutes; 2004
Watch the movie.

Questions to Ponder:

1. When Eyal (Lior Ashkenazi) meets Axel's (Knut Berger) mother, Eyal and the mother (Carola Regnier) are cold to each other. When the mother learns that Eyal is from Israel, she is concerned about his motive for visiting the family. Eyal knows she is the daughter of a prominent Nazi. Is her coldness to him justified? His coldness to her? Do the children of Nazis share the guilt of their parents?

2. Menachem (Gideon Shemer) wants Eyal to terminate Axel's grandfather, Alfred Himmelman (Ernest Lenart). According to Menachem, Himmelman "wiped out all the Jews from an entire area of Germany. Hardly anyone survived except me, your mother, and a few others." Will justice be served if Axel commits the murder? As he pre-

Eyal (Lior Ashkenazi) is charged with seeking justice for victims of the Holocaust in *Walk on Water* (2004).

pares to kill Himmelman, Eyal hesitates. Does Himmelman's age merit a show of compassion for a man who surely showed no compassion for his own elderly victims? Axel, instead, is the one who kills his grandfather. Why?

3. One of the most shocking scenes I have ever viewed is the one in which Alfred Himmelman appears at the birthday party of his son (Hanns Zischler). What was your reaction? Why? Though some show surprise, the guests seem to accept the appearance as a matter of course. Is that response reasonable? After all, Axel's mother claims that she and her husband have had trouble for years, being watched "like criminals to see if we were in contact with Grandfather." The guests would have known about the grandfather's role in the Holocaust.

4. When Eyal meets Axel to go to Axel's father's birthday party, Eyal says Axel looks very German. Do people "look German," "look American," or "look French"? What do Germans look like? Americans? French?

Movie 63: *Ushpizen*

Director: Giddi Dar; 1 hour, 30 minutes; 2004

Ushpizen contains a story of universal appeal, and at the same time provides an introduction to the world of ultra-orthodox Jewry in Jerusalem — a world hidden from most of us. Shuli Rand plays Moshe and Michal Bat-Sheva Rand, his real-life wife, plays Moshe's wife, Malli. Shuli Rand had been a secular actor until he underwent a radical change by becoming an ultra Orthodox Jew. He decided to make one more film, *Ushpizen*. He is also the screen writer for the film.

Watch the film.

Questions to ponder:

1. Do you think *Ushpizen* provides evidence that strong faith can help the believer endure hardships? Do you think prayer and faith can lead to hoped-for results?

2. After Moshe tells a lie in order to get his "guest" to leave, Malli feels guilty. She judges that she and Moshe are being "tested" by God. Of course, Yossef (Ilan Ganani) and Eliyahu (Shaul Mizrahi) are disgusting, but what kind of test would it be if the guests were pleasant people?

3. Since Moshe and Malli are such admirable people, it seems a shame to criticize their claims that miracles happen to them. However, a

philosopher is not going to turn off his critical eye, merely because nice people have strong, but philosophically questionable, beliefs.

In his *An Inquiry Concerning Human Knowledge*, David Hume (1711–1776) presents an analysis of the concept of miracles. Because of the controversial nature of his arguments, that particular chapter on miracles was only added to the book posthumously. Here are some of Hume's major arguments leading to his conclusion that it is improbable that there have ever been any miracles and, thus, that a mature critical thinker will not believe in their existence:

> a. According to Hume, "a wise man ... proportions his belief to the evidence."[1] What evidence — if any — do you have that supports any claim that a miracle has ever occurred? By "miracle," Hume means an event that breaks a law of nature. Have you ever seen a huge sea part? Have you seen someone walk on water? Would you believe a friend who has always told the truth, if he now tells you he jumped to the moon the night before? If *anyone* tells me they have seen a sea part, or that they have walked on water, or that they have jumped to the moon, I would give a similar response as found in Hume's essay: "I immediately consider with myself, whether it be more probable, that this person should either deceive or be deceived, or that the fact, which he relates,

Malli (Michal Bat-Sheva Rand) and Moshe (Shuli Rand) have their faith tested in *Ushpizen* (2004).

should really have happened."[2] Which possibility do you think is most reasonable?

    b. Hume presents four reasons to be suspicious of claims that miracles have been witnessed.

        i. "There has never been found in all history, any miracle attested by a sufficient number of men, of such unquestioned good-sense, education and learning, as to secure us against all delusion in themselves."[3] Is this a fair criticism of the belief in miracles?

       ii. People tend to find more enjoyment in sensational explanations of important events, rather than in mere accounts of known facts. It is much more exciting, for example, to believe that there was a huge conspiracy and cover-up involved in the assassination of President John F. Kennedy, than to accept the fact that one, lone, crazed gunman was responsible. One of my relatives was once in a car that was heading straight toward a tree. She was convinced that it was physically impossible for the car to miss the tree. But it did miss. It was a miracle, she claims. God's hand was involved in turning the car away from the tree. Many times I have heard professional football players claim their team won the game because God had directed the football into their hands, or had directed it away from the hands of members of the opposing team. (Did you ever think that if it were true that God involved Himself in football plays, cheating would be involved? If I, as a spectator in the stands, have some machine that sends out waves that direct the football into the hands of receivers of the team I support, I should be arrested, and the results of the game should be null and void!)

     iii. Most miracles "abound among ignorant and barbarous nations; or if a civilized people has ever given admission to any of them, that people will be found to have received them from ignorant and barbarous ancestry.... (It) is strange, a judicious reader is apt to say, *that such prodigious events never happen in our day.*"[4]

     iv. While here and there a few people claim to have witnessed a miracle, scores of other people nearby never report anything strange. It is strange we do not have Egyptian accounts of the Red Sea parting. Wouldn't you think there would be reports of a huge Egyptian contingent gone missing? A person seeing a car just miss a tree would probably not say the laws of nature had just been broken.

Given the above points made by Hume, what are we to make of the claims of Moshe and Malli that God is causing miracles to reward their faith and prayers?

Movie 64: *Waltz with Bashir*

Director: Ari Folman; 1 hour, 30 minutes; 2008

Waltz with Bashir has been labeled an "animated documentary" about the massacre of Muslim Palestinians by Christian Phalangists in Lebanon in 1952. Bashir was a Christian president-elect of Lebanon, and was committed to strengthening ties with Israel. Before he could advance his agenda, however, he was assassinated. Many held Palestinian refugees responsible for the assassination, and embittered Lebanese entered the Palestinian camps at Sazra and Shatila rounding up and executing hundreds of men, women and children. Israeli forces stood by, and did nothing to save the innocent victims. Ari Folman was one of those Israelis, and he made this film to tell his story and the stories of other Israeli witnesses of the atrocities.

Watch the movie.

Questions to ponder:

1. Is "animated documentary" a contradiction in terms? Do you appreciate Folman's use of animation to tell the story? Would you have rather seen a more traditional documentary in which the people interviewed by Folman are merely filmed while telling their stories?

2. The actual footage at the end of *Waltz with Bashir* shows how terrible the massacre was. Do you think there has ever been a sizeable war in which no atrocities occurred? Or, are atrocities going to happen — and happen regularly — in any war? Does the judgment that "war is hell" refer to the fact that not only participants in the war will face hell, but so also will a significant number of civilian non-combatants?

3. Folman displays great courage in telling his story honestly. Most accounts of the Holocaust bewail the fact that far too many people turned

Waltz with Bashir (2008): An Israeli combatant recalls a massacre of Palestinians in Lebanon.

their heads when signs of genocide appeared. At Sazra and Shatila, members of the Israeli military looked the other way. The murderers additionally did something that mirrored Nazi behavior — they tried to hide the evidence by bulldozing over the bodies of the victims. Should Jews be less damning of those who were indifferent to the fate of Holocaust victims, because numbers of Jews acting under the Israeli flag acted the same way when faced with the evacuation of the Lebanese Palestinians?

4. A major theme in the film centers on problems faced by those who seek to draw from memory an account of what they experienced during a traumatic event. Do you ever struggle to regain important memories of past events?

ADDITIONAL RECOMMENDED FILMS FROM ISRAEL

Time of Favor (2000)
Kippur (2000)
Late Marriage (2001)
Broken Wings (2002)
Nina's Tragedies (2003)

IRAN

Movie 65: *Children of Heaven*

Director: Majid Majidi; 1 hour, 29 minutes; 1997

Warning: 100 percent feel good movie! No violence, no sex, no four-letter words.

Watch the movie.

Questions to ponder:

1. If only all children were as wonderful as Ali (Amir Farrokh Hashemian), his sister, Zahra (Bahare Seddiqi) and Roya (Nafise Jafar-Mohammadi), the girl who somehow gets Zahra's shoes. Do you think movies like *Children of Heaven* should be shown in schools as part of the curriculum that deals with values? What other movies would be appropriate for that purpose?

2. Aristotle (384–322 B.C.) described the virtues of a person who possesses an excellent character. With each virtue, Aristotle also gives names to match the deficient and excessive states corresponding to the virtue. Here is a partial list of virtues[1]:

Deficient State	Virtuous State	Excessive State
Cowardly	Courage	Rash
Insensate	Moderation in pleasures and pains	Self-indulgence
Avaricious	Open-handedness in giving and receiving money	Wasteful
Spiritless	Mild-tempered	Irascible
Self-deprecation	Truthful	Tending to overstate
Boorish	Witty	Buffoon
Contentious	Friendly	Obsequious

Which of the above virtues does Ali possess? Zahra? Their father (Mohammad Amir Naji)?

Ali (Amir Farrokh Hashemian, front and center) runs as hard as he can for his sister in *Children of Heaven* (1997).

Note: If you enjoyed *Children of Heaven* check out these other films by Majid Majidi: *The Color of Paradise* (1999), *Baran* (2001) and *The Willow Tree* (2005).

Movie 66: *Two Women*

Director: Tahmineh Milani; 1 hour, 36 minutes; 1999

This film is not to be confused with the much better known *Two Women* (1960) starring Sophia Loren and directed by Vittorio De Sica. You will have to overlook some clearly inaccurate subtitles, but you should be amazed that the film withstood attempts at censorship by fundamentalist powers in Iran.

Watch the movie.

Questions to ponder:

1. *Two Women* provides a clear comparison between a marriage in which both husband and wife are free and productive in society and supportive of each other, and a marriage in which the husband sees his wife as someone to be controlled. In your view, which kind of husband would

Niki Karimi and Marila Zare'i play two women with two destinies.

probably be happier — the one in the former type of marriage in which he and his wife are equals, or the one who sees his wife as a servant? Can a person who is the master of a slave feel as good about himself as he would if he were to treat that same person not as a slave, but as a respected equal?

2. We follow Fereshteh (Niki Karimi) from her joyous times at the university to her becoming diminished as a person by her dominating husband, Ahmad (Atila Pesiani). At the end of the film, after Ahmad dies from the attack of Hassan (Mohammad Reza Forutan), Fereshteh seems unstable when she says, "I feel like a free bird now without any wings." Does that mean she will never be able to "fly" again, or that she is indeed free, but will have to work to regain her wings? Has she been destroyed, or is she free again because now she will be able to return to college?

ADDITIONAL RECOMMENDED FILMS
FROM IRAN AND IRAQ

The Circle (Iran, 2001)
Turtles Can Fly (Iraq, 2005)

Movies 67, 68 and 69: *The Apu Trilogy* (*Pather Panchali, Aparajito, The World of Apu*)

Director: Satyajit Ray; 2 hours, 2 minutes (1955) / 1 hour, 50 minutes (1956) / 1 hour, 45 minutes (1959)

The three films of *The Apu Trilogy* are based on an autobiographical novel written by Bibhutibkushan Bandyopadhyay, who also wrote the screenplay with Satyajit Ray. The following are the main members of the cast:

Apu — played by separate actors as the trilogy unfolds: Subir Bannerjee, Pinaki Sengupta, Smaran Ghosal and Soumitra Chatterjee

Harihar Ray (Apu's Father) — Kanu Bannerjee

Sarbojaya Ray (Apu's mother) — Karuna Bannerjee

Durga (Apu's sister) — Uma Das Gupta and Runki Bannerjee

Chunibala Devi (the old "auntie") — Indir Thakrun

Aparna (Apu's wife) — Sharmila Tagore

Pulu (Apu's best friend) — Swapan Mukherjee

The haunting music was composed by Ravi Shankar.

Watch the trilogy.

Questions to Ponder:

1. Of the three films, *Pather Panchali,* in particular has little plot. Its scenes seem to have little connection, except that they capture episodes in the life of a family living in poverty in an Indian forest. James Joyce once wrote that "there is more drama in the ordinary events of any single day in Dublin, Ireland — or in any human community — than is contained in an adventure story." Thus he wrote his great work *Ulysses* on one day in the life of Dublin, Ireland. Satyajit Ray seems to have striven to achieve something similar with his film *Pather Panchali.* In one scene, children are excited that the man who sells sweets is coming to their village. Apu,

not having money to buy sweets, will always keep that memory. Seeing a train for the first time provides another memory. The shock of discovering that a loved one has died is captured by Ray, as if a camera recorded a real event. (My earliest childhood memories are of playing with pet rabbits in my backyard, watching my mother fall and break her wrist, finding my dead dog who had fallen down our cellar steps and sitting in a circle with other children in the basement of a church listening to a man spout out hellfire and brimstone and thinking, "this man can't be serious.") A Ray-like movie could be made of episodes such as these. What memories from your childhood stand out? Can you picture a film being made of the events from those memories?

One critic, Jonas Mekas, after watching the entire trilogy in one sitting wrote, "I was born and grew up many thousand miles from (the places depicted in the films)—but it seemed to me, as I sat there through the five hours, that I recognized all those people; that [Ray] was telling my story."[1] Do you feel the same way? What characters are like people from your past?

Pather Panchali (1955) captures memorable scenes in the life of a boy from a impoverished village in India. Shown: Subir Bannerjee.

2. *Pather Panchali* was Ray's first film. Years later he wrote about the joys and hardships of making a movie. Many of his comments are very interesting. For example, he wrote that he was in awe of "the complex and fascinating nature of film making itself."[2] Many writers, composers, movie directors and other creative artists have expressed the same thing: that in some sense they did not feel they were the source of the finished work of art. Martin Heidegger (1889–1996) tackled this phenomenon of the art work creating itself. In order to understand Heidegger's account of the origin of a work of art, one must first understand his account of the nature of truth. Heidegger's theory of truth can be found in several works, including an essay entitled "On the Essence of Truth," and a section of *Being and Time*. Most philosophers accept what is called "the correspondence theory of truth." According to that theory, truth requires three things: (1) a sentence or belief (2) an external state of affairs, and (3) a correspondence between the sentence or belief, and the external state of affairs. If I believe there are two swans in the pond next to my house and there are indeed two swans in the pond next to my house, then my belief is true. If I believe that apples grow on corn stalks, then I have a belief that does not correspond to reality and, thus, my belief is false. Heidegger accepts the correspondence theory, provided that one sees it to be a theory of truth with a small "t." He argues, however, that there is a more fundamental, primordial notion of Truth — Truth with a capital "T." The ancient Greeks sought Truth according to Heidegger, but the meaning of Truth has subsequently been covered up. If Truth did not exist, then truth as correspondence would not be possible.

In the following, Heidegger points to Truth being more fundamental than truth as correspondence: "'Truth' is not a feature of correct propositions that are asserted of an 'object' by a human 'subject....' Truth is disclosure of beings through which an openness essentially unfolds."[3] In the first part of this passage, Heidegger asserts that Truth is not a correspondence. It follows from the second part that in order for "two swans are in the pond next to my house" to be true, several things must be revealed to me: swans, the pond, and my house. How are they revealed to me? It is an amazing fact that the nature of Being makes it possible for those things to show themselves in their own Being. Of course, we must allow things to show themselves. We must let them Be. Here I am, in space, separated from other things, and yet it is an awesome, phenomenal fact that things disclose themselves to me. Truth is uncovering, discovering, or disclosing. When Columbus first encountered the New World, he discovered something that had not been previously revealed to him. The New World showed itself to him.

A work of art is a particular type of uncovering. "Beauty is one way in which truth essentially occurs as unconcealment."[4] Again, a key point is that it is some awesome characteristic of Being that opens the world up for discovery by a human individual. Are you in awe that beings are uncovered in their Being by Being? Or is Heidegger's language merely "language gone on a holiday" as philosopher Bertrand Russell (1872–1970)—ever the skeptic on metaphysical matters—once said?

In his greatest work, *I and Thou*, Martin Buber (1878–1965) also stresses that artistic creativity depends on something beyond the artist: "This is the eternal origin of art that a human being confronts a form that wants to become a work through him. Not a figment of his soul but something that appears to the soul and demands the soul's creative power."[5] Though something "speaks" to the artist, what is required of the artist is that he responds with his whole being. Anything less than such a total response will lead to failure in capturing the spirit that confronts him. Though downplayed by Buber, the artist must, of course, also possess the technical skill to successfully complete the created work.

3. Satyajit Ray adds further remarks on the creative process: "Consider the process: you have conceived a scene, any scene. Take up one where a young girl, frail of body, but full of some elemental zest, gives herself up to the first monsoon shower. She dances in joy while the big drops pelt her, and drench her. The scene excites you not only for its visual possibilities, but for its deeper implications as well: that rain will be the cause of her death."[6] If you appreciated the monsoon shower scene was it because, as Ray held, it is the cause of the girl's death? In retrospect, that scene takes on added relevance. At the time of viewing it, however, it is not known that the girl's death will ensue. While watching the scene, one has no knowledge of what will happen in the near future. Is it not just a wonderful scene of healthy childhood joy? Or is Ray correct that: the meaning and value of a scene is often discovered only after the viewing of subsequent scenes?

4. Ray also makes a value judgment about the moral worth of a person increasing due to his/her engaging in creative endeavors. He asks how the artist can be sure that a piece of art has been created. "Is your own satisfaction the final test, or must you bow to the verdict of the majority?

You cannot be sure. But you can be sure of one thing: you are a better man for having made it."[7] This notion, that the creative person is a better person than one who is not creative, is a central idea in Friedrich Nietzsche's (1844–1900) philosophy. In his masterpiece *Thus Spoke Zarathustra*, Nietzsche introduces the reader to Zarathustra, who, at the age of 30, leaves his home, and goes to a mountaintop to find wisdom. After spending some time on the mountaintop, Zarathustra develops a yearning to leave the heights, in order to provide advice to those in the lowlands. He wants to help them reach a point where they can climb their own mountains. (For Nietzsche, the mountains always symbolize something majestic, and lower lands always symbolize shallowness. People who make it to the mountaintop get lots of praise from Nietzsche. Those in the lower levels are labeled members of the "all-too-human-herd.") Zarathustra leaves the clean mountaintop air, goes to the polluted realm of the lower lands and gives speeches. The title of Zarathustra's first speech is "On the Three Metamorphoses." I hold that this speech provides a key to the understanding of the major themes in Nietzsche's philosophy. Those themes include the death of God, master and slave morality, overcoming, the comparison of thisworldly thought and otherworldly thought, the distinction between the Dionysian and Apollonian elements of existence, and Nietzsche's stress on the value of creativity.

Zarathustra begins the speech with an introduction to the three metamorphoses: "the spirit becomes a camel and the camel, a lion; and the lion, finally a child."[8]

The person who is like a camel is a beast of burden controlled by more powerful people. Those doing the controlling are the lions. The camel feels disgust at his lowly life and imagines an "other world" where he will get his due, and live a peaceful life with no needs or suffering. Two examples of otherworldly camels, according to Nietzsche, are Platonists and Christians. The moral code of the camels is called "slave morality." An element of that code is the notion that being a weak camel is good. Nietzsche would be critical of the judgment from Matthew 5:5: "Blessed are the meek for they shall inherit the earth." The camels believe individuals who have become lions or children are evil.

The lion is the master. The feeling of self-worth and power leads the lion to have a different moral code from the camels. According to master morality, what is good is being a noble lion and what is bad is being a weak camel or slave.

The child is the "overman." The child is a "thisworldly individual" who has overcome both the camel's negative attitude about the world and the lion's need to control people. In *Beyond Good and Evil,* Nietzsche provides an important clue as to why he has a child symbolizing the "overman": "A man's maturity — consists in having found again the seriousness one had as a child, at play."[9] This is my favorite quote from all the philosophy I have read.

Nietzsche holds that there are two forces in nature that work well together — the Dionysian (a playful, chaotic, irrational element) and the Apollonian (the source of order and rationality). Most humans lose the healthy balance of the Dionysian (playfulness) and the Apollonian (seriousness). The child or "overman" recaptures that healthy balance. The "overman" is creative; camels and lions are not.

One cannot know how Nietzsche would judge Satyajit Ray's creative work. I imagine Nietzsche would value Ray's high regard for creative activity. Nietzsche would probably also praise Ray for capturing Truth with his trilogy. Do you agree that a creative person is in some way a better person than one who is not creative? Is creativity given too much value by Nietzsche, and perhaps also by Ray? An obvious problem is that many *evil* people are highly creative.

There is a scene in *The World of Apu* that contains certain ideas *very* similar to major Nietzschean themes. In this segment of the trilogy, Apu is writing an autobiographical novel. The main character describes himself as someone who "struggles" and "sheds superstition and prejudice. He has imagination; he is intrigued by little things. He has greatness in him, perhaps. He has the ability to create.... He doesn't turn from life, he doesn't want to escape. He is fulfilled, he wants to live." These sentiments closely parallel major ideas in Nietzsche's philosophy. All life is *struggle* according to Nietzsche. Weak people (the camels) feel crushed by this hard life. They, thus, project a God who will take the burden of suffering off of them, and reward them for their unfaltering devotion. Nietzsche asserts that people who project an imaginary perfect world, existing in some dimension beyond space and time are filled with *"ressentiment"* — deep-seated disgust with the world of space and time, and hatred of anyone who affirms and loves this world. Those filled with *ressentiment* are not at all creative. The Nietzschean "overman" (the child) is creative, accepts and loves this life and gets rid of superstitions. In fact, Apu's description of the main character in his novel — a character Apu sees as similar to himself — could well be a description of the Nietzschean "overman." Do you think a lot of utterances made by "otherworldly" people indicate both that they are filled with *ressentiment* about their life, and that they have a desire to "turn from life"? (Think of the following expressed with deep disgust: "This world is filled with sin and suffering, but a better world is coming — a world of peace, God's realm.")

5. Apu attends a school and performs exceptionally well. The headmaster (Subodh Ganguli) spots that Apu may be a special student, and prescribes to him the reading of "books about travel, lives of great men (and) books about science." He gives Apu books on such diverse topics. The headmaster says, "If you don't read such books, you cannot broaden your mind." He also says that just because he and Apu live far from famous oceans or population centers, "does not mean that (our) outlook should be narrow." I have believed for years that children whose parents read to them will pick up the love of reading, and will tend to excel in schools and college. Every semester I have many students who hate reading. These students typically have a dismal knowledge of history, literature, science, geography and other fields which a well-read person should be able to discuss intelligently. There are many exceptions, but numbers of my students cannot locate Iraq on a wall map of the world. They will put their finger on a location like Australia, and then move the finger over the map until they stumble upon Iraq. A huge number of students don't know whether the Korean War was fought before or after World War II. I can ask them to name the title of a book written by Tolstoy or Dickens, and I'll be met with blank stares. The writing ability of many students is much lower than should be expected.

Do you agree with the headmaster that reading books is necessary if one is to be literate in all types of topics, and if one is going to be a skilled writer? Can use of the Internet be a sufficient substitute for reading books? Why, or why not?

When he explains to his mother the causes of an eclipse, Apu shows the excitement of learning something on his own. I have always found that I learn things and retain that knowledge better if I learn them from my own effort and interest. Reading a book, *because* a teacher requires it, does not lead to successful learning nearly as well as reading because one is interested in picking up the book. Do you agree?

René Descartes (1596–1650) prescribed something broader than book reading if one wanted to achieve a high level of wisdom and knowledge.

As soon as I was old enough to emerge from the control of my teachers, I entirely abandoned the study of letters. Resolving to seek no knowledge other than that which could be found in myself or else in the great book of the world, I spent the rest of my youth traveling, visiting courts and armies, mixing with people of diverse temperaments and ranks, gathering various experiences, testing myself in the situations which fortune offered me, and at all times reflecting upon whatever came my way so as to derive some profit from it.[10]

Traveling to distant lands to experience diverse environments and lifestyles expands the mind far beyond what would be achieved if one spent their entire life around their hometown.

6. In one emotional scene, Ray shows the intense psychological suffering experienced by a parent who must choose whether or not to let their child "go." Apu has the opportunity to continue his studying by leaving his home and going to Calcutta. His mother is at first reluctant, but — out-of-love — she accepts what is best for Apu. Does a parent who would deny their child such a chance, truly love that child? As Apu leaves, the expression on his mother's face shows the depth of the sacrifice being made.

7. Jonas Mekas (see question 1 above), who himself directed an auto-biographical film entitled *Reminiscences of a Journey to Lithuania* (1972), judged that *Aparajito* and *The World of Apu,* while great films, do not live up to the genius of *Pather Panchali.* He holds that the way death is treated in the second and third films of the trilogy does not contain Ray's "insight into life." He gives the example of how Ray treats the death of the grandmother in *Pather Panchali,* as compared to the death scenes in the two sequels. "In the first part, the old granny dies simply and by herself, without the emphasis of camera or sound. The deaths in the other two parts seem mere necessities of plot; they come with big cinematic bangs, with floods of black birds and dramatic music. But they never say as much about death as the first one did."[11] Do you agree with Mekas' assessment?

Movie 70: *Water*

Director: Deepa Mehta; 1 hour, 57 minutes, 2005

Water is the third film in a trilogy. It stands alone by itself, but you may want to watch the other two films first. *Fire* was released in 1997, and *Earth* in 1998. *Fire* was a shocker in India because of its promotion of the gay lifestyle. Several theatres showing the film were stormed by protestors, and wrecked. *Earth* deals with the partition of India and the resulting ethnic violence. Rumors about the plot of *Water* circulated before the film began. Subsequently, 2000 protestors attacked the set, destroying it. As a result Deepa Mehta had to shoot the film in Sri Lanka.

Watch the film.

Questions to ponder:

1. If you were to write a sequel to *Water*, what would happen to Chuyia (Sarala) after she is placed on the train?

2. There are over 40,000,000 widows living in India. Laws have been passed to provide some security to widows. Under certain conditions, they are free to re-marry. They no longer must shave their heads. The fact remains, however, that they are marginalized by the majority of Indians who are still programmed to accept traditional values that favor the male population. For an update on the status of widows in India, check out http://griefandrenewal.com. Those Hindu fundamentalists who protested against both the making and the showing of *Water* wanted the film cen-

Water (2005) depicts the plight of India's widows. From left, Sarala and Vidula Javalgekar.

sored. Are there *any* good reasons for censoring a film — other than obvious cases, such as censoring a film that contains actual footage of child molestation? In the "Afterword" to his great science-fiction novel *Fahrenheit 451* about a future in which it is held to be good to burn books, Ray Bradbury wrote: "The world is full of people running around with lit matches. Every minority, be it Baptist/Unitarian, Irish/Italian/Octogenarian/Zen Buddhist, Zionist/Seventh-day Adventist, Women's Lib/Republican, Mattachine/Four Square Gospel feels it has the will, the right, the duty to douse the kerosene, light the fire."[1] Almost any book or movie will contain something that would offend someone. Great literary works such as Mark Twain's *Huckleberry Finn*, James Joyce's *Ulysses* and Vladimir Nabokov's *Lolita* have been banned numerous times. The following are just a few of the many films, in addition to *Water*, that have angered special interest groups:

    a. *Last Tango in Paris* (1972) — anal sex
    b. *The Last Temptation of Christ* (1988) — treating Jesus as too human and containing elements not found in the Bible
    c. *Babe* (1995) — pigs are seen as unclean in Malaysia
    d. *Dogma* (1999) — poking fun of Catholic doctrine, and having Alanis Morissette, the popular singer, play the role of God
    e. *Borat* (2006) — possible anti–Semitic leanings and making undeserving people seem like fools

Do the critics of *Water* — or of any of the above films — have good reason to be offended? Should we be considerate of their feelings and support their calls for censorship? Or would civilization lose too many works of creativity, if films such as these were censored?

Movie 71: *Slumdog Millionaire*

Director: Danny Boyle; 2 hours; 2008

Because *Slumdog Millionaire* is set in India and all the characters are Indian, I have concluded it should be placed in this section on Indian movies. However, the feel of the film is very Western, and it is a British production.

The acting, cinematography and Danny Boyle's direction stand out in *Slumdog Millionaire*. The plot centers on three unforgettable children from Mumbai slums. The film traces these children through three stages of their young lives, and thus, each child is portrayed by three different actors. There is Jamal (Ayush Mahesh Khedekar / Tanay Hemant Chheda / Dev Patel) his brother, Salim (Azharuddin Mohammed Ismail / Ashutosh Lobo Gajiwala / Madhur Mittal) and Latika (Rubina Ali / Tanvi Ganesh Lonkar / Frieda Pinto).

Watch the movie.

Questions to ponder:

1. At the beginning of the film, the viewer is asked a question: "Jamal Malick is one question away from winning 20 million rupees. How did he do it? (a) He cheated, (b) He's lucky, (c) He's a genius, (d) It is written."

I immediately thought Jamal had cheated. That judgment shows my pessimistic view, based on endless stories of past corruption covered in the media. In an era when heroes are not as common in films as in the past, we have come to expect movie characters to be self-serving cheaters. Did you tend towards a, b, c or d? Why?

The correct answer is d: "It is written." The entire film centers on the concept of destiny. It is the destiny of Jamal and Latika to be together.

Jamal (Dev Patel) trying to become a slumdog millionaire. Anil Kapoor appears on the right.

Do you think people are "destined" to experience what they experience? What do you mean by the word "destined"? My view is that things unfold the way they unfold because that is the way they unfold. Period.

2. I am usually turned off by plot weaknesses or wild coincidences in films. For example, one small scene in the Coen brothers' *No Country for Old Men* (2007) almost ruined that film for me. In fact, whenever I think of *No Country for Old Men*, the memory of that absurd scene immediately pops up. Llewelyn Moss (Josh Brolin) is walking across a bridge at the U.S./Mexico border. He carries a suitcase filled with money that he wants to hide. He throws the suitcase off the bridge into deep bushes, planning to come back later to retrieve it. Carson Wells (Woody Harrelson), a bounty hunter, is tracking down Moss and wants the suitcase. As Wells crosses the bridge at the border he pauses, and seems to get the idea that this would be a good place for Moss to have hidden the suitcase. He looks down at the bushes and sees the suitcase. Now, of all the million places Moss could have hidden the suitcase, Wells just thinks "Aha! It's going to be in them-thar bushes!" Hmmm.

Some critics are disturbed by the large number of coincidences in *Slumdog Millionaire*. The above mentioned scene from *No Country for Old Men* tainted the plot for me. However, for some reason I am not bothered by a significant number of improbable elements in the plot of *Slumdog Millionaire*. Did all, or any, of the following turn you off?

a. Maman (Ankur Vikal) and Javed (Mehesh Manjrekar), the two villains of the film, are both shot to death by Salim.

b. Salim's character irrationally switches back and forth from being a protector of Jamal to being extremely hurtful to him. (Salim locks Jamal in the outhouse, so that Jamal fails to see his idol; saves Jamal from being blinded by Maman; takes Latika from Jamal, probably rapes her, and pawns her off to Javed; then sacrifices his own life for Jamal and Latika at the end of the film.)

c. An uneducated "slumdog" is chosen to be on "So You Want to be a Millionaire."

d. Jamal does not know much, but he does know the answers to *those* questions at the game show.

e. Jamal guesses the right answer to the last question.

f. Salim gives Latika his cell phone near the end of the film. If he doesn't do that, when Jamal calls he will not reach Latika. In fact, why does Jamal have to go to the train station in hopes of meeting Latika after he wins the game show? He has the cell phone — he just has to call her.

   g. Jamal and Salim fall off the train. Where? Really close to the Taj Mahal of all places.

Perhaps I am not bothered by the above because the plot captures a type of story I love. At times, *Slumdog Millionaire* reminds me of a series of episodes from a Charles Dickens' novel. Jamal is an Indian Oliver Twist: the noble boy living in poverty, controlled by a Fagin-like king of thieves, Jamal struggles, and — with a myriad of obstacles hindering him at every turn — ends up happy. Throughout all his tribulations, the hero of Dickens' novels remains uncompromisingly good. *Slumdog Millionaire* is grittier, and more realistic in portraying the conditions in the slums, but it captures the spirit of the type of plot that made Dickens so beloved.

If you enjoyed *Slumdog Millionaire*, try Danny Boyle's other films: *Shallow Grave* (1995), *Trainspotting* (1996), *28 Days Later* (2002), *Millions* (2004), and *Sunshine* (2007).

ADDITIONAL RECOMMENDED FILMS FROM INDIA

Salaam Bombay! (1988)
The Terrorist (2000)
Monsoon Wedding (2001)

CHINA, HONG KONG AND NEPAL

Movie 72: *Himalaya*

Director: Eric Valli; 1 hour, 49 minutes, 1999

You have probably watched westerns that center on cattle drives. A great one that should not be missed is *Lonesome Dove* (1989). I bet, however, you have never seen a film that focuses on a yak drive. You are about to. *Himalaya* is the only film from Nepal ever nominated for Best Foreign Picture at the Academy Awards. After viewing the film, check out the special feature on the DVD about the making of *Himalaya*.

Watch the film.

Questions to ponder:

1. The characters in the film belong to a culture that accepts reincarnation. One character says that everything must die, and be reborn. What are your views of the idea of reincarnation? Is there *any* evidence to support that metaphysical position? In the 1950s, *The Search for Bridey Murphy* became a huge bestseller and convinced many people that strong evidence for reincarnation had been found. Under hypnosis, a woman named Virginia Tighe recounted details of a life she had lived one hundred years before in Ireland. Her name in that past life was Bridey Murphy. At the height of the excitement about the Bridey Murphy story, the *Denver Post* sent William Barker to Ireland to investigate the claims uttered by Ms. Tighe under hypnosis. In its March 19, 1956 issue, *Time* magazine summarized some of Barker's results, and connected the name of "Bridey" with "Blarney." Major discrepancies in Bridey's account were listed, and *Time* reported that "nobody could find a scrap of evidence that (Bridey) had ever lived." The Bridey Murphy story does not go away, however. Check out www.brideymurphy.com, for example. For a highly

Villagers must face a dangerous trek across the mountains in *Himalaya* (1999). Shown are Passang (Karma Wangel) and Norbou (Karma Tensing).

skeptical analysis of the case, see the "Skeptic's Dictionary" at www.skep dic.com/bridey.html.

2. Karma (Gurgon Kyap) believes that the calculations determining what day the caravan should start are nonsense. Tinle (Thilen Lhondup), on the other hand, takes those calculations very seriously. As it turns out, Tinle is the one who continually makes the right decisions. In spite of the dangers that lie ahead, he says, "The gods are with us. The mountains will recognize us. They are our allies." Is Tinle merely lucky in his decisions? Are his beliefs in the calculations, his reading of what was demanded by the "gods," and the messages he receives from the mountains in tune with reality?

3. In the past, a master told Norbou (Karma Tensing): "When two paths open up before you, always choose the hardest path." Does that advice make sense? Tinle seems to doubt it, but then *he* chooses the hardest path by deciding to lead the yak drive, rather than remaining safely in his village. The master's advice seems to mirror the meaning of Friedrich Nietzsche's famous aphorism: "Live dangerously."

Movies 73 and 74: *In the Mood for Love* and *2046*

Director: Wong Kar-Wai; 1 hour, 38 minutes, 2000 / 2 hours, 9 minutes, 2004

Wong Kar-Wai intended *In the Mood for Love* and *2046* to be viewed as one film. Indeed, the production of the two works proceeded over the same period of time. However, though *2046* is a noteworthy film in its own right, I almost wish Wong Kar-Wai had ended his plot with *In the Mood for Love*. *2046* takes us into the future of Chow (Tony Leung), the central male character of *In the Mood for Love*. In the first film, Chow is the noblest of men; whereas by the second film, he has undergone a severe character change. I miss Chow's earlier personality. In *2046*, Wong Kar-Wai portrays him as a self-centered playboy. However, every once in a while the original admirable personality still shines through.

Watch *In the Mood for Love*.

Questions to ponder:

1. Film critic James Berardinelli writes that if Hollywood were to remake *In the Mood for Love*, it "would have a radically different ending — one that would satisfy the standard romantic formula even as it betrays

Maggie Cheung and Tony Leung portray two lonely people tempted by forbidden love in Wong Kar-Wai's *In the Mood for Love* (2000).

the material and the characters."[1] Do you think in all probability that if there were a Hollywood remake of the film, Chow and Li-Zhen (Maggie Cheung) would hop into the sack? Another critic, Rob Nelson, judges:

> Wong Kar-Wai's *In the Mood for Love* is the sexiest film I've ever seen, and there is not a single sex scene in it. Prurient types might moan that the movie is all foreplay and no fuck. But what's wrong with that? Isn't foreplay the most creative part of sex — when you most relish your partner, savoring and suspending the intimate pleasures ahead?[2]

Was this film one of the sexiest you have ever seen? If so, what was sexy about it? (I can't get over the dresses worn by Li-Zhen — a different one for each scene. And how she looked in those dresses! Ouch!) The film centers on the choices Chow and Li-Zhen have to make. Should they have an affair — something viewed as dishonorable in their culture? Should they act like their spouses? Rob Nelson continues: "At Cannes, Wong admitted to identifying with the character's indecisions: Only at the eleventh hour did he opt to excise a sequence of Li-Zhen and Chow engaged in, as he put it, "hanky panky."[3] Should he have included that scene of hanky panky in the finished film? I think not. However, if you wish, look for it among the "Deleted Scenes" in the extras on the DVD.

Watch *2046*.

Questions to ponder:

1. Chow compares all his women to Li-Zhen, his lover in *In the Mood for Love*. In succession, each woman fails the test. Most of them will end up with the hopeless longing for Chow that Chow feels for Li-Zhen. Time after time, Wong Kar-Wai gets us to feel the pain of longing experienced by many of his characters. Lulu (Carina Lau) is filled with sadness over losing a Filipino boyfriend. Bai Ling (Zhang Ziyi) is crushed by the fact that Chow does not return the love she feels for him. Wang Jing Wen's (Faye Wong) spirit is almost broken because her father (Wang Sum) refuses to permit her to meet with her Japanese boyfriend. Does Wang fall in love with Bai Ling? She — like Li-Zhen in *In the Mood for Love* — helps him in his writing. He is kinder to her than to any other woman in his life except the original Li-Zhen. He goes so far as to help Wang communicate with her Japanese boyfriend. Wang even fictionalizes Bai Ling as an android in a story he writes. Tak (Takuya Kimura), who — it should be noted — puzzlingly also portrays Bai Ling's Japanese boyfriend, loves

the android. The android cannot return the love. Tak is clearly a fiction-alized Chow, and the android a fictionalized Wang Jing Wen.

2. Chow says to the second Li-Zhen, alias "The Black Spider" (Gong Li): "Maybe one day you'll escape your past. If you do, look for me." Both Chow and Li-Zhen are trying to escape their pasts. Why does he tell *her* to look for him?

Movie 75: *Spring, Summer, Fall, Winter ... and Spring*

Director: Kim Ki-duk; 1 hour, 43 minutes; 2003

It is not possible in a short space to present an in-depth study of major Buddhist themes. The following is a summary of the central ideas known respectively as the "Four Noble Truths" and the "Eightfold Path," the keys that can open the door to wisdom and enlightenment.

The First Noble Truth acknowledges that life is imperfect and necessarily involves suffering. The awareness of the impermanence of things

Kim Jong-ho as a child monk learning an important lesson in *Spring, Summer, Fall, Winter ... and Spring* (2003).

causes humans to feel great distress. This distress is probably the same as what is called "angst" by existentialists.

The Second Noble Truth asserts that our desires are the root cause of our suffering. We desire that things be different than they are. We desire to hold on to things that, by their very nature, can pass out of our grasp at any time.

The Third Noble Truth is that suffering ceases when desire ceases. The way to overcome self-centeredness is to rid ourselves of desire.

The Fourth Noble Truth is that by following the "Eightfold Path" humans can rid themselves of desire, and thus eliminate suffering.

The "Eightfold Path" provides a guide to the person who desires to be enlightened, showing the "right" way to be and the "right" way to do things. Here are the eight requirements that must be met, if one hopes to become wise and to live without suffering:

1. Right understanding.
2. Right thought.
3. Right speech. Cursing, gossiping, and lying are examples of speech that is not "right."
4. Right action. Vandalism, driving while intoxicated, throwing golf clubs after a bad shot, watching hours of porn each day are not "right."
5. Right livelihood. In your occupation never hurt other people, or the environment.
6. Right effort. One must be steadfast in following the eightfold path.
7. Right mindfulness. Are you open to the truth? Are you fixated on certain topics?
8. Right meditation. For this, one must learn how to engage in meditation. Meditation can lead to an awareness of reality that is categorically different from common perception. Various techniques have been proposed to help one reach a meditative state.

Watch the movie.

Questions to ponder:

1. *Spring, Summer, Fall, Winter ... and Spring* stresses the cyclical nature of life. The title and the plot of the film start with spring, and

life unfolds until spring comes again. The boy monk (Jae-kyeong Seo) grows into the young adult (Young-min Kim), and from there into the adult monk (played by the director Kim Ki-duk). The adult monk has taken on the role held by the Old Monk (Yeong-su Oh), who had been his teacher. Do you think life in all respects is cyclical?

2. The young adult monk falls in love with the ill girl (Yeo-jin Ha) whose mother (Jung-young Kim) hopes that the Old Monk can cure her daughter. The young girl is eventually cured, and is sent back to her mother. The young monk leaves to find her. Subsequently, his character changes, and in a fit of rage he ends up killing the girl. Is it civilization that has changed the young monk's character? Or, does his change have anything to do with his boyhood torturing of the frog, fish and snake?

3. Some of my students feel that the film needs more dialogue. What do you think? *3 Iron*, Kim Ki-duk's next movie after *Spring, Summer, Fall, Winter ... and Spring*—the next movie covered in this book—has even less dialogue. Check out that film! Though *3 Iron* is very different from the Buddhist fable you just watched, it is just as memorable.

Movie 76: *3 Iron*

Director: Kim Ki-duk; 1 hour, 30 minutes; 2004

I am often stunned by the amount of noise one hears when watching many of the big Hollywood hits. BANG BANG CRASH BOOM BAM BANG. In Hollywood, one thing that is not golden is silence. How refreshing it is, then, to encounter *Spring, Summer, Fall, Winter ... and Spring* (movie 75) and *3 Iron*, both directed by Kim Ki-duk, a director who knows how depth can be conveyed in silence.

Most viewers will be intrigued by *3 Iron,* but will find some scenes to be incomprehensible. I find those scenes to be illogical, but haunting and unforgettable. I *want* to make more sense out of them than I can— because I *care* about those scenes and the two characters who fill them with their presence.

Watch the movie.

Questions to ponder:

1. Kim Ki-duk has said the following about *3 Iron*:

We are all empty houses
Waiting for someone
To open the lock and set us free.

One day, my wish comes true.
A man arrives like a ghost
And takes me away from my confinement.
And I follow, without doubts, without reserve,
Until I find my new destiny.[1]

So — the question must be asked: By the end of the movie, is the drifter Tae-suk (Jae Hee) a ghost? Or has he developed the ability to stay out of the sight of people who threaten him? Is the end of the movie simply "crazy"? Two details that support the view that Tae-suk is either a ghost, or has reached some transcendental state are (1) that physical blows by the jail guard do not seem to hurt him unlike the golf balls that hit him earlier in the film and, (2) when he and his soul mate Sun-hwa (Lee Seung-yeon) stand on a scale, they do not weigh anything.

From left, Jae Hee (as Tae-suk), Lee Seung-yeon (as Sun-hwa) and Kwon Hyuk-ho (as Sun-hwa's husband) in *3-Iron* (2004). Sun-hwa is telling one of the men she loves him.

2. Near the end of the movie, is Sun-hwa saying "I love you" to her husband (Kwon Hyuk-ho) or to Tae-suk?

3. At the conclusion of the movie, the following sentence appears: "...It's hard to tell that the world we live in is a reality or a dream." Does that statement indicate that at least one character is dreaming? Which one(s)?

4. Why does Tae-suk return to some of the apartments he had "visited"? (His presence is sensed, but he is not seen by the occupants.) Why does Sun-hwa return to one of the apartments?

5. Having unwanted intruders enter your house while you are on vacation would be deeply disturbing. Your house is *your* sanctuary. How would you feel if Tae-suk were the intruder? (He would do your laundry, fix your appliances, and take care of your flowers.)

6. What can be made of the scene in which Tae-suk refuses to hit a golf ball tied to a tree when Sun-hwa steps in front of the ball? After she finally steps aside, he hits the ball and it breaks loose from its cord. The ball smashes through the windshield of a car, and kills a passenger.

Movie 77: *Tuya's Marriage*

Director: Quanan Wang; 1 hour, 26 minutes; 2006
Watch the movie.

Questions to ponder:

1. *Tuya's Marriage* opens with Tuya (Yu Nan) in a wedding dress, clearly distraught, crying. This person, we will learn, is a strong woman, who is not prone to crying. The film then takes us back a few months before the wedding, and proceeds to tell the story of a woman who will be reduced to despair. Have you viewed any other films that clearly depict the unfairness encountered by women faced with a world controlled by men? When she becomes divorced, a flood of suitors visit. It seems they see Tuya as a commodity to be owned. Should Tuya wait a bit longer to see if Sen'ge comes through? (All the male actors are non-professionals using their real names.) Was Tuya irresponsible by demanding that Bater be allowed to live in proximity if Tuya agrees to marriage? Contrary to Western culture that one enter marriage out of love, does *Tuya's Marriage* prove that — at times — marriage must be entered out of necessity?

2. *Tuya's Marriage* not only shows the extreme difficulties faced by women in a male-dominated world, but also the threat placed on traditional lifestyles by the encroachment of "civilized" society. Doesn't Sen´ge's new truck even seem out of tune with the natural environment surrounding Tuya's homestead? Baolier, who in the past was Tuya's schoolmate, has probably became a radically different person after leaving the countryside, and striking it rich in oil. As Stephen Holden observed in his *New York Times* review of the film (August 4, 2008):

> Baolier ... forces his attention on her in a roadside inn that, despite the large screen television and spacious accommodations is even more desolate than the steppe on which it looms like a modern monstrosity. The indus-

Tuya's Marriage (2006). Tuya (Yu Nan) is an independent woman who must choose a husband in order to survive.

trial landscape that may eventually usurp the primitive one is just a different kind of wasteland.

Does *Tuya's Marriage* show that an "industrial landscape" is uglier than the "primitive one"? Even if you would not choose to live in a totally natural area, do you think such areas are important things that should be protected? Why?

Movie 78: *Lust, Caution*

Director: Ang Lee; 2 hours, 37 minutes; 2007

Warning: Explicit sex. (Even before viewing the film, check out question 2 below.)

Watch the movie.

Questions to ponder:

1. Why did Wong Chia Chi (Tang Wei) warn Mr. Yee (Tony Leung) that his life is in danger? Does she love Mr. Yee? He is collaborating with the Japanese and having members of the resistance movement tortured and killed. Although at times he shows compassion for Wong, at other times he is brutal towards her. Does he grow to love her?

Tony Leung plays Mr. Yee, one who collaborates with the Japanese in World War II, in *Lust, Caution* (2007). At left is Tang Wei.

2.　In an entry in *The New York Times* (January 3, 2008), critic James Christopher raises the question most often raised by *Lust, Caution:*

> [Are the sex scenes in the film] necessary, or acceptable? ... I would argue that these scenes are justified; taken in the context of the film, they directly reference Lee's bigger concern, the tortured relations between China and Japan as reflected in the struggle and dangerous attraction between Leung and Wei.... For me, sex and explicit sex can be absolutely justified as a way of explaining character, motivation and plot.

Do you agree with Christopher's analysis? Do the sex scenes, indeed, relate to "the tortured relations between China and Japan"? After watching *Lust, Caution*, which stands out to you more: the sex scenes, or the acting of Tony Leung and Tang Wei?

3.　The film closes with Mr. Yee alone in a room. What is he thinking? Does his facial expression give us any clue about what is going on inside his mind?

ADDITIONAL RECOMMENDED FILMS
FROM CHINA AND HONG KONG

Raise the Red Lantern (1991), *To Live* (1994) and *Horse of the Flying Daggers* (2004). Three films directed by Zhang Yimou.
The Blue Kite (1993)
Farewell My Concubine (1993)
King of Masks (1996)
Xiu Xiu: The Sent-Down Girl (1998)
Crouching Tiger, Hidden Dragon (2000)

Movie 79: *Ugetsu*

Director: Kenji Mizoguchi; 1 hour, 34 minutes; 1953

"Ugetsu" is one of those great films that utilize fantasy to express truths about life. One critic wrote that this classic film "lends itself first to the simplest of readings as a parable — spiritually Buddhist and politically conservative — teaching us that we must know and accept, our place on earth."[1] Some scenes may seem ridiculous to you if you don't keep in mind that the film is a parable.

As you watch the film, notice the constant smooth movement of the camera. Compare that style with the one used by Yasujiro Ozu, the director of numerous classic Japanese films including *Tokyo Story* (1953). There is little or no camera motion in Ozu's films. At the hands of talented directors, both techniques can work.

Watch the movie.

Questions to ponder:

1. In several of his films, Mizoguchi shows real compassion for women who meet tragedy due to the foibles of men. *Ugetsu* is no exception. Genjuro (Masayuki Mori) gets so fixated on making money that he leaves his wife, Miyagi (Kinuyo Tanaka) alone in an area filled with marauding soldiers. Tobei, (Eitarô Ozawa) who isn't the brightest person on the planet, becomes obsessed with the need to become a samurai with prestige and power. In his absence, his wife, Ohama (Mitsuko Mito) is raped, becomes destitute, and is forced into prostitution. One even tends to feel compassion for the ghost, Lady Wakasa (Machiko Kyô — famous for her role in Kurosawa's 1950 *Rashoman* — see *Plato and Popcorn*, pages 16–17), because all she is seeking is a little love. Do you think *Ugetsu* is a bit extreme in its portrayal of men as creatures who tend to be greedy or easily drawn in the wrong direction by sexual desire, whereas the women are rational?

Ghosts hover in a scene from *Ugetsu* (1953).

2. In *Ugetsu*, two ghosts appear: the ghost of Lady Wakasa — and near the end of the film — the ghost of Miyagi, who appears when Genjuro returns to his devastated home. It seems these two women have very different characters. Donald Richie, in his history, *A Hundred Years of Japanese Film* wrote the following:

> The difference between the two women "is more than simply profane versus sacred love. Rather, both women died wanting love. The spirit in the haunted mansion is to be equated, not contrasted, with the loyal and loving wife. They are equal, and it is this parallel that interests Mizoguchi."[2]

That may well have been Mizoguchi's intent, but my reaction to Lady Wakasa was much different than the reaction I had to Miyagi. Would you characterize these two women in such a way that they should not be treated as "equals"? If you think they are equals, in what way?

Movie 80: *Rhapsody in August*

Director: Akira Kurosawa; 1 hour, 38 minutes; 1991
Watch the movie.

Questions to ponder:

1. Granted that *Rhapsody in August* does not rank with Kurosawa greats like *Rashoman* (1950), *Seven Samurai* (1954), or *Ran* (1985), I suspect that various scenes will stick with the viewer. The twisted jungle gym, the "eye" of the bomb, and — most of all — the grandmother (Sachiko Nurase) running in the storm as she thinks she is reliving August 9, 1945, should make you forget the poor acting of the five children, and of just about everybody else who appears. However, is the film fair to America, and to the Americans who decided to drop two atomic bombs on Japan

Sachiko Nurase as a grandmother who relives the atomic bomb over Nagasaki in Akira Kurosawa's *Rhapsody in August* (1991).

to end World War II? Are Japanese atrocities, such as the surprise attack on Pearl Harbor or "the rape of Nanking," unfairly overlooked?

As film critic Desson Howe puts it: "Aside from its artistic shortcomings, *Rhapsody* is politically inflammatory.... Kurosawa takes it as given wisdom that the United States arbitrarily decided to bring death and destruction on his innocent, peace-loving nation" (*Washington Post*, February 7, 1992). Richard Gere's character — the grandmother's nephew — even apologizes to her for the fact that his country dropped the bomb, killing her husband. Should Americans feel guilt over dropping the bombs on Hiroshima and Nagasaki?

In *Situation Ethics*, a book previously mentioned in *Downfall* (movie 38), Joseph F. Fletcher asks readers what is the "loving" decision President Harry S. Truman should have made, faced with the following facts:

a. If an atom bomb were not dropped on Japan, since "the Japanese leaders were 'blind to defeat,' [they] would continue fighting indefinitely with millions of lives lost."
b. The United States had two atomic bombs.
c. One atomic bomb could be dropped in a non-populated site to show the Japanese leaders what would happen if they did not surrender. However, there was a possibility the bomb would fail to explode.[1]

Fletcher lets the reader decide what was the morally best thing to be done. (Earlier in the book, Fletcher reveals his own judgment that Truman did the right thing: "On a vast scale of 'agapeic calculus' President Truman made this decision about the A-bombs on Hiroshima and Nagasaki."[2] The "agapeic calculus" consists of a set of factors to be investigated when deciding what Christian love demands in a certain situation.)

What is your judgment? Once the atomic bomb was dropped on Hiroshima on August 6, 1945, was it necessary to drop a second bomb three days later on Nagasaki? Should one of the bombs have been dropped on a non-populated area first? Does it matter that later intelligence indicates Japan would have surrendered within a few months, even if the atomic bombs had not been dropped?

An Additional Recommendation

For an attempt to recreate what it was like to be in Nagasaki when the atomic bomb was dropped, see *Black Rain* (1989).

Movie 81: *After Life*

Director: Hirokazu Kore-eda; 1 hour, 58 minutes; 1998

Jean-Paul Sartre (1905–1980) did not believe there was life after death. What then is going on in his play *No Exit*, when three people who die go to hell? Basically, Sartre is conveying ideas that are presented as true about humans who are alive and are like you and me. Those three people are totally incompatible and despise each other. Sartre's conclusion is that "hell is other people." Imagine being in a room with "no exit." You will never be alone. For all eternity you are going to be in that room with the person who is your worst nightmare.

In *After Life* people also apparently die. However, just as in *No Exit*, whether or not they *really* die is insignificant. They are sent to a waiting station on the way to heaven and they must then answer a question. The question asked will lead the viewer to analyze his or her own life.

Though it is unimportant whether characters in *No Exit* and *After Life* really die or not, a large majority of humans do indeed believe in life after death. Most of those people would accept the philosophical position called "dualism." A dualist believes a human is made up of two utterly different substances: mind (soul) and body. The body is a composite spatial thing. When that composite is broken up, death occurs. The mind, however, is not a spatial thing that can be broken into parts, and so the mind cannot die.

Other than (a) the feeling we may have that our minds and our bodies are radically different types of things, and that the mind is totally independent of the physical world; and (b) we have been programmed since our earliest childhood by our religious leaders, parents, and friends to believe that we survive death, there seems to be no reason to believe in life after death. Here are some of the major arguments against the notion that the mind is immortal:

1. Most philosophers who doubt there is life after death argue against the dualist position. Instead of claiming the human is part soul or mind and part body, and that the soul is immortal whereas the body is mortal, the skeptic claims that mind/body dualism is a theory filled with an immense number of insolvable problems. If mind and body have nothing in common, how do they interact? How — if there is no point of contact between my will and my arm — can the mental event of willing my arm to move cause my arm to move? The answer dualists give is that such

a causal event is impossible. How can a physical act cause a pain that is not something physical? It can't. For René Descartes (1596–1650), the impossibility that mind and body interact led him to conclude that there is a third substance, God. God is an infinite substance who has the power to make sure a pain is felt on the occasion of an arm being cut and that an arm moves when a person wills the arm to move. For many philosophers, this attempt to resolve the "mind-body problem" is absurd. How is the problem resolved by a solution that stresses an all powerful *mind* that can control the workings of finite minds and *bodies?* In Descartes' solution to the mind-body problem, the mind-body problem reappears. How is God's will able to control the workings of the things in the physical world? Someone may say that how God does what He does is a mystery to us. The skeptic will respond: How is the mysterious interaction between mind and body explained by the fact that God has mysterious powers?

The way to respond to dualism and its resulting mind/body problem is to deny that dualism provides a correct view either of the world, or of the human individual. Various philosophers have presented world views that do not utilize dualistic notions. Spinoza (1632–1677), for example, concluded that there cannot be two substances in reality. Only one substance exists, and it is "natura naturata" (Nature), which is God. Nature, for Spinoza, has all the key elements ordinarily attributed to the traditional Judeo-Christian God, except Spinoza's God is not a creator. God (Nature) is eternal, and is that out of which all things arise and on which all things depend. God is not a transcendent substance that creates things out of nothing. Things depend on God not because he creates them, but because they depend on him the way a vase depends on the clay that makes it up. The vase is one way the clay can be molded or modified. Humans and all other finite things are modifications of God. Just as the clay continues even if you destroy the vase, finite things come into existence and go out of existence, but the substance on which they depend is not destroyed. An infinite number of modifications arise from that substance. From the notion that we depend on God like a vase depends on clay, you should not conclude, however, that God (Nature) is merely physical stuff following the laws of nature. The laws of nature *are* God's laws and those laws govern the human individual. The element of a person's life that is called his mental "side" *is* the same thing as what is called his physical "side." They are two sides of the same coin.

2. Since David Hume (1711–1776), the great skeptic, would not accept claims about the existence and nature of substance, he would not accept Spinoza's central thesis. Hume argued that matter exists. However, according to him, we are ignorant about the workings of matter. Therefore, "matter, by its structure or arrangement, may ... be the cause of thought."[1] If matter or our material body is the cause of thought, and if death is the cessation of bodily functions, then there is no reason to think our mental life continues after death.

3. For me, the strongest argument against life after death is one that also comes from Hume: "Where any two objects are so closely connected that all alterations which we have ever seen in the one are attended with proportional alterations in the other, we ought to conclude by all rules of analogy, that, when there are still greater alterations produced in the former, and it is totally dissolved, there follows a total dissolution of the latter."[2] If I put a match to a piece of paper, the paper starts to burn. If, instead of using a match, I use a flame thrower — if I apply a "greater alteration" — the paper will burn more quickly. If x causes y and you increase x, it becomes ever more likely that y will occur. Here is how this principle can be utilized to prove there is no life after death: When I was about eight years old I tripped on a rug and hit my head on a hard floor. I lost consciousness. Using Hume's argument from analogy, if hitting my head leads to the temporary loss of consciousness, what would follow from having my head crushed? You can answer that question yourself.

Hume added the following criticism of the concept of life after death: "The last symptoms which the mind discovers are disorder, weakness, insensibility, stupidity, the forerunner of its annihilation. The further progress of the same causes, increasing the same effects, totally extinguish it."[3] One could add that another major problem arises even if the person continues to exist after death in some supernatural realm. If a person dies at the height of their mental powers, it would be nice for him/her to continue as a mature thinker after death. However, does it make sense to think of the undeveloped minds of young bodies going somewhere after death? Suppose someone in an advanced stage of Alzheimer's disease were to die. Would that person revert to what he was like when he was at the height of his mental powers? What reason can one have for thinking that would happen?

Watch the movie.

Questions to ponder:

1. The central idea of *After Life* is haunting. What memory would you choose to experience over and over for all eternity? *Could* you choose? The trailer asks if you would choose "love's awakening," "a tender farewell," "the promise of youth," "the reflection of age," "a moment of beauty," or "the beauty of silence"? What you choose will tell a lot about you and your values. I found that what is valuable to me cannot be captured in *one* memory. One memorable event will not contain all the people I love and have loved. Do you have that problem also?

2. Another intriguing concept from the film is the question of how you would respond to watching a tape of your life. Basically, you would be seeing yourself as other people see you. Do you come across as someone who is admirable or less than admirable, caring or uncaring, fun or dull, open-minded or opinionated, filled with hate or filled with love? Do you exhibit habits or mannerisms that do not endear you to other people? Do you do things that actually annoy you when other people do them? Would you give one, two, three or four stars to your life?

3. Suppose hell is experiencing your *worst* memory over and over for all eternity. It seems to me it would be easy to determine what that memory would be. Do you agree? If so, why is it easier? What is your worst memory?

Movie 82: *Kikujiro*

Director: Takeshi Kitano; 2 hours, 1 minute; 1999

Kikujiro contains scenes that are extremely funny, and also some that are very moving. Interspersed with those worthwhile scenes are some that are just plain stupid. The musical score is Western in style, but meshes well with the Japanese setting.

Watch the film.

Questions to ponder:

1. Does Kikujiro (Takeshi Kitano, who is also the director of the film) become a father figure for Masao (Yusuke Sekiguchi)?

2. What draws a human to search for parents they never met? If you were to write the plot for a film centering on the life of Masao's mother, what situation would have led her to abandon her child?

3. Do you feel the scene with the pedophile (Akaji Maro) seems out

Kikujiro (Takeshi Kitano, left), against his inclination, becomes a father figure to Masao (Yusuke Sekiguchi) in *Kikujiro* (1999).

of place in a film that is generally a feel-good, light comedy? Is it after that scene that Kikujiro sees Masao as a person of worth, whereas before that he is basically using Masao for his own purposes?

Movie 83: *Nobody Knows*

Director: Hirokazu Kore-eda; 2 hours, 21 minutes; 2004
Watch the movie.

Questions to ponder:

1. Kore-eda here performs a minor miracle in directing four children over the course of one year. In our daily lives, we perceive the "cute" behavior of children from the outside. In *Nobody Knows*, it seems to me, the *viewer* knows what it would be like to be in the same situation that these children are in. Do you agree? Or do you think I am merely *imagining* what it would be like to be one of these children? Do you feel these are four children you want to help, but can't? Regardless, Kore-eda's accomplishment is stunning. Part of the success of the film is the acting of the children; part is the direction and the camera work. In the year of filming, the apartment gets dirtier, and the children age one year's worth.

2. *Nobody Knows* is based on a true story. In 1988, a Japanese mother abandoned her children, who subsequently were not discovered by author-

ities for six months. Each of the four children has a different father. The mother, Keiko (You), clearly fails to fulfill the duties of motherhood. The harm that befalls children deserted by non-caring parents or mistreated by parents is so horrible that one must ask whether or not states should pass stronger laws governing the right to procreate. In *The Republic*, Plato asserts the following:

> The best of either sex should be united with the best as often, and the inferior with the inferior, as seldom as possible.... And I think that our braver and better youth, besides their other honors and rewards, might have greater facilities of intercourse with women given them; their bravery will be a reason, and such fathers ought to have as many sons as possible.... [T]he proper officers will take the offspring of the good parents to the pen or fold, and there they will deposit them with certain nurses who dwell in a separate quarter; but the offspring of the inferior, or of the better when they chance to be deformed, will be put away in some mysterious unknown place, as they should be.[1]

Some of Plato's recommendations will surely shock you. Given the way so many children are mistreated, are any of Plato's ideas reasonable? What are reasonable steps that should be taken to protect children from parental abuse? Do you at least agree with one critic who wrote: "...the ability to procreate does not automatically qualify you to be a parent"?[2]

The Fukushima family in *Nobody Knows* (2004): What would happen if the children would have to live on their own, without the help of their mother?

3. After viewing *Nobody Knows,* what should we think of the mega-hit *Home Alone* (1980)? Should we be disgusted with the slapstick comedy about how a child (Macaulay Culkin) survives alone in his home, and battles burglars?

4. Yûya Yagira, won the Best Actor award at Cannes for his performance as Akira. Does Akira do everything he should in his role as head of his family, when the mother disappears? Should he have gone to authorities, who surely would have split up the four children? Had he gone to the authorities, Yuki (Momoko Shimizu) probably would not have died. The children stick together and clearly continue to love each other. In *Lord of the Flies* (1963; remake 1990), the social behavior between children disintegrates when they are left alone on an island after their plane crashes. Does such disintegration occur because none of the children in *Lord of the Flies* are siblings?

ADDITIONAL RECOMMENDATIONS

Kore-eda directed two other critically praised films: *Maborosi* (1995) and *Still Walking* (2009). In his review of the latter film, Roger Ebert makes the following judgment:

> If anyone can be considered the heir of the great Yasujiro Ozu, it might be Hirokazu Kore-eda.... He has produced profoundly empathic films about human feelings. He sees intensely and tenderly into his characters.... His actors look as if they could be such people as they portray [*Chicago Sun Times,* August 26, 2009].

ADDITIONAL RECOMMENDED FILMS FROM JAPAN

The Life of Oharu (1952)
Fires on the Plain (1959)
The Human Condition Trilogy (1959, 1961). Criterion has now made this 9-hour, 34-minute epic available in a single package.
Woman in the Dunes (1964)
In the Realm of the Senses (1976). Warning: explicit sex.
The Ballad of Narayama (1983)
Shall We Dance? (1996)
Cure (2001)

In addition, you cannot go wrong with any films by Akira Kurosawa or Yasujiro Ozu, two giants in Japanese film history.

Movie 84: *Innocence*

Director: Paul Cox; 1 hour, 34 minutes; 2000

Innocence is certainly not a great movie. What is refreshing about the film is that two elderly people are seen romantically in love. The standard presentation of romantic themes in film usually centers on the relationship between some young stud and a hot young female.

The basic story of lovers reconnecting after not being in contact for decades interests me tremendously. This is in part, because my wife and I got married two years ago, after not having seen each other since we dated as teenagers 45 years before. For a series of accounts about couples who have experienced the same amazing phenomenon, see the book *My Boyfriend's Back* by Donna Hanover (New York: Hudson Street, 2005).

Watch the movie.

Questions to ponder:

1. Is it fair that neither Claire (Julia Blake) nor Andreas (Charles Tingwell) tells the other about their serious medical problems? It seems to me that Andreas particularly should "level" with Claire, because she is the one whose married life is being disrupted so much.

2. Is it clear that Claire's husband, John (Terry Norris) has not adequately fulfilled his duties towards his wife for decades? For Claire, "it's *now* that matters." Her life with John is unfulfilling; Andreas offers her greater fulfillment. Given those facts, and her belief that "what matters in life is love (and) everything else is rubbish," is she right to choose life with Andreas? Does it follow that *any* married person whose life is unfulfilled can justifiably choose a more fulfilling relationship? Life is short. Is it true that love should not be wasted by being trapped in an unfulfilling relationship?

3. At the beginning of Albert Camus' (1913–1960) novel *The Stranger,*

Meursault, the main character, finds out that his mother has died in her nursing home. Going to the home for the funeral, Meursault learns that his mother had developed a close relationship with another resident, by the name of Perez. Meursault thinks it is very strange that his mother — so late in life — had a boyfriend. Do you think it was strange that Andreas and Claire reconnected the way they did? Claire's husband thinks it is ridiculous. At the end of *The Stranger*, while waiting to be executed for a murder he committed, Meursault — who all through the novel has been cold to life because of the absurdity of everything — has a catharsis and realizes he loves the "indifferent" universe. He suddenly also realizes why his mother "had taken on a 'fiancé' — why she'd played at making a fresh start." Close to death, his mother "must have felt like someone on the brink of freedom, ready to start life all over again."[1] Claire has been a slave to a routine that involved little change or depth. Isn't the "freedom" Camus refers to the same type of freedom Clair recaptures as a result of once again developing a relationship with Andreas? Do you agree that freedom

Andreas (Charles "Bud" Tingwell) and Claire (Julia Blake) find love late in life in *Innocence* (2000).

is perhaps the highest state a person can achieve? In *Innocence*, Andreas' daughter Monique (Marta Dusseldorp) says that "so many people are dead inside." A person who achieves the freedom mentioned above is *alive* inside. Someone may reply that when a person takes marriage vows, he or she is bound by those vows, which dictate rules to be followed. Claire brings up the question of whether one should obey the rules — and deny the things that really matter — or disobey the rules, and cling to the things that really matter. I once attended a wedding which included vows that stressed certain rules should not be broken "as long as we both shall love." Years have passed, and that couple is still in a deeply happy relationship. Does the phrase "as long as we both shall love" lower the value of the wedding vows, or is it a healthy modification to traditional vows?

4. When John begs Claire to give him another chance, she responds with, "Give yourself a chance, John." What does she mean?

5. Andreas and the minister (Chris Haywood) have a debate about God. Andreas says that he can experience depth through beauty and love. The minister says that the beauty and love Andreas is speaking about is God. Andreas replies that it is not, and indicates he wishes the word "God" did not even exist. With whom would you agree more: Andreas or the minister?

6. Andreas claims that love is more real as the time of death approaches. Is Andreas correct? Think of youthful Romeo and Juliet, before they have reason to think they are soon going to die. Are they a rare exception?

Movie 85: *Rabbit-Proof Fence*

Director: Phillip Noyce; 1 hour, 34 minutes; 2002
Watch the movie.

Questions to ponder:

1. For decades, the Australian government refused to apologize for the authorized abuses perpetuated against the aborigines. Finally, in February, 2008, Prime Minister Kevin Rudd issued an apology. Do you think later generations have a moral duty to apologize for abuses that occurred earlier in a nation's history? Why? The Vatican has apologized for forcing Galileo to recant his scientific conclusions. The United States government has apologized for its past support of the institution of slavery. Germany

**Constable Riggs (Jason Clarke) takes children away from their families to
be "civilized" in a scene from *Rabbit-Proof Fence* (2002).**

finally acknowledged its central role in the Holocaust. Would it be reasonable for a person to apologize for the misbehavior of a great-grandparent? How is that different from a current government apologizing for events that occurred 70 years before? Certainly the effects of past abuses continue long into the future. Life expectancy of aborigines *today* in Australia is 17 years less than that of whites. It is the duty of a government to address such discrepancies that exist at the present time.

2. A.O. Neville (Kenneth Branagh) is baffled that the aborigines do not understand how he is trying to help them by forcing them to assimilate into the white culture. He says: "In spite of himself, the native must be helped." In America, when slavery was legal, many argued that God wanted whites to have slaves because the whites were *helping* them rise above their natural state. Hopefully, the reader is baffled at how people like Neville cannot understand that they are doing unbelievable harm. My view is that a significant number of these people *know* what they are doing is immoral. That knowledge is pushed aside, however, because of peer pressure and because no one wants to relinquish the economic rewards earned by the abusive treatment of "inferior" people. In the great documentary *Shoah* (*Plato and Popcorn*, pages 126–129), citizens who lived near

Treblinka, the notorious World War II concentration camp, are interviewed. These are people who claim they never knew what was going on in the camp. Yeah, right. Guilt starts to show on the faces of some of the interviewees, but as they verbalize that guilt, others stop them. Neville, as portrayed in *Rabbit Proof-Fence*, does not seem to have the slightest doubt about the rightness of his activities. Do you think most people involved in immoral acts against powerless groups realize that what they are doing is immoral?

Movie 86: *Look Both Ways*

Director: Sarah Watt; 1 hour, 40 minutes; 2005

Look Both Ways captures well a central theme in the philosophical movement called Existentialism — that humans are filled with deep-seated anxiety (angst) over their impending deaths. The existentialist who presented the fullest analysis of the human response to being finite was Martin Heidegger (1899–1976). The following is a summary of Heidegger's

Justine Clarke plays Meryl, who sees death everywhere she turns in *Look Both Ways* (2005).

main points about the human's "Being-towards-death." I will regularly use Heidegger's own strange vocabulary, but will try to explain in simple terms the meaning of his comments. You will notice that he used a lot of hyphens. In fact, I have heard Martin Heidegger called "Martin Hyphenator" by some turned off by his style. The word "Dasein," in the following, refers to the human individual. Dasein can be translated as "Being-There" or "There-Being." Consciousness always requires an object. The object projected by consciousness indicates *where* Dasein is at that moment. I am "there" right now, trying to find words to explain Heidegger's ideas. This evening I will be "there," watching a Philadelphia Flyers' hockey game. This morning I was "there" in a restaurant deciding how I wanted my eggs cooked. All people move from "there" to "there" to "there" to "there."

Here are some of Heidegger's comments about death from his masterpiece *Being and Time*:

1. Death is defined as "the possibility of the absolute impossibility of Dasein."[1] With this definition, Heidegger seems to be saying that, at death, it is *possible* that the individual will no longer be — or will no longer be "there" or "there" or "there." Most of the time, however, Heidegger seems to be implying that death is the *impossibility* of Dasein, period. For example, he writes that "the end of the entity *qua* Dasein is the *beginning* of the same entity *qua*, something present-at-hand."[2] There is debate about what Heidegger means by "present-at-hand being." At the least, such being refers to mere stuff that is just hanging around. Thus, after death, Dasein is no longer "there." Dasein has become a present-at-hand corpse.

2. Knowledge that death awaits us announces itself at every moment "in that state-of-mind ... called 'anxiety.'"[3] How does Dasein ordinarily respond to this overwhelming anxiety? By "falling." This Heideggerian notion of falling is similar to the Christian concept. Dasein falls out of some authentic way of being into an inauthentic state. What aids the human individual in his fall is Das Man, translated as "the they." The they "aggravates the *temptation* to cover up from oneself one's ownmost Being-towards-death. This evasive concealment in the face of death dominates everydayness so stubbornly that, in Being with one another, the 'neighbors' often still keep talking the 'dying person' into the belief that he will escape death...."[4] The they provides "a *constant tranquillization about death*."[5] The they are actually attempting to tranquillize themselves every

bit as much as they are trying to tranquillize the dying person. *They* are overcome with anxiety about their impending deaths. The dying person remains a constant reminder that *they* are going to die, and *they* fall out of facing that truth. It seems to me that Heidegger is here giving an account that can be used to explain why people watch so much TV, turn to drugs or alcohol, or allow themselves to become dominated by the other-worldly ideas of many established religions. They are tranquillizing themselves to cover up their anxiety in the face of death.

3. If "falling" is a falling into inauthenticity, it must be a falling *from* authenticity. "Our everyday falling evasion *in the face* of death is an *inauthentic* Being-*towards*-death. But inauthenticity is based on the possibility of authenticity."[6] Heidegger subsequently works towards a description of authentic Being-towards-death. In one amazing, long, wordy sentence, Heidegger presents his description: "Anticipation reveals to Dasein its lostness in the they-self, and brings it face to face with the possibility of being itself, primarily unsupported by concernful solicitude, but of being itself, rather, in an impassioned *freedom towards death*—a freedom which has been released from the Illusions of the "they," and which is factical, certain of itself, and anxious." One who achieves an authentic Being-towards-death no longer seeks the security blanket of the they. By falling, Dasein becomes enslaved by the web of the they. The authentic person breaks free of that web, stands upright on his own two feet and achieves "an impassioned freedom towards death." There is an acceptance of Being—a love of life—in spite of the fact that death is impending.

I don't think it would be fair to say that either of the two main characters in *Look Both Ways* is "tranquillized by the they." However, the last scenes seem to me to capture what Heidegger would call an "authentic Being-towards-death."

Watch the movie.

Questions to ponder:

1. Do you find such a stress on death in the film to be morbid, or do you find the way the theme is handled to be uplifting? Do you think the animated sequences add to the plot, or are they intrusive?

2. In his review of *Look Both Ways*, Roger Ebert wrote the following:

I watched the movie in a kind of fascination. It is poetic and unforgiving, romantic and stark. Death is the subject we edge around. If it is on the sidewalk, we step into the street. If it is on the telephone, we hang up. We don't open its letters. To know that we will die is such a final and unanswerable rebuke. And yet without death, we'd all be bored out of our minds, if indeed we had even developed minds in the first place. Sometimes I think the process of evolution leads up to our ability to comprehend the words: Gather ye rosebuds while ye may.[7]

Is it true that "without death, we'd all be bored out of our minds"? Did it seem to you that the central message of the film is contained in a flow of images from when Nick (William McInnes) and Meryl (Justine Clark) travel around the world "gathering rosebuds"?

Movie 87: *The World's Fastest Indian*

Director: Roger Donaldson; 2 hours, 7 minutes; 2005

The World's Fastest Indian is not a film seeped with deep meaning — it is simply a fun film to watch. Anthony Hopkins shines as Burt Munro, the real-life native of Invercargill, New Zealand. Burt wants to break the land speed record with his motorcycle, an Indian Scout. The problem is, just about everyone thinks Burt is too old and incompetent, and that his motorcycle is a pile of trash. I recently visited Invercargill. There is tremendous community pride in what Burt accomplished — he is remembered as *their* hero. Burt died in 1978. A documentary on the real Burt is included in the DVD extras. That documentary makes one aware of how amazingly Anthony Hopkins captures the spirit of the man.

Watch the film.

Questions to ponder:

1. Burt goes on a quest. The quest scenario is one of the most common of all movie scenarios. *The Lord of the Rings Trilogy* (2001, 2002, 2003) about Frodo's journey to cast that nasty ring into Mount Doom provides one of the most famous of all quests in cinematic history. The struggle of *Rocky* (1976) to prepare for a title fight is another example. Can you name any other great quest movies? What is it about quest movies that is so appealing to viewers?

Quest movies provide drama and suspense. Will the hero — against all odds — be successful? An additional value of such films lies in the possibility that they may motivate us to take risks and to go on quests ourselves. *The World's Fastest Indian* contains a number of quotes that prescribe getting off our couches and going out to live a more full life. They include the following:

a. After stating that taking risks is what makes life worth living, Burt says, "If you don't follow through on your dreams, you might as well be a vegetable."
b. "If you don't go when you wanna go, when you do go you'll find you've already gone."

Anthony Hopkins plays Burt Munro, the hero of Invercargill, New Zealand. He wants to set the land speed record with his motorcycle, an Indian Scout, in *The World's Fastest Indian* (2005).

    c. Burt asks his friend, Fran (Annie Whittle), whether or not she thinks he can make it to the Bonneville Salt Flats and break the record. She answers, "Oh, I don't know, Burt. But I don't think it really matters one way or another."

    d. Similarly, Teddy Roosevelt is quoted as saying, "It's not the critic that counts. The credit belongs to the man ... that's actually in the arena."

Concerning (a), is Burt correct that a person who fails to follow his/her dreams is like a vegetable? Concerning (c), what does Fran mean that it doesn't really matter if Burt successfully completes his quest?

ADDITIONAL RECOMMENDED FILMS
FROM AUSTRALIA AND NEW ZEALAND

Walkabout (Australia, 1971)
Utu (New Zealand, 1983)
Burke and Wills (Australia, 1985)
Starlight Hotel (New Zealand, 1987)
Proof (Australia, 1991)
The Piano (New Zealand, 1993)
Once Were Warriors (New Zealand, 1994)
Heavenly Creatures (New Zealand, 1994)
The Sum of Us (Australia, 1994)
Angel Baby (Australia, 1995)
Shine (Australia, 1996)
Oscar and Lucinda (Australia, 1997)
The Dish (Australia, 2000)
Lantana (Australia, 2001)

CANADA

Movie 88: *Black Robe*

Director: Bruce Beresford; 1 hour, 41 minutes; 1991

One could never guess that Bruce Beresford also directed three films so totally different from *Black Robe*: *Breaker Morant* (1980), *Tender Mercies* (1983), and *Driving Miss Daisy* (1989). In addition to exploring life in the Canadian wilderness during the time of Champlain, Beresford also tackled films on life in the wilds of Australia in *The Fringe Dwellers* (1986) and of Africa, in *Mr. Johnson* (1990). Though he is Australian, his recreation of the difficulties faced by priests endeavoring to convert Native Americans to Catholicism, as well as his portrayal of the lifestyle of those Native Americans, is based on solid research.

Watch the movie.

Questions to ponder:

1. Roger Ebert gives a "thumbs down" to *Black Robe*. His main complaint (see his review on www.TheMovies.com) is that the film merely offers "unrelieved despair." He bemoans the fact that almost all main characters are killed, and that the note at the end of the film indicates all the converted Indians will die within a few years and the priests will be withdrawn from the area. Thus, he raises the question: What purpose can be served by presenting a film in which nothing is left in the end? Do you agree with Ebert's assessment? I don't understand the necessity of having something positive come out of human effort. The effort itself can be something praiseworthy and interesting. If what happens to characters in the film happened to real people, it is a worthy project to recreate those events.

2. Many Native Americans protested that *Black Robe* portrays their forefathers as being too savage. A little research will show, however, that the tribes involved in the story did engage in such things as torturing pris-

"Black Robe" is the name Indians gave Father La Forque (Lothaire Bluteau). Can Black Robe convert the Indians to Christianity?

oners. Should those tribes be condemned for elements of their lifestyle, or should it reasonably be acknowledged that they did what they did because of the survival value involved? In the harsh life of the wilderness, there can be no sign of weakness, or survival would be most difficult.

As a viewer, it seemed to me I was being exposed to the events being portrayed through the eyes of Father LaForque (Lothaire Bluteau). Does that viewpoint lead us to sympathize more with the priest, rather than with the Native Americans? Does Beresford remain neutral by refraining to make judgments about the relative values of such things as the Native American's belief that dreams must be obeyed and the priest's faith in Jesus Christ? Is there any reason to believe that either side has the "better" belief? Are both sides merely guided by fanatical beliefs that have no connection with reality?

RECOMMENDED READING

Francis Parkman's seven volume *France and England in North America* is one of the great works by an American historian, as well as being a literary masterpiece. The first two volumes cover the period depicted in *Black Robe.* Those volumes are entitled *Pioneers of France in the New World* and *The Jesuits in North America.* (Some critics now justifiably point out inappropriate terms used by Parkman in his descriptions of Native Americans. He periodically uses words such as "savages" and "primitive Indians.") The entire Parkman set has been published in two volumes by the Library of America.

Movie 89: *The Five Senses*

Director: Jeremy Podeswa; 1 hour, 46 minutes; 1999

Many traditional philosophers downplayed the importance of the role of the five senses in human life. For Plato (427–347 B.C.), sense data merely give us "shadows" that we mistake for reality. True Reality cannot be found in the imperfect world of time and space; rather it must be grasped by the rational part of our soul (mind). There are two irrational parts of the soul. These parts are closely connected to our bodies, and can only give us fleeting, imperfect images of things.

Instead of admitting sense experience has an important role in human life, René Descartes (1596–1650) reduced the human being to a "thing that thinks." What is a thing that thinks? It is a thing which doubts,

Rachel (Nadia Litz) becomes easily distracted by certain things she sees in *The Five Senses* (1999).

understands, conceives, affirms, desires, wills, refuses, which also imagines and feels."[1] Shortly after this passage, Descartes attempts to show that our senses do not provide us with details that define external things. He investigates something simple — a piece of wax. We think we know what the wax is, because we use our five senses to perceive it. We smell it, touch it, see it, hear it if we tap it, and we could taste it if we wanted to. If we investigate the matter, however, we will find that we do *not* know the wax by our senses.

> This piece of wax ... has been taken quite freshly from the hive, and it has not yet lost the sweetness of the honey which it contains; it still retains somewhat of the odour of the flowers from which it has been culled; its colour, its figure, its size are apparent; it is hard, cold, easily handled, and if you strike it with your fingers, it will emit a sound.... But notice that while I speak and approach the fire what remained of the taste is exhaled, the smell evaporates, the colour alters, the figure is destroyed, the size increases, it becomes liquid, it heats, scarcely can one handle it, and when one strikes it, no sound is emitted. Does the same wax remain after the change? We confess that it remains; none would judge otherwise. What then did I know so distinctly in this piece of wax? It could certainly be nothing of all that the senses brought to my notice, since all these things which fall under taste, smell, sight, touch and hearing are found to be changed, and yet the same wax remains.[2]

For Descartes, we know the wax, not because of our senses, but because such knowledge results from an act of understanding. Our minds project "waxness" onto that thing that is hard at one time, soft at another, has a particular shape at one time and loses that shape when heated, etc. All of our giving of names to things that we perceive works the same way. Though it seems that I "see men who pass in the street, I really do not see them, but infer that what I see are men, just as I say I see wax."[3] Such an analysis certainly provides a foundation for skepticism because the things I understand to be men from the qualities I perceive might possibly not be men at all — they may be robots!

John Locke (1632–1704) was clearly influenced by Descartes "wax example." When I am aware of a physical thing, I am aware of a bundle of sensed qualities. According to Locke, there are qualities that *are* "inseparable from the Body, in what estate soever it be; such as in all the alterations and changes it suffers, all the force can be used upon it, it constantly keeps, and such as Sense constantly finds in every particle of Matter," and these are called "primary qualities." No matter what happens to Descartes' wax as it is heated it still is made up of primary qualities. Whether I am truly perceiving men, or robots I judge to be men, I am aware of certain qualities that are inseparable from the things I perceive. "Take a grain of wheat, divide it into two parts, each part has still *Solidity, Extension, Figure* and *Mobility*; divide it again, and it still retains the same qualities; and so divide it on, till the parts become insensible, they must retain still each of them all these qualities."[4] In addition to solidity, extension, figure and motion, Locke will add number, position, distance and bulk to his list of primary qualities. Things that are not being perceived occupy a certain position at certain distances from other things, come in varying sizes and shapes, and are at motion or at rest.

The activities of the primary qualities affect our sense organs and cause us to perceive qualities that we incorrectly judge to be qualities of objects external to us. For example, we see colors, smell odors and hear sounds. Though I use the word "qualities" to describe such things as colors, odors and sounds, Locke calls them "ideas" and distinguishes these ideas from their causes which reside in the activities of the primary qualities of things. These activities generate "powers" that cause us to perceive the "ideas" of color, sounds, etc. Instead of calling those powers "secondary qualities" as Locke does, I will attribute that designation to colors, sounds, tastes. Clearly, for Locke, colors, sounds, odors and tastes are not qualities of things external to us. Even if no one perceives material thing x, x still has size, solidity, and the other primary qualities, but x does *not* have a color, or any of the other secondary qualities. What reasons are there for denying that secondary qualities are qualities of things not being perceived? Take color, for example. Most of us would probably believe that the yellow of a banana peel and the red of a rose are "out there" on those things. But ask yourself the following: where are the colors perceived by color blind people? Are they "out there" on things? No one would answer that question affirmatively. Suppose fate had led the majority of humans to see the colors color blind people now see. Would we call ourselves "color blind," or would we say the colors we see are "out there"? The colors which we now say are only "in the minds of color blind people," we would then say are "out there." You might respond: "But there are lightwaves out there traveling to our eyes and they are not relative." You are correct — light waves are the cause of color, but they are themselves colorless. The light waves traveling to perceivers are the same whether the perceiver is color blind or not.

A similar analysis shows that sound is not a quality that exists unperceived out in the world. Thus, we can answer the question that probably everyone asks at one time or another: "If a tree falls in the forest and there is no one there to hear it, is there any sound?" The answer is "no!" Sound is a secondary quality. There are soundwaves out in the world but they are not sound — they are the cause of sound. Someone might say that there is an unperceived sound made when the tree falls because if you placed a tape recorder there it would pick up the sound. That is incorrect. There are no sounds on a tape. Put a tape, or a CD, or a vinyl LP record to your ear. Do you hear any sounds? No. When the tree falls and crashes to the ground, it causes disturbances in the atmosphere around it. The waves sent out from the tree hitting the ground can affect the tape in the tape recorder. The vinyl LP may provide the best example to see what it going on. An LP of Beatles' songs does not have those songs in it. Look at it. If a needle is placed on the grooves of a rotating record, sound waves will travel out of an amplifier like the sound waves created when the Beatles actually performed.

In short, color and sound are secondary qualities, as are tastes and odors. If there were no perceivers, the universe would lack color, sound, taste and odor. There is no chocolate taste in a chocolate bar and an unperceived dead skunk does not stink. In addition, feelings such as the feeling of warmth, or the feeling of roughness are nothing in the things themselves, but primary qualities that act on our senses in certain ways.

Plato, Descartes, Locke, and numerous other philosophers have argued that the data yielded by the five senses is relatively unimportant in the gaining of knowledge. For Plato and Descartes, reason — not sense experience — is the chief source of knowledge. For Locke, the data we gain from sensing primary qualities does convey accurate information about the world, but qualities like color, taste, odor and sound are, in general, scientifically insignificant.

In the film *The Five Senses,* colors, sounds, odors, tastes and the feeling of touch are not viewed as uninteresting, insignificant qualities. Such qualities have deep significance in the lives of the characters portrayed. The philosopher I find to best capture the deep significance of the data of the five senses in our lives is Maurice Merleau-Ponty (1908–1961). Merleau-Ponty indicates that my being is inseparable from what I sense. What I am, and what I perceive are often indistinguishable. "The sentient and the sensible do not stand in relation to each other as two mutually extended terms and sensation is not an invasion of the sentient by the sensible." For example, when I look at a beautiful blue sky, "my consciousness is saturated with the limitless blue."[5] Monica M. Langer, a commentator on Merleau-Ponty's greatest work, *Phenomenology of Perception*, categorizes the main thesis of that book to be "to show that perception is not *imposition*—whether of an objective *datum* on a passive subject or a subjective structure on an unknown object—but rather, pre-reflective *communication* ('dialogue') *between* the perceived world and the perceiving body—subject."[6] Such an analysis of sensory perception provides insight into the experiences of the five main characters of *The Five Senses,* including the character who immerses himself in the sounds of beautiful songs, and the character who engages in touching other people in her occupation as a massage therapist.

William James (1842–1910) also rejected the traditional notion that what we passively perceive is a mere juxtaposition of qualities. He provides several examples to show that perception is different from "naked sensation." One example in particular is amazing and very funny. Try the following: Lie on a floor. Have another person stand behind your head so you can see his or her face. Ask them to talk without stopping. Watch them talk. You won't believe your eyes! "His lower lip here takes the habitual place of the upper one upon [your] retina, and seems animated by the most extraordinary and unnatural mobility."[7] James' conclusion is that "whilst part of what we perceive comes through our senses from the object before us, another part (and it may be the larger part) always comes out of our own mind."[8]

Watch the movie.

Questions to ponder:

1. Robert (Daniel MacIvor), is the gay, professional housekeeper and friend to Rona (Mary-Louise Parker), who gives her advice about falling in love. He says she should never fall in love with anyone who:

    a. lives more than a bus ride away
    b. is under 30
    c. you meet on a vacation
    d. has never been in love
    e. has never been dumped
    f. drinks too much
    g. doesn't drink at all

> h. is self-righteous
> i. lies
> j. cries too much
> k. is too good looking

Are there any good reasons to agree with Robert about characteristics (a)–(k), or are they just silly?

2. Is it possible for love to have an odor the way Robert thinks it does?

3. Richard (Phillipe Volter) is terrified of his impending deafness. Does Gail (Pascale Bussières) his escort/friend provide him with hope that he will be able to *feel* sounds?

4. It seems that one of the messages intended by the filmmakers is that we regularly take our senses for granted unless we have problems with them. That much is clear about Richard's deafness. The sense of touch is important to Ruth (Gabrielle Rose), the massage therapist. Her daughter, Rachel (Nadia Litz), is the character on whom the theme of sight is centered. (She can't keep in sight the child entrusted to her, but enjoys watching gays kiss and her friend Rupert, played by Brendan Fletcher, dress in female clothing.) The character of Rona centers on the sense of taste, and Robert centers on odor. Do you think the themes of the five senses are well-developed in the portrayal of these five characters, or are those themes undeveloped?

Movie 90: *The Fast Runner*

Director: Zacharias Kunuk; 2 hours, 52 minutes; 2001
Warning: Nudity
Watch the movie.

Questions to ponder:

1. *The Fast Runner* captures many traditional Inuit customs that may seem odd to some viewers. Belching at meals is common. Men have multiple wives. Are there any customs captured in the film that you think are disgusting? Or, do you simply chalk such customs up to being part of a foreign lifestyle? What about the way the two males fight for the right to marry the female? Each man passively receives blows to the head from the other until one falls. If two of our countrymen did that, we would judge them to be insane. What kind of woman would want her husband cho-

Natar Ungalaaq and Pakak Innuksuk star in *The Fast Runner,* an adventure story focusing on Inuit culture (2001).

sen in this way? The Inuit men kick their dogs. In the United States, that would constitute animal abuse. Shouldn't we equally judge that such kicking in the Inuit culture is abusive?

ADDITIONAL RECOMMENDED FILMS FROM CANADA

Down the Road (1970)

Mon Oncle Antoine (1971)

The Rowdyman (1972)

The Apprenticeship of Duddy Kravitz (1974)

The Decline of the American Empire (1986)

Leolo (1993)

The Saddest Music in the World (2003) and *My Winnipeg* (2007). Two films directed by Guy Maddin. There is no way to describe Maddin's films. "Surreal," though not very helpful, may be the best descriptive word. Creative, weird, superb editing of a flow of images. Wacky!

Borderline (2008)

Adoration (2008). Directed by Atom Egoyon. See also Egoyon's *The Sweet Hereafter* (1997) and *Felicia's Journey* (1999).

Movie 91: *Double Indemnity*

Director: Billy Wilder; 1 hour, 47 minutes; 1944
Watch the movie.

Questions to ponder:

1. *Double Indemnity* is one of the earliest films in the uniquely American movement called "film noir." Some other great film noir titles are *Notorious* (1946), *The Third Man* (1949), *Strangers on a Train* (1951), *The Night of the Hunter* (1955), and *Touch of Evil* (1958). The following are some of the characteristics usually associated with film noirs:

   a. Lots of shadows appear on the screen. Faces of characters are often partially blacked out by shadowing. Most are black and white films.

   b. Very often a narrator leads the viewer through the plot. Walter Neff (Fred MacMurray) provides that service in *Double Indemnity.*

   c. All film noirs involve crime. Usually a criminal is the main character, and he becomes trapped in one way or another. As the film unfolds, the question the viewer asks is, "How will that character fall?" Aware of the danger he is in, the main character tends to be pessimistic, and filled with dread. Often it is a conniving woman that is at the root of a male character's downfall.

   d. Most film noirs take place in cities. The shadowy streets and the huge buildings of the city tend to make the main characters seem victims of something bigger than themselves.

What is it about the above list of characteristics that would generally be appealing to Americans, and make film noir an *American* movement?

Barbara Stanwyck and Fred MacMurray plotting the perfect crime in *Double Indemnity* (1944).

2. Walter Neff and Phyllis Dietrichson (Barbara Stanwyck) plan "the perfect crime." They think they have found a way to murder Phyllis' husband, and claim a large amount of money from his life insurance policy — a policy written by Neff. What goes wrong with their plan? Can you tweak the plot so that they get away with the crime?

Movie 92: *Oleanna*

Director: David Mamet; 1 hour, 29 minutes; 1994

I strongly considered not including *Oleanna* as one of the 95 films covered in this book. Critic Mark Bourne reviewing *Oleanna* for dvdjournal.com, blisteringly blasts it, but in doing so raises exactly the questions that I find give the film significance. Bourne's comments will give away some of the plot, but in this case I think viewers are better served if told something about what they will encounter. William H. Macy plays a professor accused of various wrong-doings by his student, Carol (Debra Eisenstadt). Bourne writes:

The play *Oleanna* was often criticized for an anti-feminist tone. There's no question that Mamet stacks the deck in John's favor, even if John is self-important and exhibits little we can hang our sympathy on. We *know* Carol's allegations are false, and she speaks only in the rote dialectics of a campus Student Center pamphleteer, so "the woman's point of view" is given to a dim girl who is either a vile manipulator or a deranged "empowered" cultist. There is no intellectual sparring because each combatant, in his or her own way, comes unarmed and unskilled for such a rumble. Carol is the script's fatally weak link. Her off-screen transformation from a mousy student to a fulminating manifesto-spouter goes unexplained, a cheat on Mamet's part. Because we end up despising (for good reasons) both characters, what we're supposed to take away from *Oleanna* is perplexing. That ruinous false accusations of sexual harassment exist? That WASP men might suddenly explode with "inner male" primalness under pressure? That academia represents society's thin tissue of civilized behavior? All too pat and obvious, even for Mamet. That language is an inadequate means of human communication? If so, it would be ironic given this script's inadequacies as a vessel of clear expression, but in any case it's rendered moot by Carol's obvious defects as a human being.[1]

Given Bourne's negative evaluation, you may want to skip what many think is a minor work by David Mamet. If you are adventurous, however, give the film a chance. It may stick with you, as it has with me.

If you have now decided to give *Oleanna* a chance, be prepared for one other thing that may distract you while viewing the film. David Mamet feels that actors add nothing to a film's value. In both *Oleanna* and his great film *House of Games* (1987) — see *Plato and Popcorn*, pages 14–16 — Mamet has his actors and actresses speak in monotone. You've been warned!

Watch the movie.

Questions to ponder:

1. Prior to his becoming violent, does the professor do anything that would merit the charge of sexual harassment? Does he do anything else that a professor should not do? He *does* touch Carol. Is that inappropriate? While a student was present, should he have spoken on the phone about his problems connected with purchasing a house?

2. Carol argues that she should not receive a low grade in John's course. Here is what she says: "I sit in class. I take notes ... I'm doing what I am told. I bought your book. I read your.... It's difficult for me. Lots of

A professor (William H. Macy) and a student (Debra Eisenstadt) fail to communicate in *Oleanna* (1994).

the language ... I have problems. I come from a different social — a different economic ... I have to pass this course."

I have heard words almost identical to the above from a number of students over the years. If you were a professor, how would you respond?

Movie 93: *The Woodsman*

Director: Nicole Kassell; 1 hour, 27 minutes; 2004
Warning: Disturbing topic; some nudity
Watch the movie.

Questions to ponder:

1. *The Woodsman* traces a pedophile's attempt to "become normal." Walter (Kevin Bacon) is the pedophile. Did you tend to sympathize with Walter's struggle? Did he cause disgust in you? Pedophilia is a taboo subject. Can you think of any other taboo subject that might, if handled carefully, be appropriate for the screen?

2. The title *The Woodsman* is derived from comments made by Sgt.

Kevin Bacon, as Walter in *The Woodsman* (2004), is someone you would probably not want to live next door.

Lucas (Mos Def). He brings up the story of Little Red Riding Hood and the Wolf, and ends with the line, "There's no fucking woodsman in the world anymore." What point is he making?

3. The second time Walter and Robin, the little girl (Hannah Pilkes), meet in the park is an unbelievably powerful, but disturbing scene. On the DVD, a deleted scene presents a different picture of Walter than that shown in the final cut. Walter, seeing Robin experiencing deep psychological pain due to her father's inappropriate behavior, asks Robin if she has told her mother what was happening. Robin says she can't do that. Walter then tells her she should tell her favorite teacher. The goal is to stop her father. He'll be angry for a while; people will say nasty things about him, but he will always love Robin, and he can become a better father. One side of me prefers including this scene in the finished film, and one side thinks it is better that we don't see Walter being that morally responsible with Robin. Which version do you prefer?

Movie 94: *Doubt*

Director: John Patrick Shanley; 1 hour, 44 minutes; 2008
Watch the movie.

Questions to ponder:

1. Do you think Father Flynn (Philip Seymour-Hoffman) is guilty of child molestation? Does Sister Aloysius (Meryl Streep) handle the situation in the best possible way? What motivates Sister Aloysius' prejudice against Father Flynn? Is it because he is too "liberal"? She admits that she has lied to Father Flynn about contacting a nun at his previous church. Was she wrong to have lied? Why did she not just call someone from that church? Was she afraid her belief that Father Flynn is a pedophile would not be corroborated? Is Father Flynn's decision to leave the parish an admission of guilt? Does he leave because, though innocent, he realizes there is no defense against Sister Aloysius' assault? Why doesn't Sister Aloysius directly question Donald (Joseph Foster) about what happened in the rectory?

2. Is Donald gay? If he is, would that fact have any special significance in the plot of the film? The following comment submitted by "p-francis" to IMDb on March 2, 2009, begins with a quote by Donald's mother (Viola Davis):

"Forget it then. You're the one forcing people to say things. My boy came to your school 'cause they were going to kill him in the public school. His father don't like him. He come to your school, kids don't like him. One man is good to him. This priest. Then does the man have his reasons? Yes. Everybody does. YOU have your reasons. But do I ask the man why he's good to my son? No. I don't care why. My son needs some man to care about him and to see him through the way he wants to go. I thank God, this educated man with some kindness in him wants to do just that."

I am a gay man who grew up in the Catholic school system at exactly the time this movie was set. As a student I was never approached by a priest as a mentor, adviser, confessor, friend, confidante, lover or molester. Mrs. Miller's speech moved me to tears because for years I ached for an educated man with some kindness to come to me and tell me it was okay to feel how I felt. That I wasn't alone. That I was loved. I had no man to care for me and see me through. It certainly wasn't going to come from my father. As a result, I remained closeted, ashamed, afraid of discovery. I hated myself, because I thought I was a bad person, a freak.

Even today, kids don't understand being different. And when that difference can be hidden as easily as sexuality can, shame and fear will continue to drive kids into a closet unless we build a bridge. Let them know there are good, kind, caring gay priests and gay teachers and gay parents out there. Give them some role models and let them be loved. It would have made a world of difference for me.

Is it possible that Father Flynn is showing great kindness and understanding to Donald?

1. If you have seen *Oleanna* (movie 92), what similarities do you notice between the situation faced by the main male character in that film, and the one faced by Father Flynn?

Doubt (2008): Is Sister Aloysius (Meryl Streep) a saint or sinner?

Movie 95: *Up*

Directors: Pete Docter and Bob Peterson; 1 hour, 36 minutes; 2009

I concluded *Plato and Popcorn* (page 189) with an up-lifting film: *Cinema Paradiso* (1989). Few films are more up-lifting than Pixar's animated *Up*. Not only does *Up* contain high-quality animation and continually fascinating fantasy; it includes humor and a timeless love story. Some plot elements do not make sense. The role played by the explorer, Muntz (voice of Christopher Plummer), is problematic. Muntz is seen by Carl (voice of Ed Asner) when the latter was a young child. At the time of their later encounter, Muntz would have been about 110 years old when Carl was 79. However, who cares about such trivial irrationalities when such magic is being presented?

Watch the movie.

Questions to ponder:

1. Many comments appear on IMDb about the apparent similarity between Carl and Spencer Tracy, on one hand, and Muntz and Kirk Douglas on the other. Do you see those similarities? Is there some similarity between Carl and Walter Mathau? How about Muntz and Howard Hughes, or Muntz and Charles Lindbergh?

Nothing will keep Carl down in *Up* (2009).

2. Carl and Ellie (voice by Elie Docter) have an ideal loving relationship. They seek adventures, but end up with the greatest adventure life has to offer — authentic love between two people. After Ellie dies, Carl decides to honor her memory by flying away to Paradise Falls. Though 79 years old, he decides not to give up living — he is going to live fully. There are so many messages for us shown in the story of Carl and Ellie. Have you and your significant other — if you don't have a significant other, get to work — given up striving for joyous times? Why not set up reasonable, worthy goals for the two of you. If you have children, do things with them! Read to them, take them hiking in the wilderness, take them to see *Up*. Don't just sit them down in front of the television or computer. What have you done to guarantee you, your significant other, your children or your friends have a fulfilling life? Fly to your own Paradise Falls and help them fly to theirs.

ADDITIONAL RECOMMENDED
ANIMATED FILMS

In addition to the great American productions from *Snow White and the Seven Dwarfs* (1937) to *Wall-E* (2008), see:

Animal Farm (United Kingdom, 1957)

My Neighbor, Totoro (Japan, 1988)

Princess Mononoke (Japan, 1997)

Spirited Away (2001), *Howl's Moving Castle* (2004), and *Ponyo* (2008). Three stunning works of animation by the Japanese master Hayao Miyazaki.

The Triplets of Belleville (France, 2003)

Notes

Introduction

1. Vachel Lindsay, "The Photoplay of Action" in *Roger Ebert's Book of Film*, edited by Roger Ebert (New York: W.W. Norton, 1997), pp. 355–357.

2. Quentin Crisp, "How to Go to the Movies" in *Roger Ebert's Book of Film*, edited by Roger Ebert (New York: W.W. Norton, 1997), p. 636.

3. Gareth Higgins, *How Movies Helped Save My Soul: Finding Spiritual Fingerprints in Culturally Significant Films* (Lake Mary, FL: Relevant, 2003), pp. 7–9.

Movie 1

1. Albert Camus, "The Myth of Sisyphus" in *Basic Writings of Existentialism*, edited by Gordon Marino (New York: Modern Library, 2004), p. 491.

2. Camus, p. 492.

3. Aristotle, *Nicomachean Ethics*, translated by Sarah Brodie and Christopher Rowe (Oxford: Oxford University Press, 2002), p. 104.

Movies 3 and 4

1. David Hume, "Of the Immortality of the Soul" in *Writings on Religion*, edited by Antony Flew (LaSalle, IL: Open Court, 1992), pp. 36–37.

2. David Hume, *An Enquiry Concerning Human Understanding* (Indianapolis: Hackett, 1993), p. 78.

Movie 6

1. Frederick Elliston, "In Defense of Promiscuity" in *Philosophy and Sex*, edited by Robert Baker and Frederick Elliston (Buffalo, NY: Prometheus, 1975), p. 236.

Movie 9

1. Jeff Long, *Duel of Eagles* (New York: William Morrow, 1990), pp. 28–35.

Movie 13

1. David Hume, *A Treatise of Human Nature*, 2nd ed. (Oxford: Oxford University Press, 1978), p. 252.

2. Roger Ebert, *Awake in the Dark: The Best of Roger Ebert* (Chicago: University of Chicago Press, 2006), pp. 279–282.

Movie 14

1. Dennis Lim, ed., *The Village Voice Film Guide: 50 Years of Movies from Classics to Cult Hits* (Hoboken, NJ: John Wiley and Sons, 2007), pp. 278–279.

2. Martin Heidegger, *The Question Concerning Technology and Other Essays*, translated by William Lovitt (New York: Harper and Row, 1977), p. 12.

3. Heidegger, pp. 18–19.

4. Heidegger, pp. 18–19

5. Heidegger, p. 28.

Movie 15

1. John Stuart Mill, *Utilitarianism*, 2nd ed. (Indianapolis: Hackett, 2001), p. 9.

2. Arthur Schopenhauer, *The World as Will and Representation*, Vol. I, translated by E.F.J. Payne (New York: Dover, 1969), p. 111.

3. Schopenhauer, p. 197.

Movie 17

1. Søren Kierkegaard, *Kierkegaard's Attack Upon Christendom,* translated by Walter Lowrie (Princeton, NJ: Princeton University Press, 1956).

Movie 21

1. St. Thomas Aquinas, "*Summa Theologica,* Second Part of the Second Part, Question 64, Article 5 in *The Problems of Philosophy*, 3rd ed., by William P. Alston and Robert R. Brandt (Boston: Allyn and Bacon, 1978), p. 290.
2. David Hume, *Writings on Religion*, edited by Antony Flew (LaSalle, IL: Open Court, 1992), p. 41.
3. Hume, p. 44.
4. Hume, pp. 47–48.
5. Hume, p. 49.

Movie 26

1. Aristotle, *The Basic Works of Aristotle,* edited by Richard McKeon (New York: Random House, 1941), p. 245.
2. Aristotle, p. 246.

Movie 27

1. William Paley, "The Teleological Argument" in *From Socrates to Cinema: An Introduction to Philosophy* by Jeffrey R. DiLeo (Boston: McGraw Hill, 2007), p. 11.
2. This cake example is borrowed from Henry C. Byerly, *A Primer in Logic* (New York: Harper and Row, 1973), p. 62.
3. Jonathan Miller, "March of the Conservatives: Penguin Film as Political Fodder," *New York Times*, September 13, 2005.

Movies 29 and 30

1. "The New Testament" in *The Revised English Bible* (Oxford: Oxford University Press, 1989), p. 156.

Movie 32

1. Immanuel Kant, *Foundations of the Metaphysics of Morals,* translated by Lewis White Bear (Indianapolis: Bobbs-Merrill, 1969), p. 12.

Movie 34

1. Sean Burns, Review of *Lilya 4-Ever* in www.philadelphiaweekly.com/view.php/id-5704.

Movie 38

1. Joseph Fletcher, *Situation Ethics: The New Morality* (Philadelphia: Westminster, 1966), p. 74.
2. Fletcher, p. 165.

Movie 44

1. Friedrich Nietzsche, *Thus Spoke Zarathustra*, translated by Walter Kaufmann (New York: Viking, 1966), pp. 156–158.

Movies 45, 46 and 47

1. Danusia Stok, ed., *Kieslowski on Kieslowski* (London: Faber and Faber, 1995), p. 217.
2. Stok, pp. 217–218.
3. Annette Insdorf, *Double Lives, Second Chances: The Cinema of Krzysztof Kieslowski* (New York: Talk Miramax, 1999), p. 177.
4. Stok, pp. 219–220.
5. Plato, *Symposium,* translated by Robin Waterfield (Oxford: Oxford University Press, 1994), pp. 25–27.

Movie 51

1. Randy Thornhill and Craig T. Palmer, *A Natural History of Rape: Biological Bases of Sexual Coercion* (Cambridge, MA: MIT Press, 2001), p. 2.
2. Thomas Hobbes, *Leviathan* (Cambridge: Cambridge University Press, 1996), p. 89.

Movie 52

1. *The Revised English Bible* (Oxford and Cambridge: Oxford University Press/Cambridge University Press, 1989), p. 3.

Movie 53

1. Judith Jarvis Thomson, "A Defense of Abortion" in *Philosophy and Sex*, third ed., edited by Robert R. Baker, Kathleen J. Wininger, and Frederick A. Elliston (Amherst, NY: Prometheus, 1988), pp. 232–233.

Movie 55

1. Martin Heidegger, *The Origin of the Work of Art* in *Poetry, Language, Thought*, translated by Albert Hofstadter (New York: Harper and Row, 1971), p. 33.
2. Heidegger, pp. 33–34.
3. Heidegger, p. 34.

Movie 57

1. Roger Ebert, *Roger Ebert's Four-Star Reviews, 1967–2007* (Kansas City: Andrews McMeel, 2007), p. 75–76.

Movie 58

1. Albert Camus, *The Stranger,* translated by Stuart Gilbert (New York: Random House, 1946), p. 1.
2. Camus, p. 15.
3. Camus, p. 153.

Movie 59

1. Posted on May 10, 2008, and updated May 16, 2008.

Movie 63

1. David Hume, *Enquiries Concerning Human Understanding and Concerning the Principles of Morals*, 3rd ed. (Oxford: Oxford University Press, 1975), p. 110.
2. Hume, p. 116.
3. Hume, p. 116.
4. Hume, pp. 119–120.

Movie 65

1. This list and the particular translation of the names of the virtues and their deficient and excessive states is obtained from Aristotle, *Nicomachean Ethics,* translated by Sarah Brodie and Christopher Rowe (Oxford: Oxford University Press, 2002), pp. 118–120.

Movies 67, 68 and 69

1. Jonas Mekas, "The Apu Trilogy" in *The Village Voice Film Guide: 50 Years of Movies from Classics to Cult Hits*, edited by Dennis Lim (Hoboken, NJ: John Wiley and Sons, 2007), p. 20.
2. Satyajit Ray, "A Long Time on a Little Road" in *Roger Ebert's Book of Film,* edited by Roger Ebert (New York: Norton, 1997), p. 494.
3. Martin Heidegger, "On the Essence of Truth" in *Martin Heidegger: Basic Writings,* edited by David Farrell Krell (San Francisco: Harper Collins, 1993), p. 127.
4. Martin Heidegger, "The Origin of the Work of Art" in *Martin Heidegger: Basic Writings*, p. 181.
5. Martin Buber, *I and Thou,* translated by Walter Kaufmann (New York: Simon and Schuster, 1970), p. 60.
6. Buber, p. 497.
7. Buber, p. 497.
8. Friedrich Nietzsche, *Thus Spoke Zarathustra*, translated by Walter Kaufmann (New York, Viking, 1966), p. 25.
9. Friedrich Nietzsche, *Beyond Good and Evil*, translated by Walter Kaufmann (New York: Vintage, 1966), p. 83.
10. Rene Descartes, *The Philosophical Writings of Descartes, Volume I*, translated by John Cottingham, Robert Stoothoff, and Dugald Murdoch (Cambridge: Cambridge University Press, 1985), p. 115.
11. Mekas, pp. 19–20.

Movie 70

1. Ray Bradbury, *Fahrenheit 451* (New York: Ballantine, 1979), p. 165.

Movies 73 and 74

1. James Berardinelli, *Reel Views* (Boston: Justin Clark, 2003), p. 252.

2. Rob Nelson, "In the Mood for Love: A Fine Romance" in *The X List: The National Society of Film Critics' Guide to the Movies That Turn Us On*, edited by James Bernard (Cambridge, MA: Da Capo, 2005), p. 135.

3. Nelson, p. 140.

Movie 76

1. Quoted in www.spiritualityhealth.com/newsk/items/moviereview/item_9727.html. This site contains a movie review by Frederic and Mary Ann Brussat.

Movie 79

1. Gerald Peary, "Ugetsu" in *The A List: The National Society of Film Critics' 100 Essential Films* (Cambridge MA: Da Capo, 2002), p. 299.

2. Donald Richie, *A Hundred Years of Japanese Film*, rev. ed. (New York: Kodansha International, 2005), p. 130.

Movie 80

1. Joseph F. Fletcher, *Situation Ethics* (Louisville, KY: Westminster John Knox, 1966), pp. 167–168.

2. Fletcher, p. 96.

Movie 81

1. David Hume, *Writings on Religion*, edited by Anthony Flew (La Salle IL: Open Court, 1992), p. 30.

2. Hume, p. 35.

3. Hume, pp. 35–36.

Movie 83

1. Plato, *The Republic*, translated by Benjamin Jowett (New York: Vintage, 1991), pp. 182–183.

2. Roger Moore, *The Orlando Sentinel*, June 17, 2005.

Movie 84

1. Albert Camus, *The Stranger* (New York: Random House, 1946), p. 154.

Movie 86

1. Martin Heidegger, *Being and Time*, translated by John Macquarrie and Edward Robinson (New York: Harper and Row, 1962), p. 294.

2. Heidegger, p. 281.

3. Heidegger, p. 295.

4. Heidegger, p. 297.

5. Heidegger, p. 298.

6. Heidegger, p. 303.

7. Roger Ebert review of *Look Both Ways* at www.rogerebert.com.

Movie 89

1. René Descartes, *The Philosophical Works of Descartes*, Vol. I, translated by Elizabeth Haldane and G.R.T. Ross (Cambridge: Cambridge University Press, 1972), p. 153.

2. Descartes, p. 154.

3. Descartes, p. 155.

4. John Locke, *An Essay Concerning Human Understanding* (Oxford: Oxford University Press, 1975), p. 135.

5. Maurice Merleau-Ponty, *The Phenomenology of Perception*, translated by Colin Smith (London: Routledge and Kegan Paul, 1962), p. 214.

6. Monika M. Langer, *Merleau-Ponty's Phenomenology of Perception: A Guide and Commentary* (Tallahassee: Florida State University Press, 1989), p. 158.

7. William James, *Writings 1878–1899* (New York: Library of America, 1992), pp. 297–298.

8. James, p. 310.

Movie 92

1. http://www.dvdjournal.com/reviews/o/oleanna.shtml.

BIBLIOGRAPHY

Alston, William P., and Robert R. Brandt. *The Problems of Philosophy*, 3rd ed. Boston: Allyn and Bacon, 1978.

Aristotle. *The Basic Works of Aristotle*, ed. by Richard McKean. New York: Random House, 1941.

______. *Nicomachean Ethics.* Translated by Sarah Brodie and Christopher Rowe. Oxford: Oxford University Press, 2002.

Badhwar, Neera Kapur, ed. *Friendship: A Philosophical Reader.* Ithaca, NY: Cornell University Press, 1993.

Baker, Robert R., and Frederick A, Elliston, eds. *Philosophy and Sex.* Buffalo, NY: Prometheus, 1975.

Baker, Robert R., Kathleen J. Wininger, and Frederick A. Elliston, eds. *Philosophy and Sex*, 3rd ed. Amherst, NY: Prometheus, 1988.

Berardinelli, James. *Reel Views.* Boston: Justin Clark, 2003.

Blessing, Kimberly A., and Bernard James. *Society of Film Critics' Guide to the Movies That Turn Us On.* Cambridge, MA: Da Capo, 2005.

Blessing, Kimberly A., and Paul J. Tudico. *Movies and the Meaning of Life.* Chicago: Open Court, 2005.

Bradbury, Ray. *Fahrenheit 451.* New York: Ballantine, 1979.

Buber, Martin. *I and Thou.* Translated by Walter Kaufmann. New York: Simon and Schuster, 1970.

Camus, Albert. *The Myth of Sisyphus.* Translated by Justin O'Brien. New York: Knopf, 1955.

______. *The Stranger.* Translated by Stuart Gilbert. New York: Random House, 1946.

Canby, Vincent, Janet Maslin, and the Film Critics of the *New York Times. The New York Times Guide to the Best 1,000 Movies Ever Made*, Peter M. Nichols, ed. New York: Random House, 1999.

Cook, David A. *A History of Narrative Film*, 3rd ed. New York: W.W. Norton, 1996.

Crouse, Richard. *The 100 Best Movies You've Never Seen.* Toronto: ECW, 2003.

______. *Son of the 100 Best Movies You've Never Seen.* Toronto: ECW, 2008.

DeRose, Keith, and Ted A. Warfield. *Skepticism: A Contemporary Reader.* Oxford: Oxford University Press, 1999.

Descartes, Rene. *The Philosophical Works of Rene Descartes, Volume I.* Translated by Elizabeth Haldane and G.R. Ross. Cambridge: Cambridge University Press, 1972.

Dileo, Jeffrey. *From Socrates to Cinema: An Introduction to Philosophy.* Boston: McGraw-Hill, 2007.

Dixon, Wheeler W. *A Short History of Film.* New Brunswick, NJ: Rutgers University Press, 2008.

Ebert, Roger. *Awake in the Dark: The Best of Roger Ebert.* Chicago: University of Chicago, 2006.

______. *The Great Movies.* New York: Broadway, 2002.

_____. *The Great Movies II*. New York: Broadway, 2005.

_____. *Roger Ebert's Book of Film*. New York: W.W. Norton, 1996.

_____. *Roger Ebert's Four-Star Reviews, 1967–2007*. Kansas City: Andrews McMeel, 2007.

_____. *Your Movie Sucks*. Kansas City: Andrews McMeel, 2007.

Falzon, Christopher. *Philosophy Goes to the Movies: An Introduction to Philosophy*. London: Routledge, 2002.

Fletcher, Joseph. *Situation Ethics: The New Morality*. Philadelphia: Westminster, 1966.

Fumerton, Richard, and Diane Jeske. *Introducing Philosophy through Film: Key Texts, Discussion and Film Selections*. Chichester, UK: Wiley-Blackwell, 2009.

Giannetti, Louis. *Understanding Movies*, 11th ed. Upper Saddle River, NJ: Allyn and Bacon, 2007.

Heidegger, Martin. *Being and Time*. Translated by John Macquarrie and Edward Robinson. New York: Harper and Row, 1962.

_____. *Martin Heidegger: Basic Writings*, ed. by David Farrell Krell. San Francisco: Harper Collins, 1993.

_____. *Poetry, Language, Thought*. Translated by Albert Hofstadter. New York: Harper and Row, 1971.

_____. *The Question Concerning Technology and Other Essays*. Translated by William Lovitt. New York: Harper and Row, 1977.

Higgins, Gareth. *How Movies Helped Save My Soul*. Lake Mary, FL: Relevant, 2003.

Hobbes, Thomas. *Leviathan*. Cambridge: Cambridge University Press, 1996.

Hume, David. *Enquiries Concerning Human Understanding and Concerning the Principals of Morals*, 3rd ed. Oxford: Oxford University Press, 1985.

_____. *An Enquiry Concerning Human Understanding*. Indianapolis: Hackett, 1993.

_____. *A Treatise of Human Nature*, 2nd ed. Oxford: Oxford University Press, 1978.

_____. *Writings on Religion*, edited by Antony Flew. LaSalle, IL: Open Court, 1992.

Insdorf, Annette. *Double Lines, Second Chances: The Cinema of Krzysztof Kieslowski*. New York: Talk Miramax, 1999.

James, William. *Writings 1878–1899*. New York: Library of America, 1992.

Langer, Monika. *Merleau-Ponty's Phenomenology of Perception: A Guide and Commentary*. Tallahassee: Florida State University Press, 1989.

Kael, Pauline. *I Lost It at the Movies: Film Writings 1954–1965*. London: Marion Boyars, 1994.

Kant, Immanuel. *Critique of Practical Reason*, 3rd ed. Translated by Lewis White Beck. New York: Macmillan, 1993.

_____. *Foundations of the Metaphysics of Morals*. Translated by Lewis White Beck. Indianapolis: Bobbs-Merrill, 1969.

Kaufmann, Walter, ed. *Existentialism from Dostoevsky to Sartre*. New York: Meridian, 1975.

Lane, Anthony. *Nobody's Perfect: Writings from the New Yorker*. New York: Vintage, 2002.

Lewis, Jon. *American Films: A History*. New York: W.W. Norton, 2007.

Lim, Dennis, ed. *The Village Voice Film Guide: 50 Years of Movies from Classics to Cult Hits*. Hoboken, NJ: John Wiley and Sons, 2007.

Litch, Mary M. *Philosophy through Film*. New York: Routledge, 2002.

Locke, John. *An Essay Concerning Human Understanding*. Oxford: Oxford University Press, 1975.

Malcolm, Derek. *Derek Malcolm's Per-

sonal Best: A Century of Films. London: Tauris Parke, 2000.

Marino, Gordon, ed. *Basic Writings of Existentialism*. New York: Modern Library, 2004.

Merleau-Ponty, Maurice. *The Phenomenology of Perception*. Translated by Colin Smith. London: Routledge and Kegan Paul, 1962.

Mill, John Stuart. *Utilitarianism,* 2nd ed. Indianapolis: Hackett, 2001.

Nietzsche, Friedrich. *Beyond Good and Evil.* Translated by Walter Kaufmann. New York: Vintage, 1966.

_____. *Thus Spoke Zarathustra.* Translated by Walter Kaufmann. New York: Viking, 1966.

Nowell-Smith, Geoffrey. *The Oxford History of World Cinema.* Oxford: Oxford University Press, 1999.

Peary, Gerald. *The A List: The National Society of Film Critics 100 Essential Films.* Cambridge, MA: Da Capo, 2002.

Plato. *Plato: The Collected Dialogues.* Edith Hamilton and Huntington Cairns, eds. New York: Pantheon, 1961.

_____. *The Republic.* Translated by Benjamin Jowett. New York: Vintage, 1991.

_____. *Symposium.* Translated by Robin Waterfield. Oxford: Oxford University Press, 1994.

Porter, Burton F. *Philosophy Through Film,* 2nd ed. Upper Saddle River, NJ: Prentice Hall, 2009.

Richie, Donald. *A Hundred Years of Japanese Film*, rev. ed. New York: Kodansha International, 2005.

Rutsky, R.L., and Jeffrey Geiger, eds. *Film Analysis: A Norton Reader.* New York: W.W. Norton, 2005.

Sartre, Jean-Paul. *Nausea.* Translated by Lloyd Alexander. New York: New Directions, 1964.

_____. *No Exit and Three Other Plays.* New York: Random House, 1949.

Schopenhauer, Arthur. *The World as Will and Representation, Volume I.* Translated by E.F.J. Payne. New York: Dover, 1969.

Solomon, Robert C., ed. *Existentialism.* New York: Random House, 1974.

Stok, Danusia, ed. *Kieślowski on Kieślowski.* London: Faber and Faber, 1995.

Thompson, Kristen, and David Bordwell. *Film History,* 3rd ed. Boston: McGraw Hill, 2009.

Thomson, David. *Have You Seen...?: A Personal Introduction to 1,000 Films.* New York: Alfred A. Knopf, 2008.

Thornhill, Randy, and Craig T. Palmer. *A Natural History of Rape: Biological Bases of Sexual Coercion.* Cambridge, MA: MIT Press, 2001.

Turan, Kenneth. *Never Coming to a Theater Near You: A Celebration of a Certain Kind of Movie.* New York: Public Affairs, 2004.

INDEX

www.ingramcontent.com/pod-product-compliance
Ingram Content Group UK Ltd.
Pitfield, Milton Keynes, MK11 3LW, UK
UKHW041354190726
13851UKWH00014B/108